OPEN A NEW WINDOW

THE BROADWAY MUSICAL IN THE 1960S

The Golden Age of the Broadway Musical

The Broadway
Musical
in the 1960s

ETHAN MORDDEN

palgrave
macmillan

OPEN
A NEW
WINDOW

To Joe Spieler

First published in hardcover in 2001 by palgrave
First PALGRAVE MACMILLAN™ paperback edition: November 2002
175 Fifth Avenue, New York, N.Y. 10010 and
Houndmills, Basingstoke, Hampshire, England RG2 16 XS.
Companies and representatives throughout the world.

PALGRAVE MACMILLAN is the global academic imprint of the Palgrave Macmillan
division of St. Martin's Press, LLC and of Palgrave Macmillan Ltd. Macmillan ® is a registered trademark in the United States, United Kingdom and other countries. Palgrave is
a registered trademark in the European Union and other countries.

ISBN 1-4039-6013-5

Library of Congress Cataloging-in-Publication Data available from the Library of Congress.

A catalogue record for this book is available from the British Library.

First PALGRAVE MACMILLAN paperback edition: November 2002

10 9 8 7 6 5 4 3 2 1

Printed in the United States of America.

CONTENTS

Praise for Ethan Mordden's series of books on the golden age of the Broadway musical:

"A breezy, thoroughly diverting delight . . . Mordden is such a vivacious guide that, by himself, he can make the old shows sing . . . Authoritative without being syrupy or stuffy."
—*The New York Times Book Review*

"Mordden writes fiction, too, which must account for his ability to reimagine and render a period he never surely knew, but brings to life with the immediacy of an eyewitness hanging over the balcony railing."
—*The Los Angeles Times*

"Not only is this author the recognized authority on American musicals, but he has a clear, informative, insightful, and often humorous writing style that will surely provide more than one evening's entertainment."
—*American Music*

"Mordden has found the ideal idiom for discussing musical theater. It's literate, casual, jokey, and bold."
—*InTheater*

"Deploying a novelist's subtlety, the author brings long-ago stars and stage business affectionately to life. Though impressively informative, *Make Believe* doesn't deconstruct or desiccate its subject into submission. Mordden never forgets what he is analyzing is entertainment."
—*Boston Globe*

"As always, Mordden is vastly knowledgeable, witty, and incisive in his judgments. His best writing is as sexy and slangy as a Cole Porter lyric."
—*Kirkus Reviews*

ACKNOWLEDGMENTS

To my copyeditor, Benjamin Dreyer, a one-man *New Yorker* editing squad; to Madeline Gilford, Amanda Johnson, Alan Bradshaw, and Doric Wilson; to Jeremy Megraw and Roderick Bladel of the New York Public Library Theatre Collection; to my good friend and colleague Ken Mandelbaum, who knows this field as no one else does; and to my super editor, Michael Flamini, who knows Mahanoy City as no one else does.

What's In It For You?

The Shows of 1960

It's easy to see why Frank Loesser wanted to make a musical out of *Greenwillow*. B. J. Chute's novel of life in a village located somewhere between Brigadoon and the first act of *Allegro* is bewitching, loving, wise, bemusing, and above all lyrical. It begs to sing: of the Briggs family, cursed with a wanderlust that afflicts the firstborn son of each generation; of Gideon Briggs' love for Dorrie; of two parsons wrestling for Gideon's soul, one devoted to damnation and the other to salvation; of the Greenwillow folk themselves, with their picturesque traditions and colorful dialect. "Where's my chawing turnip?" cries Gramma Briggs. "They's people at the door."

By 1960, a good musical needed a characterful score and plenty of comedy and ensemble dancing, all blended sensibly into an interesting story. But, above all, a musical needed feelings, and Chute's Neverland is loaded with them: as Gideon struggles between wanting Dorrie and wanting not to hurt her when he wanders away; as the village enthusiastically accommodates itself to the dueling reverends, for the gentle one is a newcomer to the town; as Gramma schemes to lure a much-needed cow out of mean old Thomas Clegg on his deathbed; as the Briggses try to hold together as a family even as they know that Gideon will abandon them when they most need him. Above all, there is Micah, Gideon's ten-year-old brother and virtually Greenwillow's emcee. An anxious, curious, garrulous boy, Micah interprets Greenwillow for us simply by never ceasing to ask it questions—interview it, so to say. And it is Micah who brings about the novel's climax, confronting the Devil that has cursed the Briggs family men. In fact, it is the lovable reverend, not the Devil, whom the confused Micah attacks (and is Saved by), showing us that it is love of God rather than fear of hell that holds Christianity together. The curse thus ends, Gideon stays put, and the Good Father slips out of town, His work done.

It's a beautiful story delightfully told. But without the restless Micah, it would lack energy, even a story line. *Micah* is the story. So when Loesser and his co–book writer, Lesser Samuels, decided to downplay Micah in favor of the youngest Briggs, Jabez, they limited their show. True, Micah is a literary more than a dramatic conceit; true as well, their Jabez, five-year-old John Megna, was an ace in the hole, a scene-stealer who added to rather than detracted from his scenes.

It was Megna who introduced us to Greenwillow, zigzagging happily across the stage of the Alvin Theatre bare-ass in a long shirt as villagers gathered for the opening chorus. A honey of a piece in tricky $^7/_4$ rhythm, "A Day Borrowed From Heaven" announced a score for the ages, perhaps Loesser's greatest set of music and lyrics—yes, even after *Where's Charley?* (1948), *Guys and Dolls* (1950), and *The Most Happy Fella* (1956). They's people at the door, all right, in a series of character pieces that, like all of Loesser's scores, invents its own sound style. It's folk music *for* rather than *by* folk, in the pounding defiance of Gideon's "Summertime Love" and his keening "Never Will I Marry"; in the off-kilter modal scales of Dorrie's "Walking Away Whistling" and "Faraway Boy"; in the reverends' battle of worldviews as they simultaneously extemporize for the pulpit in "The Sermon"; in the leaping ninth that distinguishes the show's anthem, "The Music of Home"; and in *Greenwillow*'s oddest number, Gramma and Clegg's "Could've Been a Ring," a kind of deadpan barn dance. Folding himself into Chute's idiom, Loesser expanded and even improved upon her, with Gideon's bitter invocation of the "flimsy-dimsy looking for true love," or Gramma and Clegg's "cozy-close to mostly."

So the novel sang after all, with George Roy Hill directing, Anthony Perkins and Ellen McCown as the lovers, Cecil Kellaway and William Chapman as the reverends, and Pert Kelton and Lee Cass as Gramma and Clegg. Joe Layton laid out the dances, mainly to bring forth the flavor of Greenwillow folk life—courting, Hallowe'en, and the like. However, it was not a great staging. Perkins did reveal an unexpected singing voice to match McCown's operetta soprano, and he turned "Never Will I Marry" into an aria with country-style wails, true Greenwillow. And though Kell-away's unsteady, toneless voice did not match Chapman's opera baritone, Kellaway had charm. But Peter Larkin's sets and Alvin Colt's costumes never told us where Greenwillow is—some of the chorus women looked like *Kiss Me, Kate*rs wearing the Islamic chador—and Hill should have forced Loesser and Samuels to trim their horribly verbose book. It has Chute's ring:

> JABEZ: Gideon! I've had a cookie this big! Big as the moon! And then another cookie, two rowdy buns, a bilberry tart, and Dorrie kissed me twice and I'm ready to go home.

However, its attempts at humor don't really land:

> GIDEON: Mr. Clegg, might I ask you a puzzling question?
> CLEGG: Many people do.
> GIDEON: Why are you so mean?
> CLEGG: That's the one many people do.

No, *Greenwillow*'s virtue is its score, the only medium through which Chute's novel can communicate to a theatre audience. A fable made of whimsy and atmosphere is readable, not playable. Onstage, it becomes too real, as real as . . . well, Brigadoon.

The critics were unable to parse the show on its March opening, in a season that had already seen *Take Me Along, The Sound of Music*, and *Fiorello!* before 1960 began. There was no pressure to discover a hit, only Kellaway and John Megna got the reviews, and *Greenwillow* lasted but three months, at that entirely on its advance sale.

It might have made an odd but lovely movie in 1956 or 1957, when the novel was enjoying its vogue, perhaps with Perkins and Kellaway them-selves, for the former was hot and the latter a beloved veteran. Today, *Greenwillow* is nothing but a cast album. Still, it stands out as a score burst-ing with feelings in a decade that seems all too often to be making musicals without any—*Let It Ride!, Mr. President, I Had a Ball, Baker Street, Breakfast at Tiffany's, How Now, Dow Jones, Sherry!, Golden Rainbow, Jimmy.*

Greenwillow was of course a Major Production—thus the big advance—but six weeks after it opened, in mid-April, came a Sleeper and a major hit, *Bye Bye Birdie*. If *Greenwillow* was a Rodgers-and-Hammerstein-era musical play, on the serious side and living within its singular enlightening reality, *Bye Bye Birdie* was a Rodgers-and-Hammerstein-era musical comedy. It had consistency of style and told a more or less believable tale. But it was also fast, satiric, and made for nothing but contemporary fun: Elvis gets drafted, kids war with parents, new director-choreographer plays host to new stars and new writers, and no one knows anyone who doesn't like it.

Actually, Gower Champion wasn't new as a director-choreographer. He had been dancing on Broadway as far back as 1939, in a talent-filled theme revue called *The Streets of Paris*, and directed and choreographed another revue, *Lend an Ear*, in 1948. But such a tidy little show had hardly any need of a master showman, and Champion won no réclame. During the 1950s, Champion and his wife and dancing partner, Marge, were largely performing for MGM. Again, he entirely staged a small revue, *Three For Tonight* (1955); but this is not how history is made. *Bye Bye Birdie* was the turning point, for now Champion was returning to Broadway to launch a career as a musical-comedy super-director. And, indeed, Champion's approach to the look and pacing of the form was brand-new. He liked scripts to zip from one number to the next. He liked songs to be staged, not just sung. And he liked the vocals not to cap a scene on a blackout but to take us from one scene to the next, the view changing as we watch.*

So, for instance, *Bye Bye Birdie* has one of the speediest expositions in the musical's history: Dick Van Dyke, songwriter, publisher, and manager of teen idol Conrad Birdie** (Dick Gautier), is losing him to the army. Van Dyke's longtime, exasperated fiancée, Chita Rivera, bustles in to say goodbye forever:

VAN DYKE: (frantic) My pills, where are my pills? The little white ones I
    take when I'm overwrought.
RIVERA: Here.

---

*Changing sets behind performers in the latter half of a number was an old device. But some thought it risked credibility to uproot characters who, in real time, were supposed to be stationary. Such stagings were used sparingly. Champion used them conventionally: he wanted us to think of them not as logistical expedients (because the scenery needs changing), but as narrative gestures (because the character isn't traveling—the story is).
**Derived from Conway Twitty, a pop idol of the time.

VAN DYKE: Not so much. Break it in half.

RIVERA: You're thirty-three years old, Albert. You can take a whole aspirin.

Inside of two minutes, we have not only the plot premise but the key to the two leads: he's a doofus, while she's the strength and the smarts of the outfit. It's Rivera who dreams up a last PR shot, when Conrad will sing "One Last Kiss," plant one on a fan's lips, and march off, all on television.

We're almost ready for the next scene—but not till a little music develops this odd couple. It's Rivera's vocal, with spoken interjections from Van Dyke, "An English Teacher." Plot number and ballad at once, this is the Heroine's Wanting Song. But there's a catch to this one. She doesn't just want him. She wants him out of the music business and in academia, where they'll be not boy-got-girl but professor and faculty wife. The daydreaming Rivera and the distracted Van Dyke give Champion something to present during the singing—his endless, hapless search for some pointless object till she calmly and instantly finds and hands it to him. Still urging the show onward, Champion brings Rivera before the traveler curtain to finish the number alone while the stagehands ready the next surprise:

The kids. In "The Telephone Hour," the teenagers of Sweet Apple, Ohio, tie up the phone lines to discuss the dating status of the show's second couple (Susan Watson and Michael J. Pollard, before his eerie-nerd phase in such films as *Bonnie and Clyde*). Champion called for a stage-filling box of cubicles in which sixteen boys and girls hurled argot at the audience ("What's the story, morning glory?"), while one boy, a young Van Dyke without a Rivera, fruitlessly sought a partner for the prom in a pubescent squeak.

Next, the American family: Watson is the girl Conrad is to kiss, so he's staying at her home with her father (Paul Lynde), mother (Marijane Maricle), and little brother (Johnny Borden). Father is that favorite American character, the Irascible Curmudgeon, Mother is long-suffering, and, in a twist, Junior is no problem but a cute little guy who's always subverting Papa's tirades by being helpful and respectful. When the grown-ups are out chasing their runaway kids, Borden offers Lynde his peashooter. This is a perfect setup for the golf-cart Caligula that Lynde played for most of his career. "A peashooter?" he violently crabs. "What good's a . . ." Then, eyes tightening as his head wobbles in misanthropic glee, he cries, "Give it to me!"

This social cross section gives *Bye Bye Birdie* a structural unity that many musical comedies lack. They seem to take place anywhere and for unknown reasons, while *Birdie* deals with something that actually happened. When American kids claimed a music of their own, they also began to create their own culture: clothes, language, morality. So the show must present us with the opposing gods of the warring societies: the Rebel and the Mom.

Birdie, of course, is the Rebel, suited up in Marlon Brando's *Wild One* leather jacket and, on his first appearance, in a crowd scene in Grand Central Terminal, absolutely silent, almost totemic but for his sleazy grin. In fact, he is a piece of redneck trash, opening beer cans so they gush all over Lynde's kitchen and romancing Watson on *The Ed Sullivan Show* with "Okay, brace yourself, chick!" But when he sings, he displays the husky baritone and samba-ing body parts. Like Elvis, Conrad has It, and we see why he has inspired American girlhood to create "the Conrad Birdie scream" and to sing "We Love You, Conrad" ten thousand times as an act of devotion.

Van Dyke is not only a doofus but a mama's boy, and Mama (Kay Medford) has taken nagging and pushing to an art form. Van Dyke wants her to ride in a cab to avoid the crowded subway:

MEDFORD: Nothing is too crowded for a mother. I'll go during the rush hour, that's the worst time. Wait a minute—how many blocks is it, after all? Only a hundred and seven. I'll walk.

Naturally, Medford loathes Rivera, making numberless remarks about her ethnic background and her age:

MEDFORD: This is Rose? I can't believe it. She looks like Margo when they took her out of Shangri-la.

Conrad is there so that, when he finally departs for the army, society can be made whole again; and Van Dyke's mother is there so that Van Dyke has someone to stand up to and conquer so he can finally deserve Rivera.

One reason why *Bye Bye Birdie* was a sleeper was that, except for Champion, it was almost entirely a project of nobodies. Rivera, of course, was known for her Anita in *West Side Story* (1957). But Van Dyke, Medford, and Gautier were unestablished, and Lynde, after a solid debut in *New Faces of 1952*, got lost in minor television work and touring shows that never made New York.

Above all, composer Charles Strouse, lyricist Lee Adams, and librettist Michael Stewart were first-timers with a Broadway show all their own. Their expertise, then, is astonishing. If Stewart's book is adroit, clever, and—as Champion demanded—extra-quick on the draw, Strouse and Adams' songs are a course in how to find the emotional reality in farce while centering its sense of humor, Musical Comedy 101. The rock-and-roll spoofs, "Honestly Sincere" and "One Last Kiss," are so apt that out of context they are pure rock and roll. Similarly, "One Boy," a burlesque of the ballads teenage girls love, became a ballad on its own when Rivera sang a chorus while pondering Van Dyke and their troubled engagement.

Champion's restless staging emphasized this richness of texture, as when Susan Watson sang "How Lovely To Be a Woman" while changing from a frilly negligée into sock-hop jeans and a sweater, expanding a character song into a comic bit while underscoring the show's overall teens-against-the-world theme. Champion highlighted it in "Honestly Sincere," letting Conrad's overwhelming of the Sweet Apple girls in his skintight jumpsuit of gold lamé take in a brand-new enthusiast, the mayor's mousy wife.

Paul Lynde had his moment in "Kids," a curse upon the rock-and-roll generation wittily set to a Charleston—the rock and roll of the father's own youth. In between the lyrics were spoken assaults, such as "Why don't they lower the draft age . . . to around eleven?" Best of all is an ensemble number, "Normal American Boy," in which cynical reporters grill Van Dyke and Rivera, Conrad ogles his fans, and we get a look at the dishonesty in American celebrity marketing—yes, even from Van Dyke and Rivera, who at one point simultaneously offer bizarrely contradictory stories of Conrad's past.

Bye Bye Birdie is without question a fine composition. But it was Champion who assured the piece its first success. Aside from the speedy playing tempo, the cartoon-bright designs, and such novelties as the overture's starting with a vocal of "We Love You, Conrad" and continuing with footage of the singer in action, there was the choreography itself. This took in a cheer-up dance for Van Dyke and two bereaved Birdie fans after "Put On a Happy Face," an ensemble number for "A Lot Of Livin' To Do," and two ballets for Rivera and the men dancers, "How To Kill a Man" (by firing squad at first, but also guillotine, poison, knife, bomb, and a mob hit) and an orgy at a Shriners' convention.*

Topping all this was the simplest dance possible. Yet it was another novelty even so. With the plot wound up and the stage cleared of all but Van Dyke and Rivera, the pair sang "Rosie." They danced a bit. And then—after all that generation war and culture war and Paul Lynde wanting to murder everyone under forty—the two embraced and the music went *yes* and the curtain came smiling down.

Even without Champion, *Birdie* went on to classic status. London liked it, Hollywood and television have made their versions, and isn't it time for a revival? Tommy Tune almost gave us one, in a touring package for him and Ann Reinking (later Lenora Nemetz) in 1991. Tune as doofus is an odd proposition. He's not even the protagonist of his own story. Yes, he's the lead: but his girl friend runs the show. Originally, Rivera had most of the numbers. Even Van Dyke's one real love song, "Baby, Talk To Me," was staged around her, in a bit of set representing a bar, where four men in close harmony backed Van Dyke (singing over the phone) while Rivera vacillated at the center of the action.

Isn't Tommy Tune a bit too . . . well, successful for the role? Working with the 1991 director, Gene Saks, Tune evened up the two leads somewhat by dropping "How To Kill a Man" and adding a solo and dance for himself, "I Took a Giant Step," after he squelches his mother. He also brought Mother into the score (Kay Medford—and Michael J. Pollard, by the way—never sang a note in 1960) with a second new number, "He's Mine," a challenge duet for her and Rose. Further, Tune found a place for the title tune, first heard in the film, sung under the credits by Ann-

---

*Note that the grown-ups in this show have their bacchanalia to match the kids' didoes. Musical comedy—unlike the sterner musical play—makes no value judgments. Its credo is: everyone is equally not guilty of everything.

Margret. Tune's tour did good business to appreciative audiences, yet it never ventured into New York.

A week after *Birdie*, the third Broadway musical of 1960 appeared, to close after two and a half weeks, *From A To Z*. Virtually the last of its kind, this was a revue built around a headliner, with an ensemble of fourteen fresh faces and an anthology of writers including Woody Allen, Jerry Herman, Fred Ebb, Mary Rodgers, Jay Thompson, and Marshall Barer. The headliner was Hermione Gingold and the ensemble included singers Stuart Damon and Paula Stewart, dancers Michael Fesco and Nora Kovach, comic Bob Dishy, Alvin Epstein miming a man changing into a bathing suit on a beach under a raincoat, Elliott Reid spoofing television coverage of a political convention, Kelly Brown trying out another of those nostalgic soft-shoe numbers, and so on. The first-act finale observed a venerable revue tradition by spoofing a current hit show; *From A To Z* chose *The Sound of Music*. Gingold was the nanny, to six of the boys and a pigtailed Stewart, all in sailor suits. Generally, the evening was the great Gingold and some good-enough talent in indifferent material, much too underpowered an offering in an age that enjoyed multi-star revues at home on television.

A week after Gingold came an operetta starring Maureen O'Hara, *Christine*. The times were as hostile to operetta as to revue, so *Christine* billed itself as "a new musical." Sorry: *Greenwillow* and *Bye Bye Birdie* were new musicals. *Christine* was a new operetta, with opera-weight voices, an exotic setting, and a few comic specialists to handle the humor while everyone else emotes melodically with extreme prejudice.

Of course, it's easy to mock a show that *today* sounds like an impossible dream: whites playing Asian Indians in dark makeup, a plot blended of *The King and I* and *Happy Hunting*, actors with names like Bhaskar, Mai-Lan, and Jinja. But *Christine* in fact embodies a notion that the musical had been toying with since the 1940s, especially after *Oklahoma!*: "good" ideas for musicals create mediocrity, while offbeat ideas create unique shows.

Based on Hilda Wernher's novel *My Indian Family*—and with a book co-written by Eastern guru Pearl S. Buck—*Christine* tells of an Irishwoman traveling to Akbarabad to visit her daughter, who has married an Indian doctor (opera baritone Morley Meredith). But here's a shock: the daughter is dead, and soon enough the mother, too, is attracted to the doctor.

Movie star Maureen O'Hara had never done a stage musical and sang but little in Hollywood. Still, like Anthony Perkins she revealed a trump instrument. That's odd, and this is odder: composer Sammy Fain and lyricist Paul Francis Webster had never created anything more musically expansive than Fain's *Flahooley* (1951) or Webster's words to Rudolf Friml's new tunes in the 1954 *Rose Marie* movie remake. Perhaps most typical of the pair were their movie pop hits, "Secret Love" and "Love Is a Many-Splendored Thing." Yet for *Christine* they conscientiously created a dense and soaring score, eighteen separate numbers plus reprises and dances. There are floppo songs—"How To Pick a Man a Wife," "The Lovely Girls of Akbarabad"—but there is also music of urgent melodic power, not least when Meredith charged up to a high G flat at the climax of the line "All life is beauty born of pain!"

A show without appeal, then, *Christine* played only 12 performances, more because of the unattractive subject matter than the quality of the piece itself. It is worth noting that Columbia's A and R man, Goddard Lieberson, recorded *Christine* even after its terrible reviews, in an extremely full reading that made it one of the longest cast albums of the LP era.

The next full-scale show came in at the start of the 1960–61 season, and this one offers a bit of breakaway. Of our book shows so far, *Greenwillow* was earnest musical play, *Bye Bye Birdie* pure musical comedy, and *Christine* a lot of very grand singing: all traditional genres. But *Irma la Douce* marked the emergence of not so much a form as an identity: the West End hit. True, Broadway had hosted many an English title around the turn of the century; *Florodora* and its fellows colonized Broadway. But by 1920, visitations were few. *The Boy Friend*, in 1954, was the exception that proves the rule.

Irma la Douce changed that. Originally a French show (the title means "Irma the Sweet") with words by Alexandre Breffort and music by a frequent composer for Edith Piaf, Marguerite Monnot, *Irma* went to London in translation in 1958 under Peter Brook's direction. It was a smash. Still, it might not have come to New York but for David Merrick's habit of importing English plays—*Look Back in Anger* (1957), *The Entertainer* (1958), and, in this same season, *Becket* and *A Taste of Honey*. Merrick had never brought over an English musical. Nobody was bringing them over, because they were thought too parochial, bizarre, or just plain twee.

But this one wasn't even English, was it? Set in Paris, it tells of the love of a prostitute and a law student, comically and erotically and without the slightest taste of the avant-garde in its staging. That is, the show itself is not unconventional: its attitude is. It treats underworld folkways from the viewpoint of the underworld. These are to an extent the people of *The Threepenny Opera*—only here they're supposed to be lovable.

This is a "naughty" piece, not a political one. The score is integrated, melodious, delightful. Using a few key French slang words such as *mec* ("pimp")* and *grisbi* ("dough"), the adapters—Julian More, David Heneker, and Monty Norman—often strayed far from Breffort's lyrics, in effect creating an English musical that is somehow trashy and elegant at once, or perhaps simply an elegant showcase for trashy characters. "Très Très Snob" (rewritten as "Sons of France" for New York) introduces a den of cutthroats with such élan that one is suckered into finding them harmlessly amusing. By the time naïve young Nestor finds his Irma, the audience is rooting for them as surely as for *Birdie*'s Rosie and Albert.

Elizabeth Seal, Keith Michell, and Clive Revill were the principals as in London, with an ensemble of thirteen men, for Merrick wanted to bring Brook's staging over just as it was, with those wonderful André Popp orchestrations and that crazy Piccadilly Montmartre spirit . . . and new choreography, new lyrics, new vocal arrangements, new snow in the Christmas scene . . . you know. Still, it was essentially London's *Irma la Douce*; and it was a hit here, too, inaugurating the present era of émigré English musicals. This, ironically, has led us from such parochial and twee events as *Lock Up Your Daughters* (closed in Boston in this very year of

---

*Actually, *mec* once denoted any male involved in illegal sex activity, including not only those who agented for prostitutes but those who prostituted themselves. Over the years, the word lost its edge and became an affectionate term; it is now in French dictionaries, virtually the equivalent of our "guy." The rest of Irma's argot was *poule* ("chicken"=prostitute), *milieu* ("underworld"), and *"Dis-donc"* ("So tell me . . ."), along with a few standard words such as *amour*. The pointillistically applied lingo and an accordion in the pit gave *Irma* such atmosphere that no one seemed to notice the strong British inflection in such phrases as the song title "She's Got the Lot" (originally "Elle a du Chien": "She's Not Half Bad").

1960) and *Pickwick* (a fast flop in 1965) to the ecumenically successful pop operas of Andrew Lloyd Webber and the two French guys.

Two and a half weeks after *Irma la Douce*, *Tenderloin* arrived. This was what we might call an "encore" show, the second by a team that found its first collaboration stimulating. The classic such instance is the reuniting of Rodgers and Hammerstein, director Rouben Mamoulian, choreographer Agnes de Mille, and the Theatre Guild management for *Carousel* (1945) after *Oklahoma!* (1943). *Tenderloin* encored *Fiorello!* (1959): composer Jerry Bock, lyricist Sheldon Harnick, book writers Jerome Weidman and George Abbott, director Abbott, and producers Robert E. Griffith and Harold S. Prince trying another period piece on municipal corruption in New York City (and even bringing along *Fiorello!* players Eileen Rodgers and, out of the chorus, Ron Husmann). Their source was Samuel Hopkins Adams' lengthy 1959 novel of the same name, based on a real-life crusade by the Reverend Dr. Charles H. Parkhurst to close down the system by which the authorities connived at the proliferation of gambling dens and brothels. To quote the doctor himself: "The polluted harpies, under the pretense of governing a city, are feeding night and day on its quivering vitals. They are a lying, perjured, rum-soaked and libidinous lot."

Such words from the Christian pulpit were sensation, and Parkhurst did instigate a thorough cleanup of the police department and an end to the Tenderloin. One can see why all concerned saw in this a dandy show: Puritan grays and blacks against the riotous colors of the demimonde, an opportunistic but likable young man working for both sides, the minister's spy mission into an underworld rookery dressed as a punter, hymns stacked against odes to Baal . . . it sounds terrific.

And it was. *But:* because the minister was the star role (for Shakespearean Maurice Evans), and because the heroine of the main plot and the hero of the secondary love plot were on the Puritans' side, one was constantly asked to sympathize with the wrong people. Police corruption is indefensible, yes—but the do-gooders weren't fun and the Tenderloin folk were. Typically, the prostitutes and touts had the captivating numbers, such as "Little Old New York," the ironic "Reform," and the epic first-act finale, "How the Money Changes Hands." The Christians' main musical portion was "Good Clean Fun," whose patter section praises games like "musical chairs" and "the parson's cat." Are you kidding? One of the reasons why *Irma la Douce* found enchantment in a Parisian tenderloin was the lack of any challenging morality. *Irma*'s cast included a corrupt cop—"Oh, it's you, Inspector," said Clive Revill as George S. Irving slipped into Revill's den of thieves; "I thought it was the police"—but no crusading minister or well-intentioned parishioners.

So *Tenderloin* was something odd: an extremely well wrought show with a character disorder. One could greatly admire but not always enjoy it, despite a score that actually improves on *Fiorello!*'s. Look at how cleverly the authors start their piece: three characters, all from the Tenderloin, appear one after the other, spotlit in darkness, to speak briefly of why each is part of this shell game of a subculture, each ending with the reminder that America is "the land of opportunity." Now the church choir is seen, singing "Bless This Land," a psalm on the theme of "opportunity for all." The Reverend himself shows up at his pulpit, denouncing and exhorting. "People of New York City," he concludes, "we must close down the Tenderloin"—but, as he vanishes, the Tenderloin people reappear in their spotlights, more and more of them, till at last the stage fills with rowdies and slumming swells, drunks and pickpockets, the hefty bordello madam and the crooked cops, all slamming home "Little Old New York" as an anthem of freedom, especially from crusading reverends.

It's fine showmanship, a unique start to a unique show; but didn't the authors see the trap they'd sprung on themselves? *Fiorello!*, also about a crusading good guy, isolates the bad guys. We dislike the little we see of them. But *Tenderloin* is very much about the bad guys, and they aren't bad. They're outlaws, but mainly because they don't want to play the parson's cat. They gamble, drink, and have sex. That's bad?

Even the show's outstanding number, "Artificial Flowers" (a hit record for Bobby Darin), was sung by Ron Husmann, as the young opportunist who bridges the two worlds. Though the church choir sings backup for him, the song really is a put-on at their expense, a story ballad goofing on the kind of poor-but-honest tragedy that church choirs believe in. And, indeed, how does the show end? In Detroit, whither the disgraced minister has carried his crusade. Once more we see him preaching about "the good fight"—and once more the whores and lowlifes roar out of the darkness to sing him down with: "Little Old Detroit."

He has the right, but they have the art. *Tenderloin*'s skewed morality irritated most of the critics, and it lasted only 216 performances. Like *Greenwillow*, it was nothing more than a cast album for cultists—till Encores! brought it back in 2000 in the usual slimmed-down concert. It played well, especially when Tenderloiners Debbie Gravitte and Yvette Cason were strutting around—but then, isn't that always to be this show's problem? Moreover, one of *Tenderloin*'s original glories was Cecil Beaton's lavish *fin-de-siècle* designs, with the picture hats and *Police Gazette* tights and riding clothes. Take these away—and Joe Layton's evocative dances—and your concert is false history. Some musicals don't really need the décor. This one reveled in it.

The next musical of 1960 arrived on November 3. It was another star vehicle, though for this one the star had to be discovered first: Tammy Grimes in *The Unsinkable Molly Brown*. Meredith Willson's return to Broadway after *The Music Man* (1957), this piece was comparably sunny, antic, and loving, and not without some good old country wisdom. *Tenderloin*'s cynical wrestling match between God and the Devil introduces us, however lightly, to a growing use of adult and even wholly dark themes in the sixties musical: *I Can Get It For You Wholesale*'s anti-hero, *Man of La Mancha*'s Inquisition, *Cabaret*'s Nazis, *Maggie Flynn*'s race riots, the hopelessness of *Golden Boy*'s boxer or even of *The Happy Time*'s photographer, so important to others yet so worthless to himself. But *Molly Brown* is one of those sit-back-and-enjoy-it shows. Tragedy tomorrow.

We expect something unconventional from Willson (as before writing music and lyrics but now assigning the book to Richard Morris) after *The Music Man*'s songs made of train conversation, con man's pitch, piano lesson, and ladies' gossip nonsense. The title role, too, will be out of the ordinary, for while Grimes has a leading man, Harve Presnell, she is seldom off the stage during a very long show.

Understudy and vacation replacement to Kim Stanley in William Inge's *Bus Stop* (1955) at the age of twenty-one, Grimes first played a musical's title role in 1956, in *The Amazing Adele*, an out-of-town casualty, so obscure that it is unknown even to those who can sing their way through all six of Barbara Cook's flop musicals. One revue and jobs in straight plays then led to *Molly Brown*: and here was Grimes heading her own big-budget show at the Winter Garden, albeit with below-title billing (and thus, by the absurd rules of the day, a Best *Supporting* Tony). As the real-life girl from nowhere, Missouri, who marries a miner, accidentally burns up $300,000, tries and fails to crash Denver society, conquers Europe, and commands a lifeboat at the sinking of the *Titanic*, Grimes was a hellion with allure, a grande dame with "ain't," and the toast of Broadway.

But then, the show itself is solid. It's a good story, because Molly's rise is vexed by love for Presnell, a decent, rough-hewn guy who doesn't enjoy social climbing the way she does. And yet she's not a climber, just curious to see what else there is besides Missouri. So behind all the high riot of the miners' saloon, the suave color of the Parisian and Monte Carlo beau monde, and Act Two, Scene Eight—"The mid-Atlantic. Shortly after 2:30 A.M., April 15, 1912"—there is that favorite American love story of two people perfectly suited but for a single gigantic little hitch.

Presnell was one of the strongest performers ever to partner a musical-comedy heroine in *her* vehicle, a fine big presence with a voice to match. After these two, there is no more in the huge cast to cite here, for unlike *The Music Man*, with its folklore and village grandees and grieving little brother, *Molly Brown* is a two-person story elaborated by Sights and Sounds. It's a busier *Annie Get Your Gun* (whose plot, by the way, is very similar: she needs, he resents, she gives in). Dore Schary was *Molly Brown*'s director, but choreographer Peter Gennaro, designers Oliver Smith and Miles White, and dance-music arranger Sol Berkowitz were very crucial in the construction of this patchwork, especially in a replica of the turkey trot called "Up Where the People Are," a dazzling dance played by one of the hottest bands since George Olsen's boys sat in the pit for *Whoopee* in 1928.

As for Willson, *Molly Brown*'s score is not on the level of *The Music Man*'s but retains many of its odd features—the use of leitmotifs, speaking in rhythm over orchestral punctuation, a stream-of-consciousness soliloquy (for Presnell in "Leadville Johnny Brown"), a male quartet (just once, and in a number accompanied solely on guitar), and those odd lyrics that border on dada ("Keemo kimo derro art"). The hit was *Molly*'s ambitious Wanting Song, "I Ain't Down Yet." But the music is full of fetchingly strange pieces, as in the miners' number, "Belly Up To the Bar, Boys," in which all the solo lines are pitched at the uncomfortable top of the tenor range; or in "Dolce Far Niente," a seductive waltz for two opposing voices that sounds like any composer *but* Willson. Look at it this way: *The Music Man* is about Iowa. *Molly Brown* is about Being a Crazy Musical-Comedy Hit on Meredith Willson's Unique Terms.

Yet another star vehicle happened along in mid-December, *Wildcat*. This was Lucille Ball's Broadway debut, as an energetic but unreliable oil driller in the old Southwest. She has one point of vulnerability, a lame sister. Ball gets involved with a champion drill-team boss who may or may not have killed a man in El Paso. He has a point of vulnerability, too: he has invented a Girl Back Home as an emotional crutch. He also has a sidekick to go with Ball's sister.

In short, this was musical comedy of an older type, the kind that can compete with *Birdie* or *Molly Brown* in its production values but not in its story, a hodgepodge of Devices: the bickering leads who finally love; the "Here I Come, You Musical-Comedy World!" number ("Hey, Look Me Over!"); the sidekick soothing the sister's shyness with a dance lesson; the leads' challenge duet ("You're a Liar!"); the cheer-up number ("El Sombrero") when Ball makes a fool of herself at a fiesta; and so on. N. Richard Nash wrote the book, Cy Coleman and Carolyn Leigh wrote the score, Michael Kidd staged the whole piece, designer Peter Larkin devised a spectacular oil strike for the finale, and Keith Andes, Paula Stewart, and Clifford David filled out the leads.

The evening never quite came together, and it was nobody's fault but Ball's. The tuneful score, the able supporting players, and Kidd's leadership are what musical comedy thrives on; and even the ridiculously unbelievable script is not unworthy of musical-comedy tradition. I assure you, *Lady, Be Good!* (1924), the original *Anything Goes* (1934), and *Something For the Boys* (1943) are even more unbelievable. By 1960, however, the better musical comedies really were good stories well told.

Consider this confrontation scene from *The Unsinkable Molly Brown*— a good-time show, I say again, but a show with a center:

MOLLY: We're goin' *home* to Europe.
JOHNNY: (on to her) Oh, no . . . We're goin' home all right—to Leadville.
MOLLY: (marching right up to him) The hell ya say. I ain't livin' in Colorado. The air is much too thin.

JOHNNY: Better learn to breathe it 'cause we're livin' in Colorado.

MOLLY: *I'm* livin' in Europe.

JOHNNY: (the law) No, yer not. You're my wife and you'll live under the roof I give ya and by God, it's gonna be in Leadville.

The mention of God brings Molly's father into the scene. A pious man, he is horrified by Molly's defiance of her own marriage. "To hell with him," she says, and then, goaded beyond reason: "To hell with the Church."

At which, her father cracks her a real bad one right across the face. "May God have mercy on you," he says, not meaning it, and he storms out of the room, leaving Molly and Johnny in such angry despair of each other that they (temporarily) part.

It's good, strong writing: real people in real trouble. There is absolutely nothing like this in *Wildcat*, though it deals with the same two characters: she wants to *be* and he's content with what he *is*. *Wildcat* never set the two in any genuine conflict. "You're a Liar!" was the most of it, as he rejects her and she bawls out Lucy Ricardo's *"Waaah!"*

Wildcat's worst problem was Ball's lack of formal savvy. She couldn't sing—*really* couldn't sing—and while at some point in the run she dropped two of her six numbers (the title song and "That's What I Want For Janie"), her rasp remained a test. Nor, truly, was this the right *kind* of musical for a clown. Ball shouldn't have tried a conventional two-roman-tic-couples story show, but rather something with the daffy opportunities of the sort that made her television series classic—the Vitameatavegamin commercial, the assembly-line chocolates, the Italian wine making. In one *Wildcat* moment, Ball had a scene with a fat sheriff. The two were standing stage right, at the door to the jail. He invited her inside. She eyed him with sardonic mistrust for a long moment, and finally said, "D'you ever know a guy named Fred Mertz?" It was a cheap and dishonest laugh, and it typified Ball's appearance in a form unsuited to her gifts.

To her credit, she tried to make a go of it, running the show on badly mixed notices and the one hit tune for five months, till she collapsed onstage and the show folded. At least no backer lost out: Ball was the show's sole investor.

Ten days after *Wildcat* came a fourth star vehicle, *Do Re Mi*. Here's another old-fashioned two-couples structure—comic leads Phil Silvers and Nancy Walker are married, and young lovers John Reardon and Nancy Dussault will be. But *Do Re Mi* is up-to-date in the authorship of its songs, for Jule Styne and Betty Comden and Adolph Green produced four scores in this decade. *Do Re Mi* also shows a slight tendency toward the edgy, serious sixties style of musical, looking in on mob infiltration of the music industry. More, it offered in Silvers a hero who is a pathetic bottom-feeder. Not a cute dithering nincompoop like *Bye Bye Birdie*'s Albert Peterson, but a loser endlessly scheming to Win Big. "All I need is an angle," he keeps telling us, as he neglects his patient wife, subjects himself to absurd humiliations, flatters and pushes and connives. It's based on the character that Silvers had been playing since *High Button Shoes* (1947) and had perfected in his two television series. But that character was blithely comic, and this character, *Do Re Mi*'s Hubie Cram, was very nearly tragic. For all his angles, he's a man who finally comes to realize that he has nothing . . . except a really wonderful marriage.

The teaming of Silvers and Walker was inspired, especially in a script (by Garson Kanin, who also directed) that gave them something to bite on. Silvers was the protagonist, no question, and Walker did disappear for stretches while an increasingly bizarre plot worked its way through a satire on pop music (from rock and roll to folk). But two domestic scenes made the Crams alarming and irresistible. Act One had the alarming, in "Take a Job," when Walker nagged at Silvers to get into something secure while he plotted and fumed: dueling monologues. Act Two offered the irresistible, in the couple's bedtime, each reading a newspaper. "Did a turtle bite a woman in Asbury Park in yours?" Walker asked. Then came her set piece, "Adventure," one of the grandest comedy songs ever, as he alternately prompted her and dozed. Here we learn that she, at least, already knows that it's a wonderful marriage, because it's never boring. "You should have married Seymour Brilkin!" Silvers sang; and Walker answered in the mock-recitative that opera buff Green loves to sneak into his shows. And, indeed, came then a Mad Scene—a bolero complete with trumpets pealing out like the band in the Plaza del Toro on corrida day and woodwinds tripping up the scale with the flash of a hundred capes. The scene's self-spoofing pastiche is a reminder that, even in this time of dark new realism, musical comedy is supposed to be silly.

But if musical comedy is getting darker here and there, does its very look have to change? *Bye Bye Birdie*, in typical early-sixties realism, was all pastels. *Tenderloin*, as befits its period flair, bore the look of old engravings and posters. Boris Aronson's sets for *Do Re Mi*, however, sought an impressionistic feel for its nightclubs, bars, Zen Pancake Parlor, and recording studio. Aronson's original plans decorated the studio with Warholesque drawings (of such icons as *Mad* magazine's Alfred E. Neuman) and an explicit spelling-out of "[Ka]ndinsky." Even more unusual was the first scene, at the Casacabana club, where the back tables were occupied by drawn figures rather than actors and, here and there, a drawing paired with an actor who would "talk" to and even fondle the drawing.

Do Re Mi ran a year but failed to pay off, a sign of how expensive it had become not only to mount but to maintain a musical. In 1955 or so, a year's run invariably paid off. This show was a bit ahead of its public in any case. Aronson was not appreciated till two classics later in the decade, *Fiddler on the Roof* and *Cabaret*, and the Sondheim-Prince musicals of the 1970s. And, aside from "Make Someone Happy," the score did not popularize the show as it had done for the three songwriters' *Bells Are Ringing* (1956). Yet this is a better score. Not as much fun, perhaps, but richer in plot and character numbers. Of course, *Bells Are Ringing* doesn't have characters. The playwright with writer's block? The composer-dentist? The sleazy bookie? Types out of the catalogue. What *Bells Are Ringing* had was Judy Holliday, character enough to keep a show running for twenty-seven months.

What *Do Re Mi* had was, mainly, the con man who cannot make it and doesn't get it: *Pal Joey* without the sex. "It's Legitimate," a musical scene in which Silvers located three old cronies (each in his own set insert), pooled their talents, and incorporated, is an impressive construction, a real case of music eating up the script to sing and dance the plot; and "Ambition," a duet for Silvers and Dussault, his new singing discovery, found lively musical correspondence for his spiel and her naïveté. There was nothing this creative in *Bells Are Ringing*. But then, on *Gypsy* (1959), Styne had been exposed to lyricist Stephen Sondheim's prodding musical genius. Styne had long been a facile tunesmith; now he was a composer. *Do Re Mi*'s score is notable for the large amount of fake pop—"All You Need Is a Quarter," the folky, minor-key "Cry Like the Wind," the novelty jest "What's New at the Zoo?," and some scene-setting bits—abutting all those nervy story numbers, as if two different teams wrote the score. The music is so rich that the best number is a throwaway, the opening, "Waiting."

It's a shocker, in a way. The overture was played to Aronson's bizarre show curtain of seven jukeboxes lined and piled up to create one huge jukebox, as intricate and powerful as the god of a primitive people. As the overture ended, this curtain rose on the Casacabana to a punishing drum beat broken into by jazzy brass solos, and . . . oh, there was Nancy Walker, alone and unhappy at a table stage left. She's waiting—as always, we learn—for Silvers, on their tenth wedding anniversary. The brass punctuate her lament, an exasperated bagatelle of a piece that rhymes only twice and at one point goes into nonsense syllables. It's over within two minutes, yet it tells us what to expect from story and score, gives us one of those nifty Star Entrances Without an Actual Entrance, and prepares us for an offbeat musical comedy, very funny but at times uncomfortably honest in its delineation of character. This is the decade of *Gypsy*'s children.

Do Re Mi came in on Boxing Day, the last musical of 1960, but let us slip just a bit into 1961 for one more show, the Carol Channing revue *Show Girl*. This started as *Show Business*, in 1959, on a fourteen-month tour that ended with this stand in New York. Trim and inexpensive to run, it made money, but it was not good news for the revue as a form. Written almost entirely by Charles Gaynor, *Show Girl* was Carol Channing's nightclub act expanded by one comic (Wally Griffin out of town and Jules Munshin in New York) and Les Quat' Jeudis ("The Four Thursdays"), a French singing quartet. Everyone had his spots—Munshin did a sketch-and-song spoof of the international classical-stuff impresario Sol Hurok (as "S. Eureka Presents"). There were also teamings, as when Channing and Munshin portrayed Lynn Fontanne and Alfred Lunt in a witless sketch about actors maintaining the theatres named after them, or when Munshin joined the Thursdays to sing a bawdy march called "The Girl Who Lived in Montparnasse."

But the evening really was a one-hander. The curtain rose on Channing, upstage, preening to her applause and then striding forward to sing "I want to be a show girl . . ." in those amusingly unscrupulous bass tones of hers; the best thing all night was Channing's impersonation of Marlene Dietrich's nightclub act; and the all-important first-act finale was given not to the ensemble but to Channing alone.

As always, this was a burlesque. "Carol's Musical Theatre" purported to lampoon the change from old-time musical comedy for the tired businessman to today's "significant" (as she said) musical plays "for the tired nuclear physicist." There were three Before and Afters, on the opening chorus, the ballad, and the New Dance Sensation.* So the twenties-flavored "Join Us in a Little Cup of Tea (boys)" is challenged by the opening of a musical treating the Johnstown Flood, *Turbulent Waters'* "This Is a Darned Fine Funeral." The "Tea" number is uninspired as parody, and the "Funeral," despite a vaguely Rodgers and Hammerstein flavor, doesn't relate to anything one had actually seen in a musical by January 1961. Similarly, "In Our Tiny Little Weeny Nest For Two" is dreary, whereas such old songs were in fact loving and tuneful. (Think of *The Boy Friend*'s "A Room in Bloomsbury," a much better parody.) The modern correspondence, "Love Is a Sickness," is just stupid. As for the dance numbers, "The Yahoo Step" catches the vapidity of the originals but not their paradoxical tang—these were, after all, song hits, for example "Charleston" and "The Varsity Drag"— and the modernist "Switchblade Bess" is ridiculous. "I'm a cat," Channing sang. "I'm a kook." This is the world of the beats, not of musical comedy.

Yet Gaynor was on to something. It hadn't happened yet fully enough to call for purgative burlesque—there are switchblades in *West Side Story*, but uniquely so. Still, the American musical was indeed going to go out of sheer fun into mixed feelings. As I've noted, we've had the merest soupçon already. But it is in 1960 that two writers who had moved from musical comedy to operetta and the musical play decided to try something truly serious. Their show stands on the short list of classics, though it was reviled in its day and is still regarded with suspicion. Its score protects it; I place it with *Show Boat*, *Carousel*, and *Follies*. Still, cynics loathe its romanticism, fascist lefties rage at its democratic idealism, and intellectuals scorn its simple solutions to complex problems.

*All three Befores were culled from the first-act finale of Gaynor's revue *Lend an Ear* (1948), Channing's first big break. This finale was itself a spoof of the twenties musical, called "The Gladiola Girl." Interestingly, what in 1948 was thought commentative was now, in 1961, representative. That is: in 1948, Gaynor was goofing on old musical comedy. In 1961, he was simply reviving it by using the same material.

But it offers no solutions. On the contrary, this show says that the solution is something one can try to implement but never successfully execute, because its plot derives from perhaps the most misanthropic novel ever written. The show remains, with *Cabaret* and possibly one or two others, one of the essential sixties musicals.

2

TWICE AS MUCH GRIEF

CAMELOT

What do Alan Jay Lerner and Frederick Loewe write after *My Fair Lady* (1956)? Not since Rodgers and Hammerstein had to follow *Oklahoma!* and *Carousel* was a writing team so scrutinized and the jealousy of some show folk so pointed and waiting. *Gigi* (1958) seemed wise: a film, first of all, far out of the Broadway battleground, and, second, a highly Parisian affair, so in contrast to Shavian London. True, Lerner and Loewe were once again giving us the non-courtship of an unformed young woman by an older man who talks his songs. True as well, *Gigi* was a gigantic hit, so Lerner and Loewe *still* had the Encore Problem: how to avoid being compared unfavorably with themselves.

How far can one get from *Pygmalion? The Good Earth?* The Koran? How about a medieval legend about the guy who invents democracy while his best friend screws his wife? A legend, moreover, told with anachronistic references to Mafeking Night, algebra, Freud, and Victorian fox hunting side by side with long-dead tricks of dialect; with brutal violence, wit, poetry, and comedy?

T. H. White's *The Once and Future King* appeared in 1958, although, like another English epic in which good citizens take on the fascist beast, J.R.R. Tolkien's chronicle of Middle-Earth, it was written and partly published in the late 1930s. White based his saga on Thomas Malory's *Le Morte Darthur*, whose "central theme," White declared, "is to find an antidote to war." *The Once and Future King* is so long that White broke it into separate books. *The Sword in the Stone*, on young Arthur (called Wart), was prankish enough to become a Walt Disney cartoon. But *The Queen of Air and Darkness, The Ill-Made Knight*, and *The Candle in the Wind* grew increasingly sophisticated and anguished. Part Five, *The Book of Merlyn*, was so irately gloomy that it didn't appear until 1977, thirteen years after the author's death.

The work in full is well over six hundred pages, so bursting with invention that an adapter might lose his nerve wondering what to leave out. Novels—even slim ones—were not yet standard source material for musicals. Plays had long been favored, for the manifest conveniences. But adapting more or less all of a full-length novel was relatively new in the 1950s, in such works as *A Tree Grows in Brooklyn*, *Three Wishes For Jamie*, *The Pajama Game*, *Damn Yankees*, and *Candide*.* Looking back at our first chapter: of the seven American book shows, four came from novels.

Clearly, the Rodgers and Hammerstein influence was broadening the musical's scope—and, ironically, connecting all the way back to what Hammerstein and Jerome Kern had attempted in 1927 with another work based on a novel, *Show Boat*, expanding the musical's *content*.

So *Camelot* was possible, especially since White's giant tapestry of life and times is elementally a Greek tragedy, in which a family curse brings down a hero and all his society. King Arthur imposes a moral code upon a barbarian world, and it works—until his own barbarism rears up at him. Having sired a son on his half-sister, he tries to erase the shame by killing all babies born at the likely time. Of course, one escapes: *his* baby, Mordred. And just as Arthur is Herod, Mordred will play Hitler to Arthur's democracy.** Oh: and Guenever and Lancelot are reluctant adulterers. Just leave out the baby murder, and one could do it all in a three-hour musical, right?

Well . . . four hours, actually, as a panicky Lerner realized on the first leg of the tryout, in Toronto. Then director Moss Hart suffered a heart

---

*Cinema also, for the first time, inspired musicals in the 1950s—*Carnival in Flanders*, *Fanny*, *Hazel Flagg*, *Oh Captain!*. Even *The King and I*, though nominally drawn from a book, *Anna and the King of Siam*, more truly drew on material devised for the 1946 film version.

**This is a crucial point in the novel. In an episode in *The Book of Merlyn* (transposed into *The Sword in the Stone* in 1958), Arthur learns what fascism is by being turned into an ant and placed in an ant colony, where the only rule is "Everything not forbidden is compulsory." White puts forth, as the ants' anthem, a song unmistakably borrowed from the Nazis; and Mordred's Thrashers are meant as a parallel to Hitler's Brownshirts.

attack. Luckily, *Camelot*'s two leads, Richard Burton and Julie Andrews, were great sports about all the pruning and replacing, Burton an infectious stimulator of company spirit and Andrews a soother of company anxiety. Choreographer Hanya Holm stoically bore the elimination of her ballet "The Enchanted Forest" (which wasn't working well anyway because the magical-animal costumes hid most of the dancers' bodies), set designer Oliver Smith neglected lucrative other assignments to play Christmas Uncle, and the musical staff—conductor Franz Allers and orchestrators Robert Russell Bennett and Philip J. Lang—remained professional throughout.

Now, why did I name them all? Because, except for Burton (and costume designers Adrian and his protégé, Tony Duquette), this is the *My Fair Lady* team from top to toe. We even got Robert Coote—yes, *Fair Lady*'s Colonel Pickering, the affable and dauntless and perhaps even beloved "Cooter," was on hand in another of his touching cameos, as King Pellinore. And of course Burton did indeed seem to echo Rex Harrison's singing style, though Burton had the more resourceful instrument, and even managed to sing harmony (in thirds) with Andrews at the end of "What Do the Simple Folk Do?"

It was just as well that Lerner had a troupe he could trust, for he was now carrying the vast production single-handedly and had to throw out more than a ballet. The Lancelot, Robert Goulet, had a lengthy solo anthologizing the knightly quests so intrinsic to Malory and White. That could go.* A number of scenes detailing Mordred's seizure of power— legal, like Hitler's—were telescoped into an exciting chorus number, "Guenevere." This gave some narrative drive to the second act, as the queen is led to the stake to be burned alive, her eyes meeting Arthur's on the way. Lancelot of course rides to save her—but not before Mordred gloats over a stricken Arthur, nailed to the cross of his own ethics. Thrilled by the way a talky book scene was now taking fire *within* a musi-

---

*With that number omitted, the preceding dialogue scene between Lancelot and Guenevere (in the show's respelling) could be converted into music, and Lerner and Loewe created "Before I Gaze at You Again." This was so late in tryouts that Andrews would have to sing it for the first time at the first of two previews before the full-dress New York premiere in front of critics, celebrities, and public. Most stars wouldn't. Andrews said, "Of course, darling, but do try to get it to me the night before."

cal number, Lerner recalled Arthur's zoological metamorphosis in *The Sword in the Stone* and gave Burton the line "Merlyn! Merlyn, make me a hawk! Let me fly away from here!" When the new pages were distributed, Burton spotted the line, grinned at Roddy McDowall, the Mordred, and said, "Well, love, it's every man for himself." Meaning, I'm going to rip the house up with that one!

They were all fine, in fact. Burton's Arthur was on a par with Alfred Drake's Kean and Angela Lansbury's Mrs. Lovett as a one-of-a-kind portrayal, not so much Best Sung or Best Acted as Largest Than Life. The way Burton varied his delivery, now relishing notions and now awed by them, his Shakespearean palette of colors—note the withering scorn for Arthur's critics mingled with injured self-esteem, all in one *"Please!"* in his first number—and his beautifully extended characterization, from schoolboy to monarch, conveyed the great irony of tragedy, that it falls upon those who deserve it least yet do the most to bring it about. Julie Andrews was the ideal Guenevere, as wise and self-assured as Burton was bewildered and struggling. It is often said of Andrews that co-workers don't get to know her in any real sense, and she brings a touch of that to the stage—a dignity, a privacy. Elegance. Robert Goulet was not in their class. Though a wonderful singer, he was too wooden an actor—but, after all, all the show's characters do say that Lancelot is something of a stick.

Coote's role of Pellinore is one of *Camelot's* problems. Though he eventually becomes useful as a spokesman for old-fashioned common sense (in opposition to Arthur's idealism), in his entrance he is that old terror of operetta, the Ridiculous Person. Blundering on with a vast white sheepdog in search of "the questing beast," Pellinore is right out of *The Once and Future King* but a very soggy jester. His endless repetitions of the word "What?," in the style of the silly-ass Brit of twenties musical comedy, are very trying. Worse, at one point Coote even imitated flamenco dancing, always—when an anachronism—a sign of a comic in desperation.

At any rate, the weeks in Toronto and then Boston, with Lerner carefully chipping away at anything that he thought he could lose while keeping the work's grandeur and comedy and lyricism in balance, forged a sound company esprit. Best of all, the tremendous physical production was working without flaw. At the two New York previews, the jokes were landing and the songs enthralling. Then came opening night, at the Majestic Theatre on December 3, 1960, and *Camelot* went *thud*. The critics were very divided, all the way from the *Daily News*' "magnificent" through grousings about its expense (Robert Coleman of the *Daily Mirror* said they were calling it "Costallot") to the *Times*' inference that the authors "badly miss their collaborator—Bernard Shaw."

One wonders if the reviewers were antagonized by the intense public interest in the show. After all, it was not only *My Fair Lady*'s follow-up but the biggest show yet—fifty-six in the cast, thirty-three in the orchestra,* extremely lavish visuals, and a rumored cost of more than half a million dollars. The most expensive musicals of the 1950s—*The King and I* and *Candide*, for example—didn't even reach four hundred thousand. Then, too, there was *Camelot*'s gigantic advance sale, always a provocation to people who think their job description includes deciding what gets to run. Another problem was the delay in the release of the cast album. With a score of this quality, home and radio play become their own set of rave reviews, but Columbia (as with *My Fair Lady* the show's sole investor) wasn't able to rush the album into stores in time for Christmas shopping. The firm substituted the lame novelty of "*Camelot* tokens," to be exchanged for the discs when they became available: buy now, play later.

Meanwhile, Moss Hart had recovered, and he and Lerner decided on emergency surgery. They sharpened here and there and actually cut two numbers that had, till now, seemed absolutely integral to the action. "Then You May Take Me To the Fair" showed Guenevere inducing three knights to challenge Lancelot—and, of course, defeat him. The number emphasized the strangely impulsive nature of her distaste for him—explaining, through irony, that she has in fact fallen in love with him at sight and is trying to exorcise her feelings. The other number, "Fie on Goodness!," a chorus with solos for the knights, underscored the atavistic nature of man that such models as Arthurian democracy must endlessly

---

*Lerner always recalled forty. Actually, the thirty-three played forty instruments, through the usual pit expedients of doubling and tripling. One man, for instance, played guitar, lute, and mandolin. Twenty-two was the more usual number of players, mainly because the Big Sing shows were becoming fewer and orchestrators were thus using fewer—some even no—strings.

strive to overcome. Also, both numbers were comic in part, and thus had helped lighten the increasing darkness in the story.

Camelot was the poorer without them, but the show's pacing picked up tremendously, and audiences were less restless than before. Word of mouth must surely have been spreading. Yet tickets were not selling even when the recording finally was.* *Camelot* might turn into another *Candide*—a town topic, a big December opening, a hit cast album, and a sudden closing after a few months.

Then a wonderful thing occurred. Ed Sullivan wanted to devote his entire hour to Lerner and Loewe, on the occasion of *My Fair Lady*'s fifth anniversary, in March 1961. You see how nationally important the musical was then? Lerner got Sullivan to program four numbers from *Camelot*, in stage costume against miscellaneously medieval sets. The next day, a line stretched from the Majestic's box office way up Forty-fourth Street. *Camelot* eventually lasted a little over two years, and might have gone for three but for its unprecedented running costs.

What a success story: but then why is *Camelot* the least respected of the classic musicals, the "pretentious" one, infantile, overdressed, and boring? Why does its association with John Fitzgerald Kennedy irk even his supporters? This is the show for which they coined the joke "You come out humming the scenery." Let me show you why I think it the most misunderstood and underrated of those classics.

Everyone agreed, at least, that it began well. The overture was short. After a fanfare on the title song and a full statement of "If Ever I Would Leave You," the lower instruments and a military drum beat out a tattoo as woodwinds let out a demented squeal on high. Then trumpets and clarinets leaped into a ceremonial wail of a tune, something primitive enough to have stirred right out of White's lurid forests. The houselights dimming to black as the march neared its end, the curtain suddenly rose to the violins' trembling on a single note: on a winter scene, with Arthur's castle shimmering in the background, a great tree at center, and snow falling on a line of courtiers extending along the stage apron. The lighting empha-

---

*The two cut numbers can be heard on the disc, taped before Lerner and Hart began their post-opening overhaul. Conversely, "The Persuasion," a duet for Mordred and Morgan Le Fay in the Enchanted Forest that was heard throughout the show's original run, was listed in the album's tunestack but left off the disc and, apparently, not recorded. To this writing, it remains the one vocal number in the score that has never been taken down.

sized Sir Dinadan (John Cullum), looking through a telescope. "My sainted mother!" he cried. Guenevere has left her carriage at the bottom of the hill, not here at the top, as tradition demands. Merlyn (David Hurst) declared a new tradition in force, of meeting the king's bride at the bottom of the hill, signaling a jaunty march during which the lords and ladies bustled and pranced past us. A line from *Gypsy* recalls itself to us: "This step is good for the costumes."

You're thinking, Uh-oh. Infantile and overdressed. Wait. The court gone, Merlyn called up to Arthur, hiding in the tree. In a scene replete with announcements and explanations, Lerner frantically crams in backstory, never easy in an epic. But now came Burton's first number, "I Wonder What the King Is Doing Tonight," a devilishly brilliant character piece, the apotheosis of anxiety yet regal and grand: the man who would be king. No sooner had it ended than Burton jumped back into his tree as Andrews raced on to "hurry music," as if pursued. Now came *her* character song, "The Simple Joys of Maidenhood," lyrical after his ranting, and secure, because even if she doesn't have what she wants, she *knows* what she wants: men fighting over her. Of course, it is one of *Camelot's* many ironies that this is exactly what she does get, and it cracks the world apart. (Note, too, that both songs, while describing earnest feelings, have their humorous touches. Lerner always said that he could tell if the show had a good audience if they laughed at Arthur's "He's wishing he were in Scotland, fishing tonight.")

Burton ventured into view, the two had a scene—Andrews took Burton for some valet or other—and this led to the title song, outwardly Burton's pitch about the attractions of the place, but really his marriage proposal. They have been under contract—that's why she'd run away—but he wants her willingly. He wants, in fact, to be well thought of and to think well of everyone. That is his problem.

What's wonderful about this scene is that we know nothing of all this subtext at first. We get three excellent numbers in a row, erasing the fey opening with the silly courtiers. We get Moss Hart's staging of "Camelot," as Arthur and Guenevere grow closer by the line till she tries to run off again and he gets in her way and she lets him. It's his solo, yet it plays as a duet.

The audience was still clapping when Dinadan returned, crying "There she is!," adding in an obeisance to His Majesty. Andrews was thunderstruck. *That's* Arthur? Delicately thudding drums launched another courtiers' pantomime, this one to a solemn rendering of "Camelot" for Guenevere's official welcome. At last the two were alone again; but by now everything had changed. As uncomfortable together as they had been intimate, they just stood there, and Arthur broke into an extremely long speech on how he pulled the sword from the stone and became a most unready king:

> ARTHUR: Until I dropped from the tree and my eye beheld you. Then, suddenly, for the first time, I felt I was King. I was glad to be King . . . I wanted to be the wisest, most heroic, most splendid king who ever sat on any throne. (There is a moment of silence.) If you will come with me, Milady, I will arrange for the carriage to return you to your father.

But now Andrews took over "Camelot" herself: accepting him. *Oh—* what would have happened if she hadn't? "War would have been declared," Burton replied. "Over me?" said Andrews. "How simply *marvelous!*"

Obviously, the joke rounds out the scene, but the whole is a perfect rounding-out of many things, the kind of writing we expect from Rodgers-and-Hammerstein-style musical plays at their best. (Think of *Carousel's* Bench Scene.) Having made one of the easiest of all libretto adaptations in *My Fair Lady*, Lerner now made one of the hardest, trying to essentialize White's epic into an operetta. Well, let's say an extraordinarily romantic musical play. Only the most romantic shows dare believe in the love-at-first-encounter musical scene we know from *The Student Prince* and *Show Boat*, from *Carousel* and *West Side Story*. But what show of any kind had to cope with the development of a hero and his political system while philosophizing on the very possibility of systems in a world that aspires to anarchy? What show had to do this while fitting in the establishing songs for the other leads (Lancelot's "C'est Moi" and Mordred's "The Seven Deadly Virtues"), the ensemble's first-act dance-and-song ("The Lusty Month of May"), the merrie old prequel to *My Fair Lady's* "Ascot Gavotte" ("The Jousts," similarly staged, with the cast lined up at the footlights to look out at the contest), the ballads, and so on? This is not to mention the all-important balance of joy and horror inherent in the story, the joy paramount (but threatened) in Act One and the horror all but taking over in Act Two.

But then, no musical had been a tragedy in the precise sense of a noble figure more or less unconsciously nourishing a weakness that must bring him—and us all—down. Arthur's weakness is that, like all liberals, he refuses to believe in evil. In White, Arthur's willingness to put not only Guenever, Lancelot, and himself but also his kingdom and its people in jeopardy simply to humor Mordred is maddening. Arthur does it, supposedly, to save civilization, but civilization collapses *because he does it.*

Lerner tempered this somewhat; he had to. What White added to Malory was a modern worldview and a fond humor but also a terrific rage at what he saw as the inferiority of mankind. The *Morte Darthur* is a romance; *The Once and Future King* is a revenge. Yet Lerner shows us, in the end, the disgraceful helplessness of the peaceful man who, confronted by the violent man, hides behind the impotent dignity of his legal code:

PELLINORE: Do you mean to say, Arthur, a chap has to wait till he's killed before he can attack [in self-defense]?

ARTHUR: (after a moment) Pelly, I'm afraid I have no answer to that.

So *Camelot* must end in despair as the Nazis kill the democrats?

Luckily, White closed on a hopeful note, when Arthur knights a young page named Tom of Warwick and packs him off to keep alive for the future the legend of Camelot's beautiful justice. White made sure we knew that this was the young Thomas Malory. Lerner omits that, making up for it with a touching envoi as Tom runs off:

PELLINORE: Who is that, Arthur?

ARTHUR: One of what we all are, Pelly. Less than a drop in the great blue motion of the sunlit sea. (He smiles. There is jubilance in his voice.) But it seems that some of the drops sparkle, Pelly. Some of them do sparkle! Run, boy!

This is of course sung to an offstage chorus' reprise of the title song. Obvious? No, logical. It may be that what so irritates *Camelot*'s detractors is the work's almost religious sense of Belief—of Grace, even. Lancelot can actually work miracles, and not just because he's the cutest baritone on

Forty-fourth Street. In White, in fact, Lancelot is the ugliest man in the kingdom. It's his *moral* beauty that sets him apart.

This sense of Belief, and the passionately ringing sounds that support it, offends some ears. Musical comedies are so easy, so . . . unimposing. A romantic show with a lot of content is a challenge. The art is as much emotional (because of the music's power) as intellectual (because of the story's profound address of certain universal themes), and some people resent the emotional tug even if they can absorb the intellectual material. It makes them feel inadequate as people, for they can't get what the rest of us so effortlessly respond to. So they strike out in anger.

Nevertheless, the score quickly became so popular that it defended the show during rough times. London's Drury Lane saw a completely new staging in 1964, reinstating the two numbers cut in New York and directed and choreographed by Robert Helpmann in John Truscott's designs. With Laurence Harvey, Elizabeth Larner, and Barry Kent, the show took an astonishing beating from the critics but filled that giant theatre for fifteen months. Then came a terrible film version and revivals with Richard Harris, Richard Burton, and a promoted Robert Goulet, each new mounting losing more of the music, the dialogue, the very passion of the piece. Arthur is one of the most difficult roles the musical has known. It takes a tirelessly resourceful actor, not an exploding mushheap like Harris or a has-been wannabe like Goulet. And Burton's appearance, as a ghost of what he had been, was an outstanding embarrassment.

Yet the show is as famous as ever, and will surely get the Major Revival treatment in due course. It shouldn't. *Camelot* is too expensive a proposition; to do it justice would easily break fifteen million in today's money. Besides, who would play it? (You're right—Davis Gaines, Laura Benanti, and John Barrowman.) It really works better as a memory—which is exactly how they saw it in the 1960s, a buzzword for a slain president, or even as the last time that the nation was focused on Broadway when a new piece by champs came to town. Today, Broadway is bathtub gin after Repeal, but in 1960 a big show was headlines. THE MOST EXPENSIVE YET. DISASTER IN TORONTO. MOSS HART FELLED.

Above all, *Camelot* is the show of serious issues, something the sixties musical was to make an article of faith. It had the oversized score that would absorb musicals in later decades, so huge that one of its loveliest numbers, "Follow Me," is virtually thrown away in plot business; so huge that a melody that might have been strongly featured in any other show is here simply a lead-in to "If Ever I Would Leave You." A fleeting wisp of glory, so to say.

Perhaps *Camelot*'s most telling quality is its marking of the breakup between Alan Jay Lerner and Frederick Loewe. They were to work again here and there in minor ways, but never gave Broadway another new show. Lerner soldiered on with others, but by 1970 there was a feeling that not only his Golden Age but the musical's, too, was over. Of Irving Berlin, Jerome Kern, Cole Porter, George and Ira Gershwin, Vincent Youmans, Rudolf Friml, Sigmund Romberg, De Sylva, Brown, and Henderson, Richard Rodgers and Lorenz Hart, Arthur Schwartz and Howard Dietz, Harold Arlen and E. Y. Harburg, Kurt Weill, and Oscar Hammerstein, most were dead or retired.

The 1960s would host new or relatively new talent: Cy Coleman, Jerry Bock and Sheldon Harnick, Charles Strouse and Lee Adams, John Kander and Fred Ebb, Harvey Schmidt and Tom Jones, Jerry Herman. But there was a concomitant falling-off in the nation's interest in this kind of music. Young people were playing guitars, not pianos. How would that affect the dissemination of theatre music? Once, when one heard an admirable song, one asked, "What's that from?" The good stuff was written for Broadway and Hollywood. All that would change in this decade.

Think of the Beatles' "Blackbird," on the so-called *White Album*. It's classic sixties pop music. But what's it from?

3

EXPECT THINGS TO HAPPEN; OR, DON'T LOOK BACK

MUSICAL COMEDY I

One odd part of the musical's history is that each decade produces more flops than the previous decade, and for the most basic of reasons: the cost of Broadway keeps rising, so shows have to run longer to pay off. In the early 1940s, a big show could easily capitalize itself at $175,000 and, with good business, pay off inside of four months. By the late 1950s, that same show would come in at something over $250,000 and pay off in eight months. In the early 1960s, the cost had jumped to $400,000 and the pay-off date was pushing a year, in some cases surpassing it.

However, the 1960s had few flops in the old "here today, gone forever" style, for the introduction of the long-playing disc in 1948 acculturated the cast album as a staple of the bourgeois listening room. Broadway hits were bestsellers, and competition among the labels to seize the next potential gold mine led them to release almost anything. This led those who follow the musical to listen to almost anything.

That created what we might call a "second history." The first history is What Happened; the second is What's Playing. For a show that can be heard indefinitely, just as it had been heard in the theatre when it was alive, cannot be called dead. Here's a dead show: the first Lerner and Loewe musical, *What's Up* (1943). Here's another: Carol Channing's first starring vehicle, *The Vamp* (1955). No cast album, no survival.

Thus, shows that in earlier decades would have permanently departed were living on in limited format. If a small number of people continue to play such recordings, the shows are called "fondly remembered." If a small number of gay men continue to play them, they are called "cult musicals." It is notable that the 1960s has vastly fewer cult musicals than the 1950s:

because there is a distinct loss of quality. The scores are sometimes less melodious—sometimes even awful—and the unique performers are fewer. The music is starting to run out.

So the typical sixties flop comprises one of two types. Type A has an enjoyable score, even if the show as a whole is not. Type B has a terrible score—and how can a musical with a terrible score be anything as a whole but terrible?

Here are three examples of Type A: *Donnybrook!* (1961), *Bravo Giovanni* (1962), and *High Spirits* (1964). *Donnybrook!* was a hit, if one believed the critics. All seven gave it a warmly favorable report, and Frank Aston of the *World-Telegram and Sun* wrote of the ingenue, Joan Fagan, "Twenty minutes after you read this, she's going to be Broadway's darling," when in fact she was going to be unemployed after *Donnybrook!* played its 68 performances.

Donnybrook! was one of the shows written and put together by—and also cast with—unknowns or veterans without major pull. Based on John Ford's film about the big bold boxer who won't fight, *The Quiet Man, Donnybrook!* had a book by Robert E. McEnroe and a score by Johnny Burke. Choreographer Jack Cole also directed for the first time on this show, joining George Balanchine, Agnes de Mille, Gower Champion, Jerome Robbins, Michael Kidd, and Bob Fosse in a forties innovation that saw development in the 1950s and exploitation thereafter. Cole was the one proved talent of the *Donnybrook!* team, having set the dances for *Something For the Boys* (1943), *Kismet* (1953), and *Jamaica* (1957), sizzling hot. Still, Cole was not famous in the way de Mille or Robbins was.

The cast, too, had its only-sort-of celebrities in comic Eddie Foy (formerly Jr.), big-hunk vocalist Art Lund, and other comic Susan Johnson, also a vocalist. The well-informed theatregoer knew Foy from *The Pajama Game* (1954) and both Lund and Johnson from *The Most Happy Fella* (1956). These are hardly the credits to inspire a box-office buying panic. Fans of the old Warner Bros. backstagers may have thrilled at the return of Clarence Nordstrom, the guy who shuffles off to Buffalo with Ruby Keeler in *42nd Street*. But heroine Joan Fagan and villain Philip Bosco were more of those *who?* names, the latter at least in 1961. In fact, *Donnybrook!* really sounds like one of those shows that get dumped at the ANTA or the 54th Street, and probably only slipped into the 46th Street because *Tenderloin* didn't run, either.

Donnybrook! has another problem, one inescapably built into the story. In brief: Lund has moved to Ireland and woos and wins Fagan, but he won't battle her quarrelsome brother, Bosco, even when Bosco flattens Lund at the wedding party itself. Blackout—and, in a silhouetted flash-back, we see Lund, a boxer in the ring, having knocked out an oppo-nent . . . and killed him.

That's why he won't fight. But his failure to stand up to Bosco threat-ens to destroy the marriage. So Lund faces Bosco down in the scène à faire, a great brutal punch-out; and Lund wins; and that's the happy end-ing.

Except isn't there something crass and stupid in judging a man's char-acter by how well he fights? Insidiously canny as always, John Ford smoothed this over in the movie by casting John Wayne as the boxer, dis-arming all judgment. Wayne is so *man* that he defines virility in whatever he does. Then, too, a great deal of outdoors Irish color and various Abbey Theatre kibitzers help separate the spectator from the plot. The film becomes a spoof of itself.

Donnybrook! turned much of this into the usual Irish caricature. (Sam-ple joke: Lund asks the local priest if he can keep a secret. *"Me?"* the father replies.) Musicals based on films are supposed to expand the films' feelings, but it's hard to expand John Ford, especially in so visually oper-atic a piece as *The Quiet Man.* Jack Cole thought of one sharp novelty in staging the overture, so that the lead characters appeared, spotlit, along with their music, the whole bonded in ensemble dancing of high caliber (even if it was exactly the sort of choreography recently made monoto-nous by *Riverdance*).

The *Donnybrook!* score deserved a better show. It has its floppo num-bers, the kind one expects from writers without taste or judgment—the tuneless title song, for instance, a cliché of villagers eager for a fight, and including the cry "Hit 'im, Bailey! With a shillelagh!" But most of the songs are quite appealing, even unusual. Susan Johnson's establishing number, "Sad Was the Day," offered deadpan comedy on the pleasures of being a widow. Lyricist Burke amusingly caught her late husband's charac-ter all in one tight line—"large moustache, hairy chest, not too clean but neatly dressed"—and composer Burke laid out the scene, for Johnson and a commentative chorus, in $4/4$ with constant infusions of $5/4$ and $3/4$. This is clever music, to match the words. Director Cole rounded it out with a sight gag: after Johnson's last words, the wearily dismissive "Ah, men!," the chorus unknowingly echoed her with a pious "Amen!," and Johnson blandly put a hand over her heart.

Though Burke had been known only as a Hollywood lyricist, he composed achingly beautiful ballads, and even some of the weaker numbers have a theatrical flair. Burke surprised that old standby the Heroine's Wanting Song by sneaking up on it with a merrily belligerent Irish jig of a verse in "Sez I," and he helped Cole cover the first set change with "The Day the Snow Is Meltin'," sung by a chorus chap as the revolving stage brought a tavern into view. It's a sweet song, of the type beloved of Irish tenors, pure atmosphere suddenly put to use in the pacing of a production.

Best of all, Burke found a way to bring Eddie Foy into the music—no easy task, for Foy was the very last of the stage comics given to ad-libbing, "breaking up" his colleagues, sudden crazy dance steps, and the like. For Foy's two duets with Johnson, "I Wouldn't Bet One Penny" and "Dee-lightful Is the Word," Burke actually devised melody to match Foy's loony prancing, and the lyrics bear the oddball eloquence—"You could never tempt me with insinuatin' queries"—that Foy loved to fondle.

Bravo Giovanni (1962) is another flop that makes for fun listening. But here it is far more for the Singers than for Milton Schafer and Ronny Graham's rather conventional songs. It was the 1950s that invented the Novelty Star, some putative non-singer from somewhere other than Broadway who would headline a musical, usually just once: Rosalind Russell in *Wonderful Town* (1953), Hildegarde Neff in *Silk Stockings* (1955), Rex Harrison in *My Fair Lady* (1956), Tony Randall in *Oh Captain!* (1958). The practice became quite common in the 1960s; we've already seen it in *Greenwillow*, *Christine*, *Tenderloin*, *Wildcat*, and *Camelot*. *Bravo Giovanni*'s Novelty Star was actually known for singing—opera basso Cesare Siepi, whose big warm voice, trim good looks, and superb English made him the ideal choice as the proprietor of a small Roman restaurant. Only nineteen at the time, Michèle Lee, the ingenue, had a wallop of a belt and physical appeal; pairing her with the senior Siepi was the one odd touch in a typically fast and loud, big-cast, lots-of-dancing musical comedy. It was Anything For a Song—the opening, a street scene, as Siepi makes a star entrance in reverse (no heralding: just out he comes) to sing "Rome"; Lee's establishing number, "I'm All I've Got"; Maria Karnilova's revival of the New Dance Sensation in "The Kangaroo"; Siepi's and Lee's respective views of their growing attraction, "If I Were the Man" and the pulsing "Steady, Steady"; a passing street singer's interpolation, "Ah! Camminare." It's all good material, very well performed, but it was musical-comedy business as usual. Which meant that *Bravo Giovanni* needed something special in its story to hold us.

So of course we get one of the most implausible librettos in the musical's history. His livelihood threatened by the opening of a restaurant-chain outlet, Siepi digs up the street to reach his rival's kitchen, where a conspirator will send *their* food to Siepi, running his operating costs down to nothing. For some reason, this co-option of mass-market cuisine makes Siepi's trattoria a smash. What, in *Italy?* This is not to mention Etruscan bric-à-brac that the digging uncovers and an ending right out of those old animal cartoons in which all the principals simply run away.

High Spirits completes this trilogy of troubled shows with pleasant music: and it's the best of the music and the worst of the shows. *Donnybrook!* comes from a movie, *Bravo Giovanni* from a novel, and *High Spirits* from Noël Coward's play *Blithe Spirit.* That sounds like a good idea, for, unlike some of the plays turned into musicals in the 1960s (such as *Picnic* and *The Man Who Came To Dinner*), *Blithe Spirit* is not done often in the United States and its film version was virtually unseen here. Authors Hugh Martin and Timothy Gray hewed closely to Coward, basically fitting songs into the existing text and graduating the character of an eccentric medium, Madame Arcati, from supporting to lead.

Flattered by Martin and Gray's scrupulous adaptation, Coward saw the show, then called *Faster Than Sound*, as a potential hit for Keith Michell, Gwen Verdon or Zizi Jeanmaire, and Celeste Holm, with Kay Thompson as Madame Arcati. Coward agreed to direct, and even gave his blessing to a new ending, in which all four leads end up dead.

Yes. For readers unfamiliar with *Blithe Spirit*: as written, it tells of a man whose second marriage is destroyed by the ghostly intrusion of his dead first wife, who wants him to join her in The Beyond but who instead accidentally kills the second wife. As Coward surely meant it, however, it presents a homosexual whose closet marriage is destroyed by the reappearance of an old boy friend. Add to this that camp favorite Beatrice Lillie (who had the success of her career as Arcati), Edward Woodward's effete husband, and another camp favorite, Tammy Grimes, as the ghost, and what is *High Spirits* really up to?

Somehow or other straight Danny Daniels got in there to choreograph, and straight Gower Champion took over for both Coward and Daniels during the usual tryout hell. Still, *High Spirits* is based on a false premise, most readily heard in the main ballad, "Forever and a Day." It's a neat plan for a musical scene: Woodward will give one nostalgic spin of the disc that Grimes played thirty times on their honeymoon night. She doesn't recognize it, he grows hissy—then she starts to sing along and so does he. We get it. She's capricious and he's Extremely Touchy For a Heterosexual, and they are still in love.* Except they aren't. This man doesn't love women, so why is he singing one a love song? Why is Grimes responding to the ballad when otherwise she is characterized by a lack of response to just about anything?

Grimes and Woodward played well together—they had in fact engagingly supplied virtually the entire cast of Charles Dyer's *Rattle of a Simple Man* in 1963. Coward thought Champion ruined Grimes' performance with overdirection; but the real problem lay in adding emotional content (in the score) to the brittle script (of the original play). Moreover, Lillie's entire part was excrescent, however much pleasure she gave making her entrance in a Bicycle Number, directing a séance, or singing a love song to her Ouija board.

In the end, Champion worked little of his usual magic, resorting to the by-now-outdated staging of Grimes' list song of the immortal dead, "Home Sweet Heaven," in one before the traveler curtain during a set change. Hadn't Champion himself outdated this usage with more vivaciously kinetic jumps from scene to scene? The first-act finale, "Faster Than Sound," ended with Grimes and a ghostly chorus flying through the clouds so unpersuasively that a number of critics troubled to complain of it.

Nevertheless, the Martin-Gray score is another of those misleading historical clues. This show *sounds* great: in the slyly syncopated quarter

---

*Add in one inside joke: the recording that Woodward played was sung by co-author Gray, in a blamelessly sweet tenorino.

notes of Woodward's "I Know Your Heart (by heart)," to a swinging vamp that Grimes vocalizes on; in the madrigal of husband and wife (Louise Troy), "If I Gave You . . ." (which is, all the same, another lying gay mess of a piece, pretty in noise but false in intention); and finally in a plot number, "What in the World Did You Want?," a waltzing sword fight for Woodward and his wives. Lillie's numbers must have been crafted for her. They are perfect matches, even if she had endless difficulty keeping text in her head, continually drying up or inventing lines and even words.*

High Spirits as a whole was not great, then. Still, it at least seemed like a hit, with all New York talking of Bea, a few months of sold-out houses, and a run of 375 performances. As we know, this tally didn't usually mark a commercial success by 1964, and the show was a failure. It is a long jump, all the same, down to our Type B shows. True, they're major projects. *Let It Ride!* (1961) was the second musicalization of John Cecil Holm and George Abbott's *Three Men on a Horse*, with Novelty Star George Gobel and, in his original role, Sam Levene, twenty-six years older. *Here's Love* (1963) was Meredith Willson's version of the film *Miracle on 34th Street*, and it was Willson's name rather than those of leads Janis Paige, Craig Stevens, and Laurence Naismith that got top billing. *Bajour* (1964) offered Chita Rivera, Nancy Dussault, and Herschel Bernardi in a tale drawn from Joseph Mitchell's *New Yorker* pieces on modern-day gypsies.

Three stinkers. Yes, television star Gobel gave a touching performance as *Let It Ride!*'s greeting-card poet who picks winning horses, and even rose to an impressive falsetto high B flat in "(Every man lives on) His Own Little Island." But this deservedly forgotten comedy about crass people bullying one of those irritating idiots savants does not deserve to sing. (It had failed on its earlier outing, too, as *Banjo Eyes*, with Eddie Cantor.)

Here's Love began with Michael Kidd's evocative suggestion of the Macy's Thanksgiving Parade; and William and Jean Eckart's set plan for a great empty stage decorated with furniture pieces against abstract backgrounds was daring. However, Willson's work had deteriorated amazingly

---

*Audiences didn't mind, for it was their first taste of Lillie in a full-scale musical since *Inside U.S.A.* (1948) and her first appearance onstage at all since her revue *An Evening With Beatrice Lillie* (1952). Five of the by-then six critics wrote her love letters, as Coward fumed at her larking about instead of playing character. The cast album preserves a bit of Lillie's haphazard rendering, in "Something Is Coming To Tea," when she parts company with the script for a few measures. "Turkish" was what Coward called it.

after *Molly Brown.* (His next and final show, *1491*, with John Cullum as Columbus and Chita Rivera as his girl friend, closed out of town in 1969.)

As for *Bajour*, how are we supposed to root for these disgusting thieves? *The New Yorker* may have found them invigorating—as did Nancy Dussault, as a sociologist who joins the band to get dissertation material. But the subject is crime; and crime is not invigorating. If Jay Livingston and Ray Evans' *Let It Ride!* songs are feeble and Meredith Willson's *Here's Love* songs boring, Walter Marks' *Bajour* songs offered a mixture of the ugly and the appealing. "Love-Line" and "Must It Be Love?" are sound ballads, "Words, Words, Words" and "Honest Man" insultingly stupid. "Soon" is haunting, the title song vulgar.

Perhaps *Bajour*'s one note of distinction lay in its unusual casting, vaunting Herschel Bernardi above the title before his days of glory as Tevye and Zorbá; presenting Dussault with a love interest in Robert Burr, fresh from understudying Richard Burton in *Hamlet*; returning to her many fans Mae Questel, the voice of cartoonland's Betty Boop, as Dussault's mother; and giving the once-and-future Rivera one of her greatest roles, reminding us that this unapproachably brilliant talent would have been short-listed with Marilyn Miller, Ethel Merman, and Gwen Verdon but for her unfortunate propensity for turning up in flops like *1491* and *Bajour.*

Interestingly, one show that went unrecorded was as enjoyable as any of these six—as tuneful as *Donnybrook!* and as funny as *High Spirits*. The first musical of the 1963–64 season, opening in very late September, it had no star names to draw attention and was stuck at that funeral home the Adelphi, at this point called the 54th Street. The show's title is *The Student Gypsy, or The Prince of Liederkranz*, and it was supposed to mark Rick Besoyan's promotion from off-Broadway to the big time.

Besoyan was the sole author of *Little Mary Sunshine* (1959), a hit at the little Orpheum for its burlesque of outmoded genre tropes from operetta to musical comedy. When he moved uptown, Besoyan brought along some of his *Little Mary* cohort: choreographer and co-director Ray Harrison, orchestrator of the cast album (the show itself made do with pianos) Arnold Goland, comic Dom DeLuise (who had taken over the second male lead), juvenile Dick Hoh (who had taken over the *first* male lead), and even some of the chorus people. Mainly, Besoyan retained his Little Mary, Eileen Brennan, here playing Merry May Glockenspiel.

It sounds a bit familiar. Why repeat a quaint off-Broadway stunt, and at Broadway prices? But wait. Merry May was no Little Mary. Instead of a simpering optimist, the heroine was now drab, friendless, and blind without her glasses. It was operetta with a clueless heroine, a new joke. Besoyan also reached out to new sources for his fun. *Little Mary* was *Rose-Marie*, *Florodora*, Rudolf Friml, Kern and Wodehouse Princess Theatre style. *The Student Gypsy* roamed more widely, from Johann Strauss to vaudeville, from Weber and Fields to *The Student Prince*, with a taste of the baby-snatching business of *Il Trovatore*. Producer Sandy Farber did not mount an elaborate production. There were only two main sets and two traveler curtains for the switches. But orchestrator Goland played some fine jests—a flat violin gumming up the overture's coda, a tuba for Germanic oomph, a set of pitched dinner bells for the second couple to play in "(I'll be your) Ting-a-Ling-Dearie," which brought the house down.

In fact, *The Student Gypsy* was an audience show all the way: not exciting or (after *Little Mary Sunshine*, anyway) unique but very melodious and vastly absurd. The plot? Merry May flees her home to seek romance, falls in love with a prince (Don Stewart), joins up with a vagabond con man (Dom DeLuise), becomes apprenticed to a Gypsy queen . . . you've been there. But where *Little Mary Sunshine* limited its action to replicas of old forms, *The Student Gypsy* occasionally *commented* on those forms. *Little Mary* is pure; *The Student Gypsy* is know-it-all. For instance:

PRINCE RUDOLPH: (seeing dancers in the wings) Look, dear Princess, the Gypsies return. (As they exit) Quickly—into the disguise I shall find for you!

Or:

PRINCE RUDOLPH: Love is the diadem on which myriad hopes come to fruition in the angelical personification of one's dreamless dream.
MERRY MAY: You don't say.

Then, too, while some of the score replays old Broadway in spoof, the rest of the score simply replays old Broadway, with no intention of spoofing. "The Grenadiers' Marching Song"; the girls and boys' "Kiss Me," bouncing with virginal bravado; Merry May and the Prince's "Seventh Heaven Waltz"; a comic male trio, "A Woman Is a Woman Is a Woman"—all point back to specific genres. But the Hero's Wanting Song, the ecstatically aspiring "Somewhere," could fit into any twenties romantic show without changing a line, a note. "Very Much in Love," the girls' explanation of courtship usage from the woman's viewpoint, is not parody but a song in its own right. And what are we to make of a character named Elsie Umlaut, a grinning idiot who never utters a word and goes around slapping a hunk of cheese into everyone's hand? "That's cheese," someone would explain; and the audience was roaring. But that isn't a takeoff: that's sound musical-comedy invention.

The sad truth is that Besoyan probably didn't want to write any more burlesques of old musicals. He wanted to write old musicals. The critics liked the show; and Brennan, a keen comic, was able to balance pretty singing with her character's clumsiness—constantly taking out a flossy handkerchief, for instance, to wave ineffectually at some invisible Prince Danilo. Still, the hard-luck theatre, the lack of star attraction, and the warm-not-hot reviews closed *The Student Gypsy* in two weeks. It was back to off-Broadway for Besoyan, who tried to reduce Shakespeare's *A Midsummer Night's Dream* to the three lead fairies, the four lovers, and Bottom in *Babes in the Wood* (1964), no spoof but a bad idea for a musical, with a truly terrible book. Sadly, Besoyan died unfulfilled at forty-five, in 1970.

It was Broadway's loss, because there weren't as many good composers in the 1960s as there had been in the past. There are great scores; but also a surprising amount of prominent mediocrity. *Subways Are For Sleeping* (1961) is a good example: not bad, really, but not good. Even: not really good, but certainly not bad. It doesn't lack anything, exactly. It just isn't special. The score is a notch below . . . well . . . the script never . . . and the cast was . . . Here's one way of putting it: among those who really enjoy musicals, some people ignore it and nobody loves it.

Subways was a major production: David Merrick presented a Comden-Green libretto to Jule Styne's music at the St. James, with Sydney Chaplin and Carol Lawrence starring and, below the title, Orson Bean and Phyllis Newman (Green's wife) as the second couple. Michael Kidd was the director-choreographer, but this was no Bob Fosse *Redhead* or Gower Champion *Bye Bye Birdie*, not to mention Kidd's own *Li'l Abner*: stylish auteur stagings. *Subways* was simply another realistic though implausible non-story with a few good songs and dances and good-enough perform-ances.

The premise, drawn from Edmund G. Love's collection of stories, is that a dispirited magazine writer (Lawrence) is doing a piece on society's dropouts. Not bums—people without an address. They live hand-to-mouth by walking dogs or playing department-store Santa, they dress well, they mooch their food at parties, they sleep in museums and under bridges, and so on. We are supposed to see them as free: but where do they wash? While they're Sydney Chaplin or Orson Bean, they're engaging enough, with the former's surprisingly ample baritone and the latter's stringy whimsy. Then, too, Carol Lawrence had been revealed as the musical's Newest Heroine in *West Side Story*, and Phyllis Newman was even newer, having played little more than the Bennet daughter who sings "I Feel Sorry for the Girl" in *First Impressions* (1959).

So far, okay. Newman spent all but one scene wearing only a towel to keep from being thrown out of her hotel room; this gave Bean a comic number near the end, in "I Just Can't Wait (till I see you with clothes on)," a list song citing the inventory she can amass, from muffler to galoshes. Meanwhile, Lawrence and Chaplin fell for each other, but he gets sore when he thinks he's been exploited for her magazine article, giving the first-act curtain something edgy to fall on. That's old stuff. Jerome Kern's *Sally* dropped its suspense curtain on just that sort of tiff in 1920: and *Sally* was old-fashioned even then. Worse—and just as in *Sally*—this problem is not resolved. It finally just stops being a problem so the show can end.

Still, there is a bit of something going on here, for this quartet of leads is, with bit parts and chorus, the entire show: and all four of them are homeless, Chaplin and Bean literally, Newman incipiently, and Lawrence in effect, because she feels so placeless in her life. As we learn in another establishing character number, "Girls Like Me," she has everything, and it's nothing. Interestingly, the song's refrain begins "Right under your eyes"—the key words from the show's title number, a bum's anthem. So home isn't an abode. Home is love, with Chaplin.

Add to this some fine material in the score—a real Styne swinger in "Comes Once in a Lifetime" and show-biz hopeful Newman's hilarious autobiography, "I Was a Shoo-in." (This comes complete with her beauty-contest talent spot, a Civil War skit about Emmalina Sue, "who perished in a fatal death so dire" while detaining Cousin Willis with mint juleps so her Yankee lover could escape.) There's a delightful surprise in "Who Knows What Might Have Been?," when Chaplin suddenly went into an imitation of Rex Harrison's Henry Higgins, the kind of out-of-character inside joke that had once been one of the musical's favorite devices and by this point was becoming rare.* And that title song, an impishly dashing waltz for four tenors, remains one of Styne's least appreciated masterbits, truly imaginative writing from this supposed pop tunesmith.

Still, most of the rest of the score is routine, as if even experts were fumbling in this era. Truth to tell, the most notable thing about *Subways* was The Ad, the greatest of all David Merrick's devious PR stunts. He'd been planning it for years: find seven men with the same names as the seven New York newspaper critics. Treat them to a lavish dinner and free tickets to one of Merrick's scorned musicals—they might balk at serious drama. Have them sign enthusiastic blurbs, and publish them in a full-page layout as if the show had actually got rave notices. One can imagine Merrick's impatience to see Brooks Atkinson retire, because there couldn't be a second Brooks Atkinson. That worthy finally withdrew, in 1960. Then came three Merrick musicals in a row—*Irma la Douce*, *Do Re Mi*, and *Carnival!*—that didn't need shell-game boosting.

But then came *Subways*, with mixed notices. ("Dull and vapid," said Atkinson's successor, Howard Taubman.) Merrick sprang into action, headlining his page "7 OUT OF 7 ARE ECSTATICALLY UNANIMOUS ABOUT SUBWAYS ARE FOR SLEEPING." Merrick's Howard Taubman called it "One of the few great musical comedies of the last thirty years." The ad even ran photos of the seven, who all looked like critics—and, lo, Merrick's Richard Watts was black, a wonderful touch. In the event, most of the papers caught on and rejected the ad. But the *Herald-Tribune* ran it and it became the talk of the town. It probably didn't sell many tickets. Like most of Merrick's japes, it seemed more a defiance of those who would thwart his will than a commercial ploy. Call it performance art.

---

*Chaplin also sang one chorus of "Comes Once in a Lifetime" in French—not well, though he actually appeared in a French production of *Sweet Charity*. Someone should have told Comden and Green that *ville* ("veel") and *Bastille* ("Bastee") don't rhyme.

With so many less-than-brilliant shows getting written, it's not surprising that the 1960s depended on star turns far more than the previous two decades had: as if a big personality might fill up the holes in the composition. A 1956 hit in Honolulu, *13 Daughters* (1961) put Don Ameche in charge of an absurd piece about the overturning of a kahuna's curse upon a marriage between a Hawaiian princess and a foreigner. The show's author, Eaton Magoon Jr., had sincerely endeavored to build something beautiful and enlightening about Hawaiian folkways, and of course it's easy to giggle at a dramatic work filled with references to kukui seeds, hoomalimali, and puka puka pants. However, like *The Student Gypsy*, *13 Daughters* was too out-of-the-way, both in subject matter and at that distant old barn of a house on Fifty-fourth Street. It was gone in three and a half weeks.

At that, Judy Holliday couldn't keep *Hot Spot* (1963) running more than five weeks at the Majestic even as a bumbling Peace Corps worker in D'hum—a kind of Kennedy-era updating of her *Bells Are Ringing* character. *Hot Spot* claimed a gloss of last-minute Sondheim in its Mary Rodgers–Martin Charnin score; but it also gave no credit to director or choreographer when it opened after a prolonged tryout, always a sign of a show that started out wrong and kept getting wronger.

Continuing to move in ascending order of quality, we come to *I Had a Ball* (1964), with a Novelty Star, comic Buddy Hackett. As Garside the Great, a sideshow clairvoyant, Hackett presided over a *Guys and Dolls*–like society on the boardwalk at Coney Island: Stan the Shpieler (Richard Kiley), man-hungry Addie (Luba Lisa), a friendly loan shark (Steve Roland), Joe the Muzzler (Jack Wakefield), and know-it-all Ma Maloney (Rosetta LeNoire), with one innocent newcomer, Jeannie (Karen Morrow). Playing a belly dancer, a performer billed as Morocco shyly wondered if she, too, might join the ranks of the mononymous great, such as Lilo and Napoléon. But *Christine*'s sadder-but-wiser Bhaskar warned her that it is not enough simply to be in a musical. To be famous, one must be in a *hit* musical, or at least invade Russia.

I Had a Ball was no hit. Like so many other sixties musicals, it ran half a year on advance-booked parties, lost its entire investment, and left behind a cast album a notch above terrible. It was a cheap show. It looked cheap and it sounds cheap, too, especially in "Coney Island, U.S.A.," the worst opening number of the decade. But Kiley's Wanting Song, "The

Other Half of Me," is intelligent, "Think Beautiful" is a hummable waltz, and Morrow's lustrous belt made "I've Got Everything I Want" and the title song sound like Jule Styne. They were the work of Jack Lawrence and Stan Freeman, another of the many sixties teamings that were suddenly there and then suddenly not there.

Other writers apprenticed themselves to the pop market or the revue in the 1950s, then came to Broadway, fully fledged, such as Charles Strouse and Lee Adams. After *Bye Bye Birdie*, their star was Ray Bolger, in *All American* (1962). This is the kind of show Broadway used to put on blindfolded: with a picturesque theme for background, the star goes all out in his specialties with lots of saucy fun and nice tunes. Bolger himself did it in *By Jupiter* (1942) as a sissy among Amazons with a Rodgers and Hart score. *All American*'s background was college football, Bolger being an immigrant professor of engineering who coaches the team to victory in his own terms: "Now, suppose the polygon in question is the Texas backfield and suppose the tangent is a kick!" Mel Brooks' embarrassingly witless book paired Bolger with Eileen Herlie, as the college dean. For the second couple, student Anita Gillette chased student Ron Husmann, and villain Fritz Weaver—he's a captain of PR, chief of Exploiters Unlimited—amusingly made his entrance only seconds before the first-act curtain.

Director Joshua Logan presented *All American* in his favorite genre of musical—big, with lots of detail. But *Annie Get Your Gun*, *South Pacific*, and *Fanny*, his three major hits (he staged *By Jupiter*, too), had a lot of personality and color—Wild West shows, World War II, the Marseille waterfront. These three were also good stories. *All American* had little personality; Bolger came with his identity ready-made, and the others had to work around him. And it wasn't a good story. A professor coaches the football team with logarithms? Logan tried to make Bolger's first trip through America, "What a Country!," a gala number, filled with zany sights: the fancy rich, a drunk, cowboys, a gorilla dressed as a bridegroom with a human bride. (They're advertising a movie.) It wasn't gala; it was silly. Logan sent the football players into the aisles of the Winter Garden to throw the ball over theatregoers' heads. It was desperate. The team was also seen in the locker room, in various stages of football dress, forming a human pyramid. It was scary. There was heterosexual eroticism as well, in "Nightlife," with Gillette and the girls in pajamas, but this hardly compared to the sight of all that locker-room beefcake, strutting to a number called "Physical Fitness" that sounded like a cross between a sarabande and a blowjob.

Logan, a homogay who tried to strangle his hungers in the netting of the closet, was an open joke on The Street. Julius Monk's cabaret revue *Baker's Dozen* (1964) was shockingly direct about the acres of male skin that Logan would obsessively uncover:

WIFE: Basketball! It's disgusting!
HUSBAND: I thought you liked watching half-naked young men leaping
　　about. (To Friend) That's where Martha and I met, you know.
FRIEND: At a basketball game?
HUSBAND: No, at a Josh Logan musical.

All the same, this is a Type A flop, lasting only 80 performances but leaving a good score behind. It lacks the character studies of Strouse and Adams at their best, but then *All American* doesn't have characters. The wonderful Eileen Herlie got a lot out of the fondly optimistic "Our Children" and "If I Were You," both duets with Bolger; and she gamely got into a vamp number in "The Real Me." Husmann had an odd number, "We Speak the Same Language"—not, as one might guess, a love song, but an expression of respect for Professor Bolger. However, "I've Just Seen Her (As Nobody Else Has Seen Her)" was pure Besotted Young Guy Thinks He Just Invented Love, a Broadway staple—think of "I Met a Girl," "On the Street Where You Live," or "It Only Takes a Moment"— here individualized by Husmann's rolling baritone and Strouse's slithery chromatic harmony.

Bolger, whose identity as a foreigner was established by his spending almost the entire evening in a tailcoat, was given the works—star entrance ("Where's Fodorski?" everyone cries, leaving an enthralled pause for Bolger to emancipate by walking on with "I forgot my umbrella"), lots of book time (even if the action didn't need it), the hit tune, "Once Upon a Time" (another duet with Herlie), and the dancing-and-clowning solo late in Act Two, "I'm Fascinating."

The problem is, he wasn't. Bolger made *By Jupiter* a huge hit, but that was an era earlier. Musicals were smarter in 1962, and audiences had higher standards. Bolger was supposed to be *All American*'s subject matter. But all the amusing things—Gillette stalking Husmann, Husmann getting roped into playing football and turning out to be a hero, Herlie's dedication to her job, and Weaver's schemes of conquering the world as a Doctor No of publicity—were the rest of the show.

Tovarich (1963) ran considerably longer than *All American*—eight months—and it's a more consistent show, yet a silly one. The source, Jacques Deval's play that conquered Western civilization in the 1930s, is a serious comedy. Deval wrote it as a satire on the Russian character: theatrical, solemn, infantile, bombastic, and mercurial enough to leap from arrogance to servility within a moment. Russian émigrés had flooded Paris after the Revolution, and though their insular community did not mix much with outsiders, the Russian aristocrat who had commanded a regiment and now drove a taxi was a Parisian running gag. Deval pictured one couple such, a grand duchess and a prince, who hire out as maid and butler, with the plot complication that the Tsar entrusted four billion francs to the prince and everyone is after it—not least a commissar who brutally used the pair when they were in his power.

So Deval's *Tovarich* is a boulevard comedy and its two leads are paragons of stereotype, but at least a very expansive one. Robert E. Sherwood translated Deval for the West End and Broadway, and it was his version that formed the basis for the musical in David Shaw's new book. *Tovarich* opened up easily. First, bring in lots of Paris with the usual hymns to its charms that Broadway seems never to run out of, right? *No*—and this is one thing that *Tovarich* got right. Shaw stuck closely to the play, though in a show of this size there would have to be a chorus, at first of émigrés with the expected jokes about who they were and what they now are, later of rich guests forming an oil cartel, an expansion of an intimate dinner in the original.

Second, Shaw changed Deval's Duponts who employ the Russian couple into visiting Americans, the Davises (George S. Irving, Louise Kirtland). Deval had already given the family a son and daughter (here, Byron Mitchell and Margery Gray); Shaw had only to give them puppy-love crushes on vivacious "Tina" (Vivien Leigh) and dashing "Michel" (Jean Pierre Aumont).

Yes, *Tovarich* had *two* Novelty Stars, and while Leigh and Aumont would clearly have been more comfortable in a straight revival of the Deval-Sherwood script, this way was more fun. Leigh danced a Charleston with Mitchell in "Wilkes-Barre, P.A.,"* and Aumont showed off his fencing skills (also from Deval). It has to be said that the two stars had a lot of charm; what's more, Leigh really did delight the critics and draw the public. She even won a Tony as Best Actress in a Musical (over *Oliver!*'s Georgia Brown, *Mr. President*'s Nanette Fabray, and Sally Ann Howes, for a City Center *Brigadoon*).

But *Tovarich* was worthy only when Leigh and Aumont were on, when Shaw and the songwriters, Lee Pockriss and Anne Croswell, had established personalities to play with. The rest was musical-comedy fill, some of it embarrassing. One rather expected a number from the émigrés called "Nitchevo" (Russian for, roughly, "So what?"), a lament in Volga tones on all they had to leave behind. And one knew that George S. Irving would throw himself into the most risible compositions as if they were Rodgers and Hammerstein; luckily, he had only two. But did there have to be a *second* émigré lament, "It Used To Be"? Did the two kids have to be so persistently around to present yet another extraneous number? The show was so unimpressive that it wasn't recorded till Leigh got her Tony, two months after *Tovarich* had opened.

Unfortunately, Leigh's unmitigated triumph became compromised by the neurasthenia that destroyed both her career and her marriage to Laurence Olivier. The tryout had been taxing, especially when the director, Delbert Mann, was replaced by Peter Glenville; it can be disorienting to be forced to make such a major adjustment when one is boxing above one's weight in the first place, not to mention playing opposite an actor one doesn't like and having one's darling Noël Coward tell one that one's show is a disaster. We have to admire Leigh for honoring her contract; some others might have walked, forcing *Tovarich* to close on the road and throwing a lot of people out of work. As it was, more than a few theatregoers will recall that the best thing that season was Leigh and the adoring Mitchell sitting at stage right while she let him down gently with "I Know the Feeling," a haunting melody of the kind Kurt Weill might have writ-

---

*This number popularized the mispronunciation of the town's second word as "Barry." The locals say "Bar" or "Barruh." While we're at it, the correct Russian for "comrade" is not *tovarich* but *tovarishch*.

ten for, say, Lucienne Boyer. Had *Tovarich* been a hit, they'd be singing it today.

Our last two titles in this chapter of flops typify the two major genres of the day, sassy musical comedy and the more adult musical play. Moreover, while every work discussed here failed to satisfy in part or whole, these two came closest to being hits, in quality if not performance tally. And this time there were no browsing celebs on vacation from some other line of work. These two shows offered stars born to see their names over the title of a Broadway musical: Robert Preston and Carol Burnett.

Preston had the musical play, *Ben Franklin in Paris* (1964), by Sidney Michaels to the music of Mark Sandrich Jr. As Franklin, Preston was playing his signature con man, Harold Hill of *The Music Man* but also Pancho Villa of *We Take the Town* (1962), which closed in tryout. This time, Preston was trying to sell the French on recognition of the United States during the winter of 1776–77, when it seemed unlikely that we would win our liberty. Michaels made a few concessions to popular taste and dramatic unity, but otherwise told a remarkable, even implausible tale taken right from the record.

The action, though quite busy, holds very tensely to the throughline of Franklin's desperate quest for French support. However, Franklin can achieve this only through the King's adviser, the Comtesse Diane de Vobrillac. A former amour of Franklin's, she thus establishes the love plot. Then, too, as Franklin travels with two grandsons, the elder of the pair can enjoy a romance with a French girl as the subplot.

Franklin Kiser and Susan Watson as the younger lovers were sound Broadway casting; and the seven-year-old grandson, Jerry Schaefer, was one of the better kid actors. But this gave the show nothing in the way of continental atmosphere, so the producers brought over Sweden's Ulla Sallert, so prominent that she was Eliza Doolittle when *My Fair Lady* took Sweden on its global rampage. Sallert was something special with Preston, sophisticated and layered in contrast with his blunt energy, yet always his helpless admirer. And he is hers. But his first love is his country:

BEN: Madame, you live in a poem and I live in a newspaper's bold type
    where the ink's still wet on the page.
DIANE: You are obsessed with posterity, Monsieur. 'Tis unmanly.
BEN: And you are drunk with power, Madame. 'Tis unfeminine.

Ben Franklin in Paris had something always unusual in the musical, an extremely good book. It was not just good storytelling, but concise and clever and romantic writing, quite worthy of its subject. Preston, of course, was brilliant, looking astonishingly authentic and obviously relishing every devious sortie in Franklin's campaign to impress, manipulate, and fool the French into giving him that crucial diplomatic accommodation.

Too restless to need a star entrance, Preston got one anyway, after an evocative opening of sailors perched high in rigging against a blue cyclorama in "We Sail the Seas." Then, in director Michael Kidd's *trompe l'oeil* staging, the crew hauled on a rope as if docking; after a blackout, we saw French harbor workers hauling on the same rope from the *opposite* side, and the lights came up on the first full set. Franklin's famous inventions—rocking chair, Franklin stove, and so on—were paraded down the gangplank. Then came Preston, part of the booty. Indeed, he broke right into "I Invented Myself," as if he were his own contraption. It was a fine start. To quote one of Michaels' lyrics, "The damn thing works."

It worked so well that it's hard to say why the show lasted only 215 performances. Perhaps it's because, when one thinks of musicals with really smart books, they more often than not come wedded to outstanding scores: *The King and I, My Fair Lady, West Side Story, Gypsy. Ben Franklin's* score is tuneful enough, but really only at its best in the songs developing the central romance: the wary reunion duet, "Too Charming"; a giddy tête-à-tête in an air balloon, "To Be Alone With You"; Diane's regretful and angry yet nobly unbitter "How Laughable It Is"; and finally a musical scene wedding his "Diane Is" and their "Look For Small Pleasures."

To learn that the first two were interpolations by Jerry Herman only emphasizes the Hermanesque feel of the score in general, for Herman's voice informed many writers' styles at this time. He would have wanted to create something like "Half the Battle (is learning to smile)," though probably in $6/8$ rather than Sandrich's $4/4$; and the lovely waltz "When I Dance With the Person I Love" gets even lovelier in its release ("and oh, if he ever should go away . . ."), a trick of song construction Herman favored.

This is not to say that there is anything derivative in the show. It's a unique piece (even if it did offer one of those Paris numbers), and was beautifully designed by Oliver Smith to collaborate with Kidd's many theatrical strokes. Oddly, for a staging by a director-choreographer, there was little dancing. In the 1950s, such a show would as a rule have had a good deal of dance—perhaps a Paris ballet or an interpretation of a Revolutionary War battle as Franklin gets the bad news. But just as dancing enlivens musical comedy, it slows a musical play—even dates it, to the Rodgers and Hammerstein days. The 1960s was the last decade dominated by traditional musical comedy. From then on, the musical play would take over, with its ever-intensifying gravity and realism. What's less grave and real than dance?

Ben Franklin in Paris preferred story to divertissement, albeit in a series of absorbing visuals. Considering that a major show of 1969 also gave us Ben Franklin and closed in a moving tableau on a bit of early-American history, we should remember that *Ben Franklin in Paris* did it first. It's a bold finale, for all the evening's energy has been pressing toward the resolution of Franklin's mission, by this time still unresolved. He is about to enter the King's court—in fact, the Hall of Mirrors at Versailles, so we know that Oliver Smith is realizing one of his devastating visuals. Preston is in one, in a plain hallway, and Michaels daringly stops the show dead to let Preston deliver a long soliloquy in Franklinese about . . . well, something apparently irrelevant yet very apropos. It really is a speech to the audience, a reminder that the freedom that they take for granted was not easily seized. Then the summons comes, Smith unveils his Versailles, and the footman announces, "The Ambassador of the United States of America!"

So he *has* won! As that opening sea chantey is heard in the orchestra, the court pays homage to our new country, the King smiles . . . and Ulla Sallert, wearing one of her famous facial expressions with about eleven ambivalent meanings and twenty-three enigmatic nuances, drops into a deep curtsy. Preston is in tears. And the curtain falls.

Carol Burnett had an even grander mission in *Fade Out Fade In* (1964): to become a movie star. In this satire on Hollywood, the authors of the almost contentless *Subways Are For Sleeping* had something to gnaw on. With George Abbott directing, spoof-hero Jack Cassidy as a matinée idol and spoof-villain Lou Jacobi as a studio chief, and plenty of dancing (by Ernest Flatt), *Fade Out Fade In* was back-to-basics musical comedy. It was so into its burlesque that it sacrificed the Boy Meets Girl to the comedy, leaving Boy Dick Patterson with very little romance to play.

No, most of this show was Burnett's misadventures and Comden and Green's Hollywood jokes: the chief's six groveling assistants (all nephews); movie titles such as *Don Juan's First Date*, *Sing, Boy, Sing*—*Smile, Girl, Smile*, and *Dance, Barn, Dance*; the intelligent black guy who goes all slow and dumb when the camera's turning; Cassidy's creepy yet glamorous narcissism; even one very funny moment when Cassidy appeared in John Barrymore tights, flowing white shirt, and sword but latched into a portable pillory, his head and hands locked into the holes as he bumped around the stage.

Burnett played Hope Springfield, A Girl To Remember (the last four words the show's original title), if only because she was tapped by accident and isn't cut out to play the roles the studio imposes on her, least of all the vamp. Patterson thinks her ridiculous—well, miscast—in her skimpy outfit, and in an allusion to Clara Bow's 1932 film *Call Her Savage*, Comden, Green, and Styne get a tasty duet out of the scene, "Call Me Savage": because Patterson won't. To lightly pounding Latin percussion and Carmen Cavallaro piano, Burnett does allure and Patterson lays plans to introduce her to Mother. Another wonderful duet found Burnett and the black actor (Tiger Haynes) doing a takeoff on Shirley Temple and Bill Robinson's numbers in "You Mustn't Be Discouraged." The song recalls with killing expertise those Depression cheer-up ditties; Burnett was made up as Temple, complete with curly-top wig and direly precocious moue.

All the best of *Fade Out Fade In* was that great musical-comedy thing, burlesque. The traditional musical play took most things seriously; only musical comedy saw everything as joke material. But the Rodgers and Hammerstein revolution had reformed musical comedy, which now took some things seriously. Or even: *all* things seriously, if in a sometimes funny way. *Donnybrook!* didn't run because it had no drawing power and no hit tune; but it also was a musical comedy without crazy fun. It was comic when Eddie Foy was on, but it did have rather a lot of love plot; the true musical comedies were too busy goofing off to do a lot of love.

So *Fade Out* was of an old fashion, though the staging was state-of-the-art, with the breezy set changes that now characterized all musicals. For instance, Burnett's first number, "(I've Never Been Here Before But) It's

Good To Be Back Home," ran on as the visuals shifted from the studio gates to on the lot, as Burnett danced with players representing Mae West, Jeanette MacDonald and Nelson Eddy, Dracula, Bette Davis, the Marx Brothers, and so on. The most elaborate staging was that of "I'm With You," the love song of *The Fiddler and the Fighter*. Burnett and Cassidy rehearsed the number at the piano, which led to a "dissolve" effect, as if the show were a movie. Then we saw the number as filmed, in Hollywood black-and-white and à la Busby Berkeley: women violinists like those in "The Shadow Waltz" (in *Gold Diggers of 1933*), men in tails plucking women dressed as violins, instruments glowing in the dark, and at last Burnett and Cassidy on risers dressed all in silver (including the boxing gloves).

Doesn't this sound like a humdinger? Why didn't it run? First, Burnett had a traffic accident and started to miss performances early in the run; and who wanted to see a Carol Burnett show without Burnett? She reportedly offered to buy her contract out for $500,000, which would have covered the show's production costs. Finally, she entered the hospital, closing the show. Arbitration found for the producers, and three months later the show reopened, with Burnett and Dick Shawn (improbably) taking over Cassidy's part and getting astonishing billing in letters as big as Burnett's and just below her name *above the title*. (Cassidy had had an "also starring" but in smaller type below the title.)

The authors had revised in the meantime, dropping the flashback frame and reworking the score. Songs were moved, dropped, and added, giving Dick Patterson a torch number, "Notice Me," to firm up the love plot. Perhaps the authors were aware that they had not produced a hit score, even a hit tune, so useful at this time when airplay and 45 singles made Broadway the wallpaper of American pop music. *Fade Out Fade In* has some sharp music—"The Usher From the Mezzanine" is one of this writing team's best character songs, hymning a girl's wish to be Somebody as a democratic right. It's de Tocqueville's worst nightmare as a musical-comedy ditty.

But much of *Fade Out Fade In* was a little too just-okay for the production to recover from the bad feeling caused by Burnett's dropping out. Some say that her career had advanced so imposingly in television that she just couldn't bother with Broadway any more. One might also consider that, as a brand-new mother and the victim of a traffic accident, she found carrying a big show overwhelming. In either case, *Fade Out Fade In* closed for the second time at a loss and at a final count of 271 performances.

Without Burnett's problems, the show would have paid off, for it had the big-show smarts that *All American* and *Tovarich* lacked, the glamour that *Bajour* lacked—Hollywood with silver costumes!—and even a believability that *Bravo, Giovanni* could not have begun to imagine. But then, more and more "successful" musicals were failing—simply not running long enough to make a profit at the new high overhead. Our next two titles are among the decade's best, and both failed. Well, of course they did: both are cult musicals starring Barbara Cook.

4

A ROMANTIC ATMOSPHERE

THE GAY LIFE AND *SHE LOVES ME*

Rodgers and Hammerstein invented the musical play: but the musical play reinvented musical comedy. Almost immediately after the appearance of *Oklahoma!* in 1943, the more lighthearted forms of musical, while staying light in tone, became more consistent in structure and more reasonably narrated. By the 1960s, some musical comedies were virtually musical plays, while unreconstructed musical comedy was becoming rare.

Let us get our bearings on these two genres that together dominated the American musical in its Golden Age:

	MUSICAL COMEDY	MUSICAL PLAY
STORY:	Can be improbable.	Must be probable; in a fantasy, behavior remains realistic
SCORE:	Light emotional content; specialty numbers having little connection to plot are permissable (for example: "Oh, Diogenes," "Zip," "Pass That Football," "Mu-Cha-Cha," "Gentleman Jimmy," "The Rhythm of Life," "That's How Young I Feel")	Strong emotional content; specialty numbers are rare; prefers unique numbers useless in any other show ("The One Indispensable Man," "Stonecutters Cut it on Stone," "Train to Johannesburg," "You Did It," "On the Farm," "C'est Moi")
COMEDY:	Plenty, especially of sarcastic, satiric, and ribald nature; out-of-story gags are acceptable (as when, in *A*	Seldom enough, and only within limits of character; no out-of-story gags

	MUSICAL COMEDY	MUSICAL PLAY
	Tree Grows in Brooklyn, Shirley Booth refers to "The Ocarina," a number in *Call Me Madam* the year before)	
CHOREOGRAPHY:	Hoofing ("The Hot Honey Rag")	Ballet or "dance" ("The Small House of Uncle Thomas")
PERFORMING STYLE:	A mélange of show-biz modes, including caricature and schtick	An integrated acting ensemble
REASON FOR BEING:	Entertainment	Enlightenment

Keep in mind that there have been many exceptions along the way, as when musical comedies such as *I'd Rather Be Right* (1937) and *On the Town* utilized ballet *and* dance; or when, again, musical comedies such as *The Music Man* and *Chicago* (1975) were able to enlighten as well as entertain. Note, too, that while the better writers of musical comedy consistently tend toward the musical play, the musical play seldom degenerates into musical comedy.

We've seen some excellent examples of pure musical comedy already in *Bye Bye Birdie*, *The Unsinkable Molly Brown*, and *Fade Out Fade In*. Now we'll have another. This one sports a plot that, decades before, would have worked only for an operetta: turn-of-the-century Vienna, romance, waltzes (actually only two), St. Stephen's Cathedral, the Hotel Sacher, the Paprikas Café, taking the waters at Carlsbad . . . *The Gay Life* (1961).*

This is an exemplary sixties musical comedy, with an unusual story and one of the most satisfying scores of the era but, in its compositional layout and physical production, absolutely conventional. Its source was Arthur Schnitzler's seven one-act plays on the love life of the Viennese dilettante Anatol, first published in 1893 and produced in 1910. The characters are

---

*The title was actually set forth within quote marks, as, generally, were titles of shows that adopted popular phrases or that indicated spoken lines. Others such were *"How To Succeed in Business Without Really Trying"*, *"A Family Affair"*, *"Nowhere To Go But Up"*, *"It's a Bird It's a Plane It's Superman"*, *"I Do! I Do!"*, and that's but a partial list. Although I have honored this practice in previous volumes, I find it irritating and unnecessary, and I am retiring it from this page onward.

Anatol; his confidant, Max; and Anatol's various girl friends. Book writers Fay and Michael Kanin drew on "Christmas Shopping" (a woman sends a bouquet to Anatol's mistress, saying, roughly, "I would gladly trade places with you, if I had the courage"), "A Farewell Dinner" (Anatol must break off his latest affair, but is flabbergasted when *she* breaks it off first), and "Anatol's Wedding Morning" (Max finds him in bed, entertaining: and it's not his betrothed).

What the Kanins mainly created was Liesl, Max's naïve young sister, who yearns for the worldly Anatol. The other leads were Max and Liesl's parents, typical Broadway nags:

LIESL: (holding up dresses) I could wear either of these. What do *you* think, Mama?

FRAU BRANDEL: (eager for control) Well, I—No, Papa is right. You should pick it out yourself.

.   .   .

LIESL: But, Mama—

FRAU BRANDEL: (firmly) It's about time you had your own opinions.

LIESL: (shyly) Well, I think . . . the blue one.

FRAU BRANDEL: With *your* complexion?

and four *maîtresses* for Anatol: a suicidal noblewoman (Anita Gillette), a sophisticated married woman (Jeanne Bal), an impudent Frenchwoman (Yvonne Constant), and an explosive Gypsy woman (Elizabeth Allen).

The Gay Life's scene plan was very contemporary: a series of backdrops laced with furniture and decorations hauled on and off from the wings, moving from larger ("The Carlsbad Drinking Pavilion"), with plenty of dancing space, to smaller ("The Terrace of the Brandel Suite"), to larger ("The Casino at Carlsbad"). As we saw in *Bye Bye Birdie*, there were no blacked-out stage waits between scenes: everything flowed together from overture to first-act curtain, and from entr'acte to bows.

The dancing, too, typified the time, with a major dance in each act. The first, following Anatol and Max's "Now I'm Ready For a Frau," showed Anatol courting a variety of girls—a tennis whiz, a mountain climber, a boating fanatic, a butterfly chaser, and so on, all in those great *belle époque* costumes and all, at the end, stretched in a line with Anatol at the center, they full of energy and he so dazed that, for the climax, he fainted. The second-act dance, biographical vignettes at Anatol's bachelor party, reviewed his affairs, to Max's narration. (As four ballerinas appeared in the famous *Swan Lake* pas de quatre, Max cried, "Ah—his cultural period!")

For, yes, Anatol is getting married, and to Liesl. It was she who sent the flowers to his mistress, wishing to trade places; she whom Anatol named when that mistress tried to dump him before he could dump her; and she who surprised Anatol in his flat with another woman on the morning of their wedding, all pretty much as in Schnitzler. But it was not the script that made *The Gay Life* special. The script was functional, no more.

It was the cast and staging staff and above all the score that made this one of the major uncelebrated shows. Producer Kermit Bloomgarden replaced director Gerald Freedman out of town with the show's choreographer, Herbert Ross, perhaps because it was Ross' dances that held the staging together, in a blending of mock ballet, narrative spoof, and grandiose hoofing. Ross provided the wit that the Kanins too often didn't; he gave them class and sex appeal. Oliver Smith, as always, summoned up the true-to-life fairyland that musical comedy wants to take place in, and costumer Lucinda Ballard won a Tony. (Given 1904 Vienna and all those glorious damsels in their stripes, ribbons, and picture hats, one would virtually have to have done.) Orchestrator Don Walker put a cembalom in the pit—a sort of Hungarian keyboard instrument that sounds like Johann Strauss wrestling a harpsichord.

And now comes the cast—Walter Chiari as Anatol, Jules Munshin as Max, and Barbara Cook as Liesl. Chiari, though a looker, was actually a gifted comic, able even in slapstick: something of an Italian Cary Grant. Munshin, whom we last saw assisting Carol Channing in *Show Girl*, may be recalled for his excruciating Salad Routine in the Astaire-Garland film *Easter Parade*; but here he was delightful, bringing almost as much continental suave to his scenes as Chiari. And Cook had in Liesl something musical comedies didn't have till Rodgers and Hammerstein reinstructed them: a substantial character to play, from kid to woman and, even, from lady to sensualist.

One odd thing about musical comedy's maturity is that as its stories get more spacious and its characters more complex, it has no trouble finding performers with the traditional virtues who can also act. Cook was one such—along with Gwen Verdon, Robert Preston, and Chita Rivera—who made confession in musical comedy rather than in the musical play while blessing the lighter form with the grander form's intensity.

This Cook did especially in the songs. Her numbers actually describe an arc, to take a shy and wistful young woman into, at first, competition for the man she loves, then something approaching confidence, then regret, and at last fury at his eternal vacillating. The key number is "Magic Moment." This is an outstanding example of the Heroine's Wanting Song, because composer Arthur Schwartz and lyricist Howard Dietz conceived something at once murmured yet passionate, embarrassed at its own erotic longing. It is amazing to consider that these two first teamed up in the 1920s, and that they went separate ways after *Inside U.S.A.* in 1948. Schwartz had been heard from only twice after that, working with Dorothy Fields; and Dietz not at all: yet they effortlessly acclimated themselves to the "new" musical comedy.

Now for a character change. Anatol gets pulled into a magician's act and disappears with the magician's captivating French co-adjutrix. No, *really* disappears. The chagrined Liesl sings "The Label on the Bottle," a diatribe on the attractions of French females while herself wishing to be one. It's a typical premise for a musical-comedy number, wordplay on a stereotype. And there in the empty casino are, of course, three waiters to support Cook in the dancing section. The modified cancan setting for the lyrics is a nice touch, a musical pun on the cliché; and the vocal takes Cook into her soprano range, at the time one of Broadway's most welcome sounds. What makes the number most enticing is how well Schwartz and Dietz wrote it *for Liesl*, with the crestfallen verse but then the vigorously complaining chorus and at length a *determined* chorus, exactly right for this one character in this one show—indeed, in this one scene. The lyrics would have been too smart for her earlier in Act One, and by Act Two she has too much self-knowledge to think that she can win Anatol as anyone but herself.

Liesl's numbers are a show in themselves. Visiting Anatol's apartment, she charms his resentful valet:

LIESL: I've been waiting for this chance to talk to you, alone.

FRANZ: (drawing himself up coolly) You needn't worry. I won't embar-

rass you. I'm quite aware that Herr von Huber will have no more
need of me after his marriage.

LIESL: Oh, but *I* will.

FRANZ: (confused) You?

She wants clues, tips, understanding. In "Something You Never Had
Before," Schwartz and Dietz give us insight into why Liesl finally believes
in her own dream. She even feels superior, now, to his many women. It's
the same old musical-comedy reason that we have known for decades:
they were pleasure, but she is true love. The music rises, soaring in the
chorus and flirting a bit in the release ("You've had gay love before . . ."),
emotions warring inside her. Then comes a patter section ("I know the
art of keeping house . . ."), as Liesl rationalizes while she wonders. Then
the orchestra returns to the main strain as Liesl investigates the apartment, tries to know it as she wants to know Anatol. And, of course,
singing again, she pauses most tensely at the bedroom door.

The rest of the score is more functional, almost circling around Liesl,
making her in effect the protagonist of Anatol's story. Chiari's character,
amusing enough in "Now I'm Ready For a Frau," only really comes alive
in his duet with Liesl, "You're Not the Type." It's a separated duet, for
they are not actually communicating: she is in her room and he—in that
very new sixties technique of cutting across time and space within a
scene—is taking a stroll through town. It's a dialogue in soliloquy, as she
finally sees how uncommitted he is and he vainly tries to reassure her. For
once, after all his clowning and prevaricating, he is deeply touched at her
alarm. His most typical attitude has been exasperation at his uncontrol-
lable power over women; now he is fearful of that power, of how it may
hurt Liesl. He tries to envision their life together, claiming that he has
had his last affair. And, in a reply of crushing honesty, she sings, "You
have not had your last affair." For these few minutes, it was musical-comedy writing as good as anything in *Brigadoon* or *West Side Story*.

It is one of the curiosities of the musical that despite the lengthy
rehearsal period, many titles open out of town with everyone stunned at
how Stuffed Full of Too Much Everything a show can be. Did Anatol
need *four* women besides Cook? Anita Gillette's role was cut out, freeing
her for *All American*, and *The Gay Life*'s first window cards were printed

without credits, as if producer Bloomgarden wasn't sure who else might have to go or come in. (At one point, the creative staff considered letting Cook play all of Anatol's women in different guises.) The critics, as so often in this decade, were very mixed. They noted the important contributions of Cook and designers Smith and Ballard, but the merely adequate script was a problem for some. Rather than stand pat, Bloomgarden called for yet more improvements—yes, *after* the opening. At the New York premiere, *The Gay Life* began with an old-fashioned chorus, "What a Charming Couple," at Anatol and Liesl's wedding. But the notoriously skittish Anatol is not there. Max rushes to Anatol's apartment, Anatol starts to explain . . . and a flashback began.

Now the flashback was dropped, and Jeanne Bal's "Why Go Anywhere At All?" was replaced by "You're Not the Type." This was completely incorrect for Bal's flighty character and vitiated the song's effect when it reappeared in Act Two. "What a Charming Couple" finally turned up during the curtain calls, showing the happy ending: a big wedding in St. Stephen's. But at least the book retained a superb conclusion: with all problems cleared away, Anatol and Liesl find themselves so hot for each other that he picks her up and starts for his bedroom. Then:

ANATOL: (shocked) What am I doing? We're being married in half an hour.
LIESL: (playfully) They can't start without us.

And, as the orchestra surged up, he carried her inside, the audience took in the ribald joke of the empty stage, and the curtain fell. Note that, while the *script* thought the throughline was Anatol Grows Up and Gets Married, the *score's* throughline was Liesl Grows Up and Likes Herself; and the two came together perfectly in the sight gag of Anatol's vacated living room.

No one can explain the failure of *The Gay Life*—or of our second continental piece. This one would have been an operetta before musical comedy got smart, *She Loves Me* (1963). A publicizing hit tune might have helped, or more consistently *pow!* reviews. However, unlike *The Gay Life*, *She Loves Me* is a well-known and constantly revived piece. It also represents, in its songwriters, Jerry Bock and Sheldon Harnick, New

Broadway (as opposed to the Old Broadway of *The Gay Life*'s Schwartz and Dietz) and is unconventional in structure.

In place of the big set–small set–big set pacing of big musical comedy, *She Loves Me* takes place largely inside and in front of a women's notions store, with one other full-scale set (a café) and some incidental partial sets. The dancing is very limited and the chorus hardly there except as body count in the café and in an ensemble, near the end, that serves as punctuation for a series of plot vignettes. *The Gay Life*'s chorus was all over the action, singing seven numbers in whole or part, constantly dressing the stage or playing roles in the two ballets, now an usher at the wedding or the magician with the French cutie, then a waiter, a doorman, more waiters. This could make for surprisingly crowded dramatis personae in the playbill. (*The Unsinkable Molly Brown* lists thirty-nine such, including "Brawling Miners," "The Grand Duchess Marie Nicholaiovna," and "Wounded Sailor.") Equity loved it, because, this way, virtually everyone in the chorus got role billing.

Oddly, big as it was, *The Gay Life* was about two people. *She Loves Me* is about the store owner and his staff of six: about them all. Maybe *She Loves Me* would have run longer if it had more openly proclaimed its source, which was not, as stated, "a play by Miklos Laszlo" but *The Shop Around the Corner*, the extremely popular 1940 movie that Ernst Lubitsch made of that play. "Nothing [of Laszlo]," said Samson Raphaelson, Lubitsch's scriptwriter, "not one scene, not one line of dialogue, coincides with the film." All that Lubitsch took was the play's idea of life in a parfumerie in the course of which two bickering people learn that they are in love.

She Loves Me comes directly from Lubitsch and Raphaelson—the "Dear Friend" correspondence of the two leads, their *Anna Karenina* and red carnation meeting signal, the boss' suicide attempt at the discovery of his wife's infidelity, even the music box that the heroine sells as an audition for her job. Joe Masteroff's book added one important consideration, uniting two of the shop's clerks in a second love plot and developing this couple so that, in contrast with the main pair, Amalia and Georg (Barbara Cook, Daniel Massey), he (Jack Cassidy) is a roué and she (Barbara Baxley) takes the available rather than the ideal man.

At first, Masteroff's second couple might appear to supply the standard musical-comedy subplot: Clifford David and Paula Stewart in *Wildcat*, or John Reardon and Nancy Dussault in *Do Re Mi*. You know—Will Parker and Ado Annie. The fun roles. In fact, Masteroff's supplementary pair helps us to understand the two leads, to sense that they're not quite the Curly and Laurey that musicals like to center on. After all, Georg and Amalia are so unable to connect with others that they've placed lonely-hearts ads. These are shy and uncomfortable people with low self-esteem levels. No wonder they start fighting as soon as they meet yet feel so close in their letters: they're insecure about how others see them on the out-side. So, in the rendezvous café, just as we feel that Georg might be about to tell Amalia that he is Dear Friend, he says, "You've never really looked at me."

It's a key line, easy to miss in the excitement of the moment: because it unfortunately gives her a cue to tell him off conclusively. Remember, she is extremely nervous about this meeting and he has been aggressively irritating her. So:

AMALIA: I'm looking at you right now—and shall I tell you what I see? A smug, pompous, petty tyrant—very sure of himself and very ambitious. But I see him ten years from now—selling shampoo. And twenty years from now—selling shampoo. And thirty years from now still selling shampoo! Because, basically, you know what he is? Just a not-very-bright, not-very-handsome, not-very-young man with balding hair and the personality of a python!

This is something new in their relationship. Thus far, they have merely been firing shots across each other's bows; this is total war. If played well, it can be stunning in the theatre. It certainly stuns Georg: he leaves without uttering a word. Because he's afraid she's right.

She Loves Me would have been unlikely in the 1950s, at least in this form. A good writer might have given us these characters as fully as Masteroff does. But would staging conventions have allowed for William and Jean Eckart's free-flowing design, which literally "opened up" the shop's exterior like a wrapped present to reveal the inside? Would the 1950s have tolerated Bock and Harnick's intimately vast score of more than twenty numbers, everything from little bits to full-out musical scenes?*

*Yes, the 1950s played host to such big scores as those of *The Golden Apple*, *Candide*, and *The Most Happy Fella*. But these are a ballet ballad, a "comic operetta," and a Broadway opera. Plain musical comedy, in the 1950s, was not so ambitious.

The first of these scenes is the opening, one of those let's-meet-the-characters anthology pieces, "Good Morning, Good Day." A brisk march that eventually opens into a sweeping ensemble without ever really changing its tune, it gives us a taste of everybody—adolescent Arpad (Ralph Williams), self-effacing Sipos (Nathaniel Frey), exploited date Ilona (Baxley) and exploiting dandy Kodaly (Cassidy), and finally Georg. Their boss (Ludwig Donath) arrives *after* the song, tipping us to his peripheral involvement in the story; and of course Amalia enters in the following scene: for that *starts* the story.

This is admirable Broadway writing. "Three Letters" is even better. I saw *She Loves Me* on a Wednesday afternoon in a sea of matinée mavens, and while this much-abused group talks too much and doesn't get the jokes, the ladies love a good story. So, when Georg, at stage left, sang out his third letter to Dear Friend and Amalia came into view at stage right singing the words along with him as she read his letter, the entire audience went "Ohhhh." The nemeses are lovers. That's sweet.

It's comic, too—but not the way musical comedies usually are. There are no gags, only character comedy, and the humor seeps into the lyrics of even love songs. A duet for Amalia and Ilona in which they compare their respective love lives gives Amalia for her main strain a delightful little tizzy of a trill followed by a rising line of aching desire. It's very lilting, yet it climaxes with "I couldn't know him better if I knew his name," an absurd concept, however true. Even "Ice Cream," which builds up to Cook's trusty high B flat, goes into comedy as she tries to write to Dear Friend and keeps getting jammed in her new, favorable impressions of Georg.

But then, this score finds music in anything. The courtesies routinely performed as customers leave the shop turn into "Thank You, Madam"—which itself turns into a plot number when Georg quits and his colleagues have to pay their respects while conducting business as usual, all in song. "Where's My Shoe?" is almost indescribable, for it isn't about what it thinks it's about. (It's actually Georg's first chance to get his hands on Amalia.) And there's one very short musical piece, in the café, in which Amalia threatens to scream if Georg doesn't leave; and he doesn't; so she screams.

Harold S. Prince directed (and co-produced) *She Loves Me*, on his first shot at seeing a work through composition, rehearsal, and performance. One senses his touch in the score's powerful sense of character. It's what any good director asks: what's happening in this song? For instance, for the day of the café rendezvous, Bock and Harnick wrote a solo for Amalia, "Tell Me I Look Nice," expressing her nervousness at being judged on her appearance. It's a fine piece. The music suggests the butter-flies-in-the-stomach feeling that she must be suffering, and the lyrics offer the calm frenzy that she customarily gets into when unsure. But the moment isn't about what she's wearing. It's about how she feels. So they wrote a new solo, "Will He Like Me?" *That's* sweet.

Prince later stated that booking this medium-sized show into the medium-sized Eugene O'Neill Theatre kept it from earning enough over its weekly costs to pay off. At 302 performances, *She Loves Me* was another example of that sixties invention, the successful flop: good notices, popular score, nice run, red ink. It did even less well in London. But its relatively small scale has endeared it to regional companies, not least because, after Amalia's soprano and Kodaly's greasy tenor, actors who can sort of sing easily fill out a capable ensemble. New York saw several stagings before a prominent revival at the Roundabout in 1993. This was greatly misconceived, even vulgarized, though the production went on to London, with a better cast headed by John Gordon Sinclair and Ruthie Henshall. The show never makes money, but it keeps being done. Is it too subtle a piece? Too intelligent? Too soft, too lovely? Can a musical be too integrated?

It's a superb story superbly told, an acknowledged glory of the day. *The Gay Life* lacks a good story, but it boasts a more outgoing score and enjoyed excellent production values. The production, now, is gone and the score just a cast album. *She Loves Me* is a classic, because it will always surprise a willing public. Remember my matinée ladies? As *She Loves Me* reaches its curtain, Georg and Amalia are leaving the store on Christmas Eve. They're about to part company. But he knows that he's Dear Friend. And we know that he's Dear Friend. Now *she* has to know. So he quietly sings to her the words of the letter she composed during "Ice Cream."

Now she knows.

And, as Barbara Cook turned to Daniel Massey with a look at once relieved, ecstatic, and terrified, the Eugene O'Neill Theatre broke into tremendous applause even before Cook reached Massey's arms for the curtain tableau.

I was waiting for that, those women were saying. You presented a lovely tale in a unique way, and I now realize that if I am to be stimulated, inspired, and touched, it needn't be a musical play that does it. Musical comedy can have magic moments, too.

5

NOTHING MORE TO LOOK FORWARD TO

OLD TALENT

The 1960s, like the 1920s, is a time of demarcation. The earlier decade saw an American form of musical theatre conclusively overwhelm European derivatives; the later decade saw virtually the last work of the surviving writers that had created this form. So the Broadway of "Tea For Two" and "Night And Day," of *Show Boat* and *Anything Goes*, of belting broads and loony clowns, of showgirls and dream ballets, was over. *Camelot* may be the closing event of that era, the last major show of the Rodgers and Hammerstein kind that this four-decade age had been striving to invent and then perfect.

There was overlap. Irving Berlin, whose first full stage score was written in 1914, offered *Mr. President* in 1962, with the producer and scriptwriters (Leland Hayward and Howard Lindsay and Russel Crouse) of his previous show, *Call Me Madam* (1950). What an idea: a look at an imaginary First Family, with President Robert Ryan and wife Nanette Fabray and Joshua Logan directing. The box office took in more than two million dollars before the show opened, and it ran 265 performances entirely on that advance, for it was not a good show. Blame unfortunately fell on Berlin, for so much had been expected of him simply because he was still showing up, at the age of seventy-four. The true culprits were Logan, a truly worthless book, and even set designer Jo Mielziner.

Mr. President looked ugly, went nowhere, and suffered a lack of charisma in its cast. Sure, Ryan seemed presidential. What natural-born musical-comedy leading man could embody better than dramatic actor Ryan the gala WASP that Stephen Decatur Henderson was supposed to be? Robert Preston would have come off as too sly—that's Wintergreen for President—and Alfred Drake too sensual. Still, Ryan appeared uncomfortable not only in the songs but in the dialogue scenes. Fabray was, as always, terrific; those who never saw her live in a musical have nothing to tell their grandchildren. The rest of the crew counted the capable, no more: Anita Gillette as First Daughter and Jack Haskell as her loving bodyguard; Jack Washburn as Haskell's rival, a duplicitous Arab diplomat; Jerry Strickler as First Son; and Wisa D'Orso as Strickler's flame, a belly dancer.

Actually, the only thing that worked in the show was Berlin's score. It is not at all impressive; but it is tuneful and it tries to create content for the silhouettes that Lindsay and Crouse gave Berlin. There was one excellent number, "They Love Me," Fabray's report on a world tour that choreographer Peter Gennaro illustrated with native islanders, Asian beatniks, the typical Kabuki lion, and a gigantic elephant. There was some pure Irving Berlin genre—Gillette's one-cute-rhyme-supports-an-entire-song comedy spot, "The Secret Service (makes me nervous)"; the two-melodies-heard-separately-and-then-together duet, in Haskell and Gillette's "Empty Pockets Filled With Love." (He sang the ballad, then she came in with the syncopated jive.) Given the show's Washington background, Berlin could hardly omit the patriotic number, even if "This Is a Great Country" seems a bit by-the-numbers. Critics carped that Berlin was doing what he always did. After half a century, what else is he supposed to do? There was an item called "The Washington Twist," but it was Berlin in protest.

Though Berlin lived twenty-seven years more, *Mr. President*'s failure pushed him into retirement. Seclusion, even. This is, in fact, another all-flop chapter, though these are almost all Type A failures, with good music. *Do I Hear a Waltz?* (1965) has suffered a bad rap from its surviving authors, lyricist Stephen Sondheim and book writer Arthur Laurents, but their dissatisfaction seems based more on the miserable time they had working with composer Richard Rodgers and director John Dexter than with any flaw in the composition. *Do I Hear a Waltz?* went through one of Broadway's best-known tryout hells, intimate to many who know the show itself hardly or not at all. There is: Rodgers' mistrust of and eventual intense distaste for Sondheim, Laurents, and Dexter; Rodgers' trashing of Sondheim's latest lyric before the entire company; Dexter's shocking lack of leadership, which forced the hiring of Herbert Ross, supposedly as cho-reographer but really to take over Dexter's job; Sondheim's famous invo-cation of Mary Rodgers' notion of the "Why? musical," meaning, Why add songs to a play that doesn't need them?; even the fact that the origi-nal stager of the musical numbers, Wakefield Poole (later billed as Ross' "choreographic associate"), became a pioneer gay-porn filmmaker in the 1970s.

The play that Sondheim says doesn't need songs is Laurents' own *The Time of the Cuckoo* (1952). But there's a song cue—and, by synecdoche, a potential score—written into its script, about an American spinster tour-ing Venice:

> LEONA: I used to think when I fell in love, I'd hear a waltz. No waltz, Signora.

However, at the end of this scene this awkwardly warm and intensely self-protected old maid is happily weeping in the arms of a tenderly amorous Italian, and Laurents' stage directions tell us that Leona finally hears her waltz.

That sounds like a musical to me, especially with all of Venice to open up into. But the authors didn't want to open up in the usual sense. Venice was suggested, by designer Beni Montresor's series of tall rectangular screens against a skyline backdrop, and by the chorus, which moved about but played no bit parts and never sang. As in *The Time of the Cuckoo*, the action centered on a few visiting Americans; on the pen-sione-keeper, Signora Fioria, and her maid; and the Venetian with whom Leona becomes involved. The casting, with one disastrous exception, was fine: Elizabeth Allen as Leona (we last saw her as *The Gay Life*'s gypsy, Magda), Sergio Franchi as her Venetian, Stuart Damon and Julienne Marie as a marital problem, Madeleine Sherwood and Jack Manning as a boring marriage, and the too-seldom-seen Carol Bruce as Signora Fioria. The score was entirely about them: Leona's startled opening, "Someone Woke Up" (for everyone is startled by his or her first sight of Venice), Sig-nora Fioria's genuflecting "This Week Americans" (and an amusing reprise, completely reversing her posture, as "Last Week Americans"), Franchi's tour de force of baritone against falsetto, "Bargaining," or the second act's first number, "Moon in My Window," with Marie's foolishly optimistic chorus, Signora Fioria's cynical chorus, and Leona's wondering chorus.

It's a fine score. Laurents expertly reworked his play. And the Ross-Poole-Montresor staging was very effective. What was wrong was Elizabeth Allen. She, too, was fine and expert: but wholly miscast. Leona is a wounded bird; Dorothy Collins would have been right, or perhaps Florence Henderson. Allen projected strength and resourcefulness: a healthy person. Leona is shy and bitter, still somewhat young but without romantic prospects, always trying not to intrude while always intruding. Even her standby mode of address, "Cookie," irritates when it is meant to soothe. In Laurents' play and the movie based on it, *Summertime*, Leona's problems were eased by the charm of Shirley Booth and Katharine Hepburn. These problems shouldn't be eased: the problems are presumably why Laurents wrote the play. Leona is not someone who simply hasn't yet heard a waltz. She's *terrified* of the waltz—after hearing it, she arranges to murder it so she'll never have to hear it again.

Allen was glad to hear it; maybe the confident title song was a mistake. The musical ends with Allen and Franchi parting, as in play and movie. So Rodgers, Sondheim, and Laurents weren't trying to "cure" Leona, just present her. "A workmanlike, professional show," Sondheim calls it, in dismissal. But a concert reading at Encores! might well reinstate it as another very good if not great show that failed simply because it didn't run.

The same can be said for the last two musicals written by Noël Coward, *Sail Away* (1961) and *The Girl Who Came To Supper* (1963). Coward had even greater seniority than Rodgers, for as actor Coward had made it to the West End when Rodgers was in high school, and as writer Coward was celebrated in London and New York for the play *The Vortex* (1924) when Rodgers and Hart had yet to attract notice. Over the decades, only five of Coward's revues, operettas, and plays with music had appeared in New York, yet he was by the 1960s more honored in America than in England, where critics wrote of him as a horrid old dinosaur.

Sail Away is a musical comedy and *The Girl Who Came To Supper* something of an operetta. This sums up the two dominant strains in Coward's music—the saucy patter number and the sweeping waltz, to confer, respectively, wit and romance upon a hurly-burly world. But now Coward was trying novelty. *Sail Away* was an attempt to write a contemporary fun show in the Broadway style, and *The Girl* was an attempt to write *My Fair Lady*.

Sail Away, too, knew tryout hell. Coward's plan was to use the setting of a cruise ship and the romance between an older woman and a younger man (the original title was *Later Than Spring*) to bind together an assortment of frivolities. These included burlesques of tourism, eccentric characters, and—making her entrance with a bouquet of balloons on a string and a dynamite aria di sortita, "Come To Me"—Elaine Stritch. As social director Mimi Paragon, Stritch would help unify the action simply by being able to turn up literally anywhere in the script. The glamorous opera soprano Jean Fenn and James Hurst had the romance, giving Coward a chance to use music yet heard only in London shows, her "This Is a Changing World" (the show's only waltz) and his "Sail Away." Alice Pearce zipped in and out as a zany novelist traveling with her niece (Patricia Harty), who takes up with a cute guy in a tank top and running shorts (Grover Dale). These two sang Coward's not entirely unsuccessful attempts to Write Young in "Beatnik Love Affair" and "When You Want Me." Charles Braswell played the ship's purser in Act One and an Arab rug-seller in Act Two, with two lyrics set to the same melody, stuffy for "The Passenger's Always Right" and whining for "The Customer's Always Right." Stritch sang the comedy spots, including one with a group of brats and an eleven o'clocker, "Why Do the Wrong People Travel?"

Out of town, the company was tense, because with so loose a narrative structure anyone might be replaced. There was also the billing problem, with eleven names to accommodate under the title: in what order? At one point, Stritch confronted Coward with the rumor that one of the woman leads was going to have her name listed last and set off in a box with the word "and" in front of it. The exasperated Coward replied, "She shall have her name listed last and set off in a box with the word '*but*' in front of it!"

Three weeks before the New York opening, choreographer Joe Layton made a suggestion. Especially not landing was the Fenn-Hurst romance, and especially landing was Stritch. Why not lose Fenn and let Stritch play opposite Hurst? Coward went for it, and it saved the show—not from financial failure, but from the disaster of not being a good piece. As a 1999 New York concert reading (with Stritch) made clear, *Sail Away* is exactly the fun that Coward planned it to be: "a revue formula with a mere thread of story running through it," as the author himself admitted. That's its charm. But some of the New York players were weak, a mistake that the London staging in 1962 seemed to admit by retaining Stritch (now boldly headlining) and Dale but bringing in young people with energy and old people with élan. Long-ago operetta diva Edith Day made a comeback after twenty years out of musicals, and the nutty novelist was that queen of twee, Dorothy Reynolds. Again, the show failed to pay off.

The Girl Who Came To Supper was a bigger failure—a bigger show, for one thing; and it did seem awfully like *My Fair Lady* in its Sprechstimme male and soprano female leads, its Edwardian London, its buskers' alley and Embassy Ball, its Tessie O'Shea doing music-hall numbers comparable to those of Stanley Holloway in *Lady*, even in its producer, Herman Levin, who had mounted the earlier show. As always blaming everyone but himself, Coward excoriated Harry Kurnitz's gag-ridden book, the oversized Broadway Theatre, and, especially, the lack of appeal in the leading man, José Ferrer. Christopher Plummer had turned it down, and Keith Michell was apparently not big enough. "He *is* ugly," Coward thought of Ferrer, "but he is also curiously attractive." Actually, he was Cyrano de Bergerac, completely wrong for a part played by Laurence Olivier and Michael Redgrave in the original play.

That was Terence Rattigan's *The Sleeping Prince*, a boulevard comedy about an American musical-comedy player dallying with an eastern European royal. Coward and Rattigan are often "twinned" in English theatre histories. But besides Coward's status as performer and songwriter, they are also very unalike in that Rattigan wrote of strong women and Coward wrote of weak men. They meet in *The Girl Who Came To Supper* because Coward saw possibilities in Rattigan's setting, diplomatic London at the time of the coronation of George V.

Possibilities there certainly are. Consider Coward's opening, a backstage look at *The Coconut Girl*. Consider the coronation ceremony, a comic ensemble for the opening of Act Two, with the aristocrats ranged before us making acid remarks while the American heroine revels in a naïve thrill. Consider *his* patter numbers, "Long Live the King (if he can)" or "How Do You Do, Middle Age?" Consider *her*, yes, sweeping waltzes, "I've Been Invited To a Party" or "Here and Now." She also gets a real tour de force in a seven-number sequence spoofing old musicals—the opening chorus, the Automobile Song, the New Dance Sensation, the Swing Song (which we saw in actual performance at the start of Act One), the harmony number in which she amusingly sings a monotonous bass line.

With Florence Henderson playing the very heart and head of The Girl, Oliver Smith and Irene Sharaff designs, and Joe Layton as director-choreographer, *The Girl Who Came To Supper* sounds like a case of Possibilities Fulfilled. Except.

Except Coward was right about Ferrer, who had Cyrano's charisma but was indeed physically unhappy. Except Tessie O'Shea's extended vocal spot had nothing to do with the story—and her *gangway!* numbers warred with the rest of the silky-witty score as Holloway's had not in *My Fair Lady*. Except the lack of sheer plot, which never held back a light comedy, stops a musical cold.

And except the assassination of John Kennedy, which occurred while *The Girl* was about to leave Philadelphia for New York, drained the amusement from an entertainment that was in part about government intrigue. Obviously, "Long Live the King"—which Layton had staged with extravagant feints and assaults from assassins in the auditorium—had to go. Coward replaced it with "My Family Tree," on a new melody for the refrain but chunking in bits of music and lyrics from "Countess Mitzi" from his 1938 show *Operette*. Still, the larger problem remained: not enough people were in the mood for this piece at this time.

It is obviously a problem for veterans that, after two decades or so, their modes may become cliché. This never slowed Cole Porter down. But how was lyricist and librettist E. Y. Harburg to pursue his Popular Front musical comedy, a form he had been exploiting since *Hooray For What!* in 1937, mostly with composers Harold Arlen and Burton Lane? One way was to team up with Jacques Offenbach in an adaptation of Aristophanes' *Lysistrata* as *The Happiest Girl in the World* (1961). Harburg's longtime associate Fred Saidy wrote the book with Henry Myers, and Harburg was a most respectful collaborator, using Offenbach's melodies very much as they were. There was none of the "adaptation" that Robert Wright and George Forrest effected of Grieg and Borodin for *Song of Norway* and *Kismet*. Occasionally, themes from two different Offenbach titles would be combined into a single new number. But *Happiest Girl*'s most important songs consisted of Harburg's new lyrics married to familiar strains purely used.

Thus, the title song is *La Périchole*'s Letter Song, slightly promoted from an Andante in $^6/_8$ to an outgoing waltz. The *Hoffmann* Barcarolle is "(Here we are) Adrift on a Star." "How Soon, Oh Moon?" is Euridice's death scene from *Orpheus in the Underworld*. About one fourth of the music came from *La Belle Hélène*,* but generally Harburg took a wide view of Offenbach's prolific career, using a few obscure tunes while favoring those that had had nearly a century in which to catch on.

It should have been a sure thing, with Harburg in fine form in a bawdy tale, given a big production and staged for low fun by its star, Cyril Ritchard. To Aristophanes' tale of women refusing their marital duties till their men renounce war, *The Happiest Girl in the World* added the caperings of war-mongering Pluto** (Ritchard) and peacemaking Diana (Janice Rule), which at least provided a lot of plot. Dran Seitz and Bruce Yarnell were Lysistrata and her Kinesias, and the chorus proved a lusty crew, a sort of co-ed burlesque show. Typical of the show's tone was the ironically leering "Vive la Virtue" (from Orestes' third-act rondo in *La Belle Hélène*), which rhymes "Vice is not averse to virtue" with "The man who would unskirt you."

That's wit; but the book lacked it. Noël Coward thought the whole thing "an orgy of frustrated sex. Naked young men lying about; no jokes above the navel; an appalling scene in a Turkish bath; and Cyril bouncing on and off the stage in ladies' wigs and ladies' hats." However, this is not to mention Harburg's adroit use of ancient Greece to comment on how differently the genders view the making of war. The critics gave the show the almost inevitable very mixed reviews: as if no one could agree on how a musical should go any more.

They did agree on *Kwamina* (1961), finding Robert Alan Aurthur's

---

*Was this an odd preview for another musical comedy with Offenbach's music, *La Belle* (1962), featuring the relentless husband-and-wife floperetta duo of diva Joan Diener and director Albert Marre? It closed in Philadelphia before reaching Broadway. Diener's costar, Menasha Skulnik, vowed to return: and did, in *Chu Chem* (1966). It closed in Philadelphia before reaching Broadway.

**Why do writers constantly use Roman names when invoking Greek deities? Indeed, Harburg meant to bring in not the god of war but the lord of the Underworld. But that worthy is Hades: Pluto is his Roman name.

romance of an Englishwoman and an educated African against the background of African tribal life trite but the dancing extremely exciting. This was good news to Agnes de Mille. She was not the first choreographer to apply dance to hoofing shows, nor the first choreographer to direct. But the astonishing history that she made in *Oklahoma!* (1943), *One Touch of Venus* (1943), *Bloomer Girl* (1944), *Carousel* (1945), and *Brigadoon* (1947) dwindled in the 1950s into filler. She seemed to be forever turning up in shows that didn't really need or deserve her distinction (such as *The Girl in Pink Tights*) or that failed to check in properly at the history desk (such as *Juno*). By the time she reached *Kwamina*, de Mille was the least influential of the generation of choreographers that she in effect had created—Robbins, Kidd, Fosse, Cole, Champion, Layton. Some said that de Mille's work in *Kwamina* was the best of her career, all the more amazing for her lack of grounding in African dance. "I have a nose," she explained. I can sniff things out, create my own authenticity.

Still, a 32-performance flop will do nothing to reacculturate one. Critics greatly liked half of Richard Adler's score—the African half, with its beguiling vamp of stamping strings and chopping woodblock for four melodies in counterpoint in "The Cocoa Bean Song"; or "Seven Sheep, Four Red Shirts, and a Bottle of Gin," whose orchestration suggests a squealing animal of the veld to the women's chanting of "Oonamakalolo." But the score's other half treats that trite romance all too faithfully, as Sally Ann Howes seemed like Julie Andrews playing Anna Leonowens to Terry Carter's King in starched slacks and button-down shirts. "You're as English As" was her Irritation Song, "Did You Hear That?" their Fight Duet, and "What's Wrong With Me" her Wondering Ballad late in Act One. Familiar numbers, alas. Not bad ones. Just same ones.

Some of the public found *Kwamina* anything but familiar. Carter and, especially, Howes got hate mail of a disgraceful savagery, though their interracial alliance was so delicately treated that it was almost platonic. It may sound strange to report today, but the two never kissed; and the moment in which Carter pushed an African bangle up Howes' arm sometimes occasioned outraged walkouts.

If Agnes de Mille is in trouble, think of Bert Lahr. Her era, that of Rodgers and Hammerstein, was still winding down. But Lahr's day was the one *before*, that of star-clown musical comedy. What happens to him in the 1960s?

Foxy (1964). Again, it's a neat idea: Ben Jonson's *Volpone* reset in the Gold Rush Yukon, with Lahr in the title role and Larry Blyden as Lahr's sidekick, the pair faking Lahr's death to bilk his associates of a fortune. In a Bert Lahr vehicle, the humor outweighs all other elements. But this was the last decade in which such shows were possible—*How To Succeed in Business Without Really Trying, Little Me, A Funny Thing Happened On the Way To the Forum*. The songs and dances and supporting talents can be excellent, if it so happens: but they don't *need* to be so long as the sheer antic hoopla obtains. And with Lahr it would; *Time* magazine hailed him as "the funniest man left alive."

However, note that the three comedy shows I cite above had qualities besides the star clown—a distinctive look, or Bob Fosse choreography, or interesting songs. There was a time when one could run a show entirely on a Lahr; isn't that time over? Lahr thought not, but neophyte scriptwriters Ian McClellan Hunter and Ring Lardner Jr. and veteran director Robert Lewis resisted his attempts to improvise gags in the old tradition. Like those insufferable hacks Lindsay and Crouse, the authors regarded their every line as a pearl, their go-nowhere structure as Shake-spearean in its balance and beauty; and Lewis supported them. Making his entrance on a dogsled amid a crowd of Eskimos, Lahr was to hand them a bag of gold and say, "Here, buy yourself a couple of fishhooks." That's not funny. Lahr changed it to "Here, buy yourself some chocolate-covered blubber." That's not funny, either—except when Lahr brings to it his characteristic loser's winning grin, his showing us how a flop thinks a hit acts.

Clearly, the authors and Lewis were working on the wrong play. With an acceptable score by Robert Emmett Dolan and Johnny Mercer, a young romantic couple, and a curvaceous saloon owner to play opposite Blyden, *Foxy* was no *Ben Franklin in Paris*, or even *Fade Out Fade In*. The script could only serve the entertainment, not embody it. Book writing for a show of this type is not a thing-in-itself. *Lahr* is the thing: or don't hire him in the first place. Or, conversely, write something really sharp that Lahr can play.

It's a heartbreaking show, because any star but this one would have walked. After more than three decades at the top of his profession, Lahr should have been treated as no less than oracular on the subject of how to make a musical funny. Ironically, Blyden understood Lahr's frustration and even sympathized with it while similarly resisting Lahr's freestyle technique. Blyden didn't want to be in Bert Lahr's carnival. He wanted to be in a musical comedy with a book by Hunter and Lardner and a score by Dolan and Mercer, directed by Lewis.

Now comes something strange. *Foxy* launched its tryout, in 1962, not in New Haven or even Detroit or Baltimore but at the Palace Grand Theatre in Dawson City, Yukon territory. True, the show partly takes place there. But imagine the difficulties if musicals had to try out where they were set. Think of *Greenwillow, Camelot, Brigadoon*. Dawson City was hardly more practical, an inaccessible hamlet that the Canadian government wanted to popularize for tourism. Its theatre, seating four hundred, was also impractical. Finally, *Foxy* was impractical, too, given the way it was put together. What Lahr should have been playing was a *Foxy* with a De Sylva, Brown, and Henderson score, the young Eddie Foy Jr. as the second banana, Ruth Etting as the saloon owner, and, say, John Steel and Queenie Smith as the love duets. In short, something from about 1929. But one takes what one gets when one's age is past; and the Canadians were to underwrite the production as long as it opened in Dawson City. This is the kind of thing that even smart producers find irresistible.

Foxy died in the Yukon, and everyone went on to other things, till David Merrick resuscitated the show in late 1963. *Foxy* was heavily revised, with seven new numbers (including the quite recordable ballads "Talk To Me, Baby" and "Run, Run, Run, Cinderella"). Robert Lewis was still directing, but the $420,000 physical production was brand-new and, except for Lahr and Blyden, so was the entire cast. Cathryn Damon now played the saloonkeeper, and John Davidson and Julienne Marie were the youngsters. After all the wrangling and tantrums, *Foxy* ended up a fit piece of fun. Of course, Lahr overwhelmed it. All the big moments were his, as when, faking convulsions and told by Blyden that he was overdoing it, Lahr snarled out, "Lemme alone, I got a hell of a finish"; or his solo with chorus, "Bon Vivant," another of those numbers in which Lahr ridicules the affectations of the debonair; or when Davidson menaced him and Lahr jumped onto the proscenium and literally climbed up it to get away. The reviews were more or less great, and *Foxy* should have run. But the out-of-the-way Ziegfeld Theatre cut down on the walk-in trade that was still quite lively when musicals hadn't yet broken a ten-dollar top. Worse, *Hello, Dolly!*, another Merrick production, had opened exactly a month before *Foxy*. With this gold mine to tend, the Merrick office simply deserted *Foxy*, and it went down after 72 performances. In 1929, it would have been the hit of the season.

Mary Martin was not as superannuated as Lahr. Her form, after all, was the more contemporary Rodgers-and-Hammerstein-era book show; she had starred in two by the boys themselves. Sometime before Lahr went trekking to Dawson City by train, boat, and, I have no doubt, dogsled, Martin had a choice of two period backstagers, one on Fanny Brice and one on Laurette Taylor. Let's look at this choice from Martin's perspective. Both are potentially worthwhile, dealing with the early life of a star in the booming show biz of an America that is like a millionaire's favorite son: rich, young, and trying everything, hot for fun. The costume plot alone will be a diva's dream. Both stories include a problem marriage, Brice's with shady gambler Nick Arnstein and Taylor's with disaster-prone producer-playwright Charles A. Taylor.

But there was a hitch in the Brice project. Naturally, you know that the Jewish Brice was a performer in the ethnic style, while Martin was plain American. That wasn't the hitch. In the early 1960s, stars got a lot of leeway in casting, whether in age, look, or ethnicity. No, the problem was that the Brice show was a pet of producers David Merrick and Ray Stark, Brice's son-in-law. Moreover, Mrs. Stark, Brice's daughter, was on hand to monitor the development of her mother's portrait. However, by this time Martin was her own producer and monitor (with her buttinsky husband, Richard Halliday), and she was not about to put *her* portrait in the power of either Merrick or the Starks.

There is another reason why Martin chose Laurette Taylor: it was to be based on *Laurette*, the biography of Taylor by her daughter, Marguerite Courtney. It's quite a book, engaging and knowledgeable and vivid in its evocation of bygone theatre. Try this look at old Seattle:

> The curative effects of the gold strike in Alaska in 1897 were not felt until the century was well over its hinge. Then . . . the assay office in a single day received nine hundred thousand dollars in gold dust and nuggets. [Producers John] Cort and [Robert] Considine . . . began programs of expansion that made them the theatre giants of the Northwest. . . . Between 1902 and 1904 eleven theatres were built in Seattle.

This time the Taylors arrived to find the veins of the metropolis well infused with gold, business booming, several stock [i.e., repertory] houses open all season, and the town looking for good entertainment.

It is the age of exotic blood-and-thunder melodrama, of *The White Tigress of Japan* and *Stolen By Gypsies*, of vaudeville, Shakespeare, touring the country and fleeing one's creditors, of becoming a star when personality was everything.

Martin must have been enchanted. But she took so long to make up her mind that Stanley Young had adapted Courtney's book as a spoken play starring Judy Holliday, also called *Laurette* (1960). This collapsed on its tryout, suggesting that so intricately comprehensive and colorful an era should have been presented as a musical in the first place. However, it was decided to fictionalize the characters of the two Taylors and J. Hartley Manners, the Englishman who married the divorced Laurette and wrote her greatest hit till *The Glass Menagerie*, *Peg O' My Heart* (1912). The heroine was now Jennie. Her husband was James O'Connor (Dennis O'Keefe), Manners was one Christopher Lawrence Cromwell (Robin Bailey), and the ancient Ethel Shutta, last seen on Broadway in a Willie Howard–Nanette Fabray flop, *My Dear Public* (1943) and next seen introducing "Broadway Baby" in *Follies* (1971), played Jennie's mother.

So far, so good, even if O'Keefe was another Novelty Star who probably couldn't sing. Sure enough, O'Keefe left the show during tryouts. But replacing him (with baritone George Wallace) was the least of *Jennie's* problems. Courtney's book "suggested" (as the posters had it) Arnold Schulman's script, yet Schulman almost entirely failed to encompass the theatre world of Laurette Taylor.

True, there were re-creations of melodrama in *The Mountie Gets His Man; or, Chang Lu, King of the White Slavers*, and in *The Sultan's 50th Bride*. *The Mountie* opened *Jennie*, with George Jenkins' spectacular waterfall set, as Martin, on a fragile tree branch at the upper left, saved a baby from going over the falls and then outwitted Chinese bad guys and a bear to save Wallace (as Randolph of the Royal Mounted Police), who was tied to a tree at the lower right. The Turkish show came way at the other end of the evening; in between was a lifeless tale of an actress who reluctantly leaves one thespian for another, looking forward to triumphing in what we presume is *Peg O' My Heart*.

Perhaps Schulman was hoping that the songs would bring in some the-atrical color. After all, he had the benefit of Arthur Schwartz and Howard Dietz, in their encore to *The Gay Life*. *Jennie*'s score is pleasant enough. It nostalgically recalls a host of old-time vaudeville numbers in Martin and Wallace's "Waitin' For the Evening Train." (Think of Irving Berlin's "When the Midnight Choo Choo Leaves For Alabam'.") And a number for tenor Jack De Lon and chorus called "When You're Far Away From New York Town" dotes on the homesickness of the ever-touring actor in two strains that then run together, a classy touch in musicals from the days of Gilbert and Sullivan on. Still, most of *Jennie*'s songs are character and situation pieces, not historical background.

Maybe Schulman thought that Irene Sharaff's costumes would fill in the script's empty spaces—Martin in going-out red with ruffled pink shawl, Martin *pour le sport* in dark brown jacket, light brown skirt, white bow, straw boater, and pencil-thin umbrella, Martin keeping house in a frilly white dress trimmed with a black bow and a mauve rose that looks as if Mainbocher might have gone to heaven in it, Martin as the Sultan's Bride, Martin in yellow and auburn, in picture hats and scarves and matching shoes. The window card featured photographs of Martin in her changes, as if admitting that they were the best thing in the show. *Jennie* lasted 82 performances and ended the career of Arthur Schwartz and Howard Dietz.

Some may wonder if failure is inevitable after a certain amount of time because styles change so rapidly in popular art. However, it wasn't Irving Berlin's age that stalled *Mr. President*; it was the dull book. And—please note—not an outdated book, but a book without a shred of imagination in its plot or wit in its execution. Nor was Coward's *Sail Away* a relic, even if Coward himself was. Musicals don't necessarily fail because everything about them is horrible and stupid. Sometimes one mistake—José Ferrer, for instance—can nail you to the cupboard door. Sometimes the public simply isn't interested: so it isn't even José Ferrer. Sometimes it's because David Merrick screamed at Laurence Harvey—but let me leave that one for the end of the chapter. Right now, let's consider a form that really was staying up past its bedtime, operetta.

Kean (1961) was Alfred Drake's project. This brilliant performer had knocked around for twelve years, both well cast and miscast in both hits and flops till he lucked into *Kiss Me, Kate* (1948) and *Kismet* (1953). After that, he was back to waiting upon the producers to come up with something suitable. Why not become one's own producer and commission the ideal property, starring oneself?

That would be a musical version of Jean-Paul Sartre's 1953 revision of *Kean; or, Disorder and Genius* (1836), by Alexandre Dumas *père*. The great Shakespearean Edmund Kean (who dominated Drury Lane in the early nineteenth century and then moved to America after a scandal) has long been a role magnet for actors. Dumas' play is itself a revision of one written at the request of actor Frederick Lemaître; similarly, Pierre Brasseur had Sartre retailor Dumas for Brasseur's public. Sartre called Kean "the patron saint of actors" for the theatricality of his offstage and the naturalism of his onstage. His life was one great performance.

No wonder actors want to play Kean; and who better than Drake to present a singing Kean, with Drake's comic bravura, his ham grandeur, so finely turned that it is in effect a spoof of ham, an end to grandeur? Sartre tidied Dumas' tangled plot, emphasizing the protagonist's involvement with two women and his rivalry with the Prince of Wales. Peter Stone's book for *Kean* followed Sartre's plan, and Robert Wright and George Forrest's score amplified Stone. Thus, the piece is replete with games on pretense and reality: "Any woman who loses her heart to an actor is chasing a mirage"; "Do not make the mistake of confusing what you're wearing with what you are"; "I do not really exist—I *pretend*, to please you, ladies and gentlemen"; and even, as the intermission curtain starts to fall, "What a magnificent first act!"

The score sets the tone for all this in Drake's first number, "Man and Shadow," which begins "One world is true and one illusion." The entire show presents Kean's attempts to reconcile the two worlds, or perhaps simply separate them. With baritone Drake and two soprano leads (Joan Weldon and Lee Venora), with plenty of legit voices in support and lots of chorus, with a harpsichord in the pit and veiled women passing through secret doors, the period setting of London lavish and low, *Kean* was one of the last operettas. An intellectual operetta, to be fair: but all the same a beautiful artifact, designed by Ed Wittstein and staged by Jack Cole to be not only one of the last but one of the best.

There was one flaw—far too much book. A smart operetta script gets to the next music as efficiently as possible. Stone didn't dawdle, but, like Sartre, he Discussed. It wasn't boring, just talky. What, a talky operetta? Don't blame Wright and Forrest; their songs absorbed a great deal of plot and character material, and were ingenious in outwitting some of operetta's traditional traps. For instance, what to write for the inevitable ball scene? After two decades of shows taking this moment to rejoice in social grace or extol the waltz, what idea is left to pursue? None: so Wright and Forrest wrote "Mayfair Affair" as a glittery chorus without a single lyric. The ensemble simply vocalizes while Cole's dancers busy our eyes.

Wright and Forrest are of course famous for "adapting," but they also wrote from scratch, and, as three earlier scores were not heard in New York,* *Kean* marked their Broadway debut as authors of their own sound. It's good work, once the characters cease their endless repartee, which not only dominates the script but seeps into the score as well. "Sweet Danger" is the traditional operetta love duet, passionate, even stormy, and rising to a fetching climax in "We'll be in love, and *we* won't care!" For musical wit, there's "To Look Upon My Love," a dialogue in song as Kean's manservant interrupts an erotic reverie with a nag about unpaid bills. (It ends with a kind of pun, a brass tag in twenties jazz-band style, reminding us that this is a modern operetta.) "Elena" is a superb ballad, haunting in its *faux*-Shakespearean choral bits, as Kean soliloquizes in his dressing room while, onstage, a high tenor (Arthur Rubin, a mainstay in such parts for nearly half a century) creates atmosphere for a performance of *Romeo and Juliet*. There was a perhaps forgivable lapse in quality in a big chorus scene, "The Fog and the Grog," one of those forced showstoppers in which the performers nudge, pose, wink, and grin their way through some noisy folderol, to show you what a great time you're having.

Kean was, in all, a grand exhibit. But 1961 was too late for operetta. With a very few exceptions—such as, in fact, *Song of Norway* and *Kismet*, the latter of which isn't precisely an operetta anyway—the form had been bombing since 1930. *Kean* closed after 92 performances. But Drake was not done: two years later, he starred in another operetta, *Zenda*. This one

---

*One of these, for *At the Grand* (1958), later made it in, with interpolations by Maury Yeston, as *Grand Hotel*, in 1989. Wright and Forrest never specified composer or lyricist billing, as they shared equally in writing words and music. They were lifelong friends as well: a unique partnership.

never made it into New York, though it euphemized its genre on the posters as "a romantic musical." That's what an operetta is, even if it's set in present-day Europe and has Chita Rivera as a Greek *favorita* for that touch of spice.

Let's face it: a musical based on Anthony Hope's 1894 novel *The Prisoner of Zenda*, however contemporary in approach, has to deal with a lot of intrigue, masquerade, sword fighting, mad sad glad love, and assorted pantywaisting. Remember, *Zenda* is the work that coined the place-name "Ruritania." Shouldn't Sigmund Romberg be writing this in the 1920s? Romberg *did* write it, as *Princess Flavia* (1925). At least 1963's book writer, Everett Freeman, purged the tale of much of the Ruritanian stuff for Drake, changing his character's name from Rudolf to Richard and making him a kind of Harry Van (in Robert E. Sherwood's *Idiot's Delight*), touring Europe with a girl act. The 1963 show even dropped Ruritania itself, pretending that Zenda was the country of event.*

Vernon Duke, who had been composing musicals since 1926 and had never had a Broadway hit, worked hard to give *Zenda* an up-to-date feel. Working with three lyricists, Duke gave good musical comedy in an operetta situation: in Drake's comically self-admiring "My Royal Majesty" when he takes over the "role" of King Rudolf (also played by Drake); in "Zenda," a soigné fox-trot version of the traditional love duet, with Flavia (Anne Rogers); in another of those ball scenes, as Rivera gets paranoid in a tango called "I Wonder What He Meant By That." Generally, it was more comedy, less romance.

Still: Ruritania, even if by another name? Commoner changes place with king? A squabble among the authors and director killed *Zenda* in Pasadena after three months on the West Coast, but how could it have run on Broadway in 1963? There is a reason why this show was one of the very last operettas, and that reason isn't Alfred Drake or Vernon Duke. Ruritania is why, even if one carefully doesn't mention it. A place called Zenda is better? "Let Her Not Be Beautiful" was Drake's number at the first-act curtain, a fine ballad of worry and need and almost on the *Kean* level of "If I play the hero, do I deserve to get the heroine *for real?*" He

---

*In Hope's novel, Zenda is a small town in Ruritania, where a distant cousin and twin of the king takes his place to defeat a coup. Flavia is the king's betrothed, who of course falls in love with the impostor, as he with her.

pleads, "Let me be unable to care." Fat chance, in an operetta. This is material to interest and even thrill some of my readers, perhaps. But it was not for general consumption at this time. One cannot modernize operetta any more than one can modernize the cathedral of Notre-Dame. What it believes in no longer exists.

So why did they try *Anya* (1965)? Here is the *last* operetta, a two-week flop at the Ziegfeld. It gives us Wright and Forrest again, this time coaxing their huge score out of Rachmaninof; but why did they and scriptwriter Guy Bolton think George Abbott a valid director for a romantic show? "The musical musical" is how *Anya* was billed, yet Abbott was no judge of music. His fortes were making sure the laughs landed, cutting down verbose scripts, and pacing the evening.

Anya's source was *Anastasia*, Bolton's version of Marcelle Maurette's play about the woman some thought to be the only surviving Romanof. Seen on Broadway in 1954 with Viveca Lindfors as "Anna" and crusty, cynical Eugenie Leontovich as her alleged grandmother, the show was old-fashioned even in its time, boulevard melodrama at its best. The syndicate supporting the girl's claims is in it for the money. They think she's an impostor. Yet she knows details that few but Anastasia could know. Leontovich scrutinizes her with the intention of exposing her, but the girl pulls out one last story, something that literally only Anastasia could know. Leontovich is frozen to the spot and melted to the core. What a moment for an actress of the Old School! She drops to the floor to hold the girl, kiss her, welcome her back from the dead. Now comes The Exit, for which star etiquette demands that Leontovich take the entire room with her, from the chandelier to the carpeting: "And please, if it should not be you . . . don't ever tell me!"

What a play for music! But did it have to be a floperetta, complete with Irra Petina as one of the émigrés of the sort we've already met in *Tovarich*? "Vodka, Vodka!" was the émigrés' chorus, as dumb as *Tovarich's* "Nitchevo"—but at least now the music was by Rachmaninof. That was *Anya's* strength, one almost entirely ignored by the critics. They could see only the hambone artifice of the story. Also, the cast was not the kind that Broadway cares about. Constance Towers played Anya, who now had one of those unfinished melodies, like that naughty Marietta and Liza Elliott; and the underrated Michael Kermoyan stepped in for Met baritone George London, who left during rehearsals. Kermoyan, who fielded an almost unheard-of low, low D in "So Proud," played the chief of Anya's syndicate, whom she eventually runs off with; John Michael King (*My Fair Lady*'s original Freddy) played the prince she disappoints; Lillian Gish played the grandmother; and the inevitable George S. Irving was there, as always, to bring on the Weismann girls.

Just keeping you alert, boys and girls. What Irving was there for, along with Boris Aplon, Ed (later Edwin) Steffe, and a rousing chorus, was to support the tale with vocal weight. This was virtually the cast of an opera, which may be why they let Lillian Gish play the Dowager Empress as an acting part, with one ditty ("Little Hands") to talk her way through. But Gish was wrong for the Empress, a bitter woman living entirely in the past, just as operetta was doing in 1965. Gish couldn't even get out a correct "Malyenkaya" (Little one), cutting corners with a blithely American "Malyenkaya." No. Operetta needs atmosphere, particularly if Lillian Gish is in it.

Still, the music stands among the best of the decade, even amid the silliness. The well-known themes were heard—the violin melody that opens the Adagio of the Second Symphony formed Anya's unfinished leitmotif, "A Song From Somewhere"; and the big warm tune for the oboes and violas from the finale of the Second Piano Concerto (known in the 1940s as "Full Moon and Empty Arms") turned up on the line "A fire that smolders low" in the duet "This Is My Kind of Love." The once-ubiquitous C Sharp Minor Prelude appeared in "That Prelude!" (Petina asked the pianist for "something gay." He banged into the familiar mournful tones. An appreciative Petina said, "That's *nice*.") Best of all, the middle section of the G Minor Prelude created "Homeward," nostalgia for Petina and the chorus that has to be the most stupendous four minutes of music in all the 1965–66 season.

As in *Song of Norway* and especially in *Kismet*, Wright and Forrest composed as much as they borrowed. It's interesting to see how just a phrase in Rachmaninof's song "Thou, My Field, My Lovely Harvest Field" grew into the haunting middle section of "Snowflakes and Sweethearts," or how the first few notes of the jumping figure that launches that G Minor Prelude grew into the a cappella chorus "Leben Sie Wohl." *Anya* is not a good show, but it has an intensely musical score, just as it promised. Anyway, had it been a good show it still would have bombed in this distinctly post-operetta age. At least Bette Midler saw it. "I never miss a Lillian Gish musical," she explained.

Now for David Merrick and Laurence Harvey. This show was, to my mind, the best of all these failures, *I Can Get It For You Wholesale* (1962). Merrick billed it as "a new musical," which generally was a euphemism for "a musical play." But the piece is basically a musical comedy with darkish undertones. Its source is Jerome Weidman's 1937 novel of the same name, about a rapacious upstart in the dress-design business. A 1951 film made him a woman, played by Susan Hayward, but for the musical Weidman recalled the tale to its origins, the rise-and-fall saga of a young man who is charming but unscrupulous. His every act appalls. Yes, he adores his mother; but the rest of the world can only be sheep to his wolf.

Laurence Harvey would have been perfect. His movie career had taken off like a skyrocket, thus to lend drawing power to a production that was not attracting stars. Harvey could sing—remember, he played Arthur in the Drury Lane *Camelot*. And he really wanted to play Weidman's Harry Bogen, through some deeply personal identification with the character, or perhaps just a desire to break out of the zombie roles that movie people were always offering him. Harvey was even willing to commit for nine months, a sacrifice for a movie actor who has just got hot. But Merrick decided to try a little brinkmanship. In his way of seeing things, all men were opponents, to be shredded if possible or respected (but constantly tested) if necessary. Harvey wouldn't play this game, so when Merrick started shouting, Harvey walked. Merrick eventually settled for the capable but unknown Elliott Gould.

Wholesale's casting in general is an odd mixture of newcomers, not-quite-getting-theres, and has-beens. The outstanding newcomer, who fell in love with and married Gould, was Barbra Streisand.* The show's

---

*Show-biz legends can be tiresome, but a number of essential ones swirl around Streisand in regard to this show, her Broadway debut after little more than a club act and an obscure off-Broadway flop. Her arrogance, her lack of interest in any reality but her own, her ability to captivate some while alienating others—all were in play, this early. Streisand's audition for *Wholesale* had the authors mesmerized and Merrick ranting. "She's too ugly for a musical!" he observed. "Those clothes!" he noted. "And those shtetl inflections!" he screamed. But a number of production associates were staring at Streisand and asking one another, Who does she make you think of? Fanny Brice. And whom was Merrick planning to do a show about at that time? Fanny Brice. They watched him sitting apart and glaring at Streisand. Doesn't he get it?

ingenue, Gould's love interest, was Marilyn Cooper, in her first lead after small parts (including the girl who yearned for Puerto Rico in "America" in *West Side Story*). Sheree North, as the showgirl whom Gould keeps, on his firm's capital, was a not-quite, having been around both Broadway and Hollywood without landing the role in which to—as choreographer Ron Field would put it—punch out. Ken Le Roy, as Gould's naïve business partner, had played Bernardo in *West Side Story* but nothing much since. Harold Lang was Gould's wary business partner, and almost a has-been. He had had the title role in the hit revival of *Pal Joey* in 1952, but then it was flops and things, a bad sign for a dancer who could actually sing and act. Bambi Linn, another dancer, had created Louise in *Carousel*; that was seventeen years before. And Lillian Roth, as Gould's mother, hailed from so far back in show biz that Hollywood had already filmed her bio.

Wholesale's great old-timer was composer-lyricist Harold Rome, return-ing to his favored haunt of the Jewish show after a decade in France (*Fanny*) and the western (*Destry Rides Again*). Rome's first success, the revue *Pins and Needles* (1937), was more or less produced by and about *Wholesale's* characters, a kind of Senior Class Play for garment workers. Callous union-busting is how Gould's character, Harry Bogen, gets his start; and labor troubles vex the show again near its end. *Pins and Needles* was a gentle if at times sharply satiric wish that all peoples and classes might live and let live. Now Rome was mature enough to know that they can't. In one of his greatest songs, "What Are They Doing To Us Now?," Streisand led the chorus in a social tract of great bitterness. It rolls out in the odd meter of $^6/_4$, what one might call a Great Depression rhythm, volatile, unstable.

All of *Wholesale* has that quality, even when it's happy (or at least unknowing), as Harry's genius for exploiting an angle stalks musical com-edy's innate sunniness. He enjoys a delightful duet early on with Cooper, a sort of childhood sweetheart, in "When Gemini Meets Capricorn." It's a typical musical-comedy charm tune: except she doesn't know that he has staged their meeting, and only to connive money out of her. Never-theless, Rome catches the innocence of *her* viewpoint, because a writer cannot lie this kind of number.* So Rome lets her beliefs run the scene,

---

*Not, that is, in a straight-on linear narrative. After *Cabaret* and the Sondheim-Prince series revise the musical's lines of communication, writers can help themselves to layers of

soaring in the release and finally hitting, in the line "Hey, you stars over the Bronx," something like an ultimate completion of old-fashioned musical comedy: the poetry of a registered Democrat.

Very little of *Wholesale*'s score reflects Harry's perspective. He has a crafty Hero's Wanting Song, egged on by snarls from the brass section, in "The Way Things Are." But the show itself finds him so horrifying that it won't let him be its protagonist. There is none. Those nine names featured under the title indicate a true ensemble. One might argue that Harry's mother, Lillian Roth, is the work's central figure. At least, she's the only one who knows what's happening, right from the start. She even has a song warning Cooper not to trust her son, "Too Soon (don't give your heart away)." And finally, after Harry has not only bankrupted his business but set up the credulous Le Roy for jail time, it is Roth who commands the scène à faire, a confrontation of mother and son. It is a duet, "Eat a Little Something." But only she sings. He speaks, in a lengthy line of swindler's rap, rationalizing his destructiveness. She is trying to understand how she could have raised this monster; he doesn't care to understand, because understanding means considering how it feels to be one of his victims. As she feeds him, she begins to loathe him. There had never been anything this brutally honest in a musical comedy. Between the sung lines, she speaks, too, in ironic distance:

MRS. BOGEN: All she thinks about, that Blanche, the only thing in her head is Meyer. All she worries about is tomorrow morning he's going to jail. . . . People who have room in their heads for only little things like that, what chance have they got to get ahead in the world? The way you did, Harry. The way I did through you.

But there is always that refrain of "Eat a little something"—so measured, quietly intense. And always Harry, sitting at the table, stunned, not moving. Yes, "Eat a little something," his mother sings. Then, speaking again: "Harry, eat. It's good. Your mother made it. Just like she made you, she made these." The moral archon has reached self-hatred. Somehow, some-

---

commentary and irony. Thus, Sondheim can give us a lying version of Rome's number in *Into the Woods*' "Hello, Little Girl" that tacks to the Wolf's disingenuous viewpoint without confusing or alienating us.

thing in her failed to check something that an amoral business world would inspire in him. What's worse than a mother loathing her son? And, on that note, the curtain fell.

In *Philadelphia*. This ending did not go over; they're lucky the audience didn't tear the theatre apart. For New York, a deus ex machina was allowed to save the innocent and even redeem the guilty. Some called it "*Pal Joey* with a happy ending." But Joey is essentially harmless, a no-talent show-biz bottom-feeder who plays women. He doesn't loot and imperil a partner with a jail term, as Harry Bogen does. Musical comedy had come so far in twenty years that, where marital infidelity and foiled blackmail were once thought shocking, now a cutthroat little tycoon whose own mother ends up hating him seemed a plausible leading man. Even *Wholesale*'s generally troubled social milieu of labor unrest and illicit business practices startled no one. (Think of how tame the same background is in 1954's *The Pajama Game*.) After all, *Pal Joey*'s smash 1952 revival proved that it is at its hardest a sardonic and earthy show, not a dark one. *I Can Get It For You Wholesale* is dark.

Even the dancing, musical comedy's most joyous element, went dark, in Herbert Ross' depiction of near-slaughter on Seventh Avenue and materialists slithering to the ring of a cash register. Peter Howard's dance arrangements caught the vexed tone, in the prologue's slamming xylophone and shoving trumpets or, in "The Sound of Money," the frantic Latin beat of strings singing in two over the bass thrummed out in three, a kind of greedy *West Side Story*.

The score does lift now and again, but seldom for pure charm. The Heroine's Wanting Song, "Who Knows?," jumps up to a radiant major ninth on the two title words, and its recitative verse limns an adorable character. Yet she's weeping before the song is over. The recitative gives us not just a person but a virtual way of life: eager to get ahead, to be educated, to appreciate the arts. "Don't you think Odets is great?" she asks Harry—a line that only Harold Rome would think of, catching a culture in six words. Such more overtly Jewish numbers as "The Family Way" (a strangers' get-together over dinner) and "A Gift Today," to a young man undergoing the rites of bar mitzvah, help fill in the folkways. But Rome's true objective is to use character numbers to present a people.

Thus, the very first vocal number, "I'm Not a Well Man," only appears to be an error. It's sung by Streisand about her boss (as "He's Not a Well

Man"), then by the boss himself (Jack Kruschen). But the boss then vanishes from the story, to reappear much later as the deus ex machina. Why
does he have a song? Why do the self-effacing Ken Le Roy and Bambi
Linn have a timid ditty in Act Two about how much they love each
other? Haven't they been established by then? Does even Streisand need
"Miss Marmelstein"—though of course it was a showstopper, and who
doesn't want to hear Streisand sing?

I believe Rome was using the songs *collectively* to summon up how these
people felt as a whole. Each number adds more information—about the
times, the garment-center workplace, the social code, the meaning of
marriage, the use of English as a translation from a babble of diaspora. So
"I'm Not a Well Man" is not merely about this particular boss, but about
the kind of relationship he has with his secretary (stern but intimate:
politically liberal, even socialist), about how his business is going (he's
being bankrupted by a strike), about his morality (he wants to survive but
secretly sympathizes with the strikers), and about how this people reveres
the creative intellect (in a line that compares his ills to the sort of play
that "Turgenev, maybe, could write"). We also get the language, the
music (in orchestrator Sid Ramin's wailing klezmer clarinet and English
horn), and Streisand, singing the first notes in her Broadway career.

I always wonder what Lillian Roth thought of Streisand, for the young
Roth had been a kind of Streisand herself, as one can see in her early
talkie musicals: raw rather than glamorous and emphatic in comedy but
an arresting presence with a grand instrument. One continuity that held
from Roth's time to the 1960s was the importance of a Broadway visit in
building a career. When Janice Rule got "money notices" in *The Happiest
Girl in the World*, her name went up on the Martin Beck's marquee and her
phone Began To Ring. We look for such continuities, for the 1960s is the
last decade in which the Broadway musical held a stable position in
American civilization. During this time, the music changed (to rock), the
status of Most Privileged Art changed (to cinema), and the capitalization
minimums changed (to prohibitive).

Yet writers continued to stretch themselves, not retrench conserva-
tively: that's a sign of both change *and* continuity. In the Rodgers and
Hammerstein era, the correct career is the unpredictable career. Harold
Rome did it in *Fanny*, Frank Loesser in *The Most Happy Fella*, Bob Merrill

in *New Girl in Town*. We've just seen Richard Adler (in *Kwamina*) and Noël Coward (in *Sail Away*) do it.

The Russians would call this Rodgersandhammersteinshchina: the typifying acts of the era in which they ruled. And they ruled that one must grow, but their time has ended. In what direction does one now grow?

6

SUMMER IS OVER

NEW TALENT

If the Golden Age is to continue, new songwriters are essential. In fact, five new sources come in at about this time. We've already met Charles Strouse and Lee Adams, and also Cy Coleman (working, temporarily, with Carolyn Leigh). Jerry Herman will appear, and John Kander and Fred Ebb. One of these sources will give us the sixties show that changed the musical's history. But that comes later; for now, let's start with Harvey Schmidt and Tom Jones, on their debut in the spring of 1960 with *The Fantasticks*.

Cats called itself "now and forever." But *Cats* closed. *The Fantasticks* is more truly now and forever, still going after four decades as I write. True, the Sullivan Street Playhouse seats but one hundred fifty-three, and, with an orchestra of piano and harp and a cast of, at first, nine,* the production is cheaply maintained. Yet it very nearly closed just after it opened, to mixed reviews and little business. It's odd to think that this international phenomenon—the influential progenitor of The Little Musical—might have been less even than a statistic. There's nothing more obscure than an off-Broadway flop.

Even odder are the origins of the piece, in Edmond Rostand's *Les Romanesques* (1894) but with suggestions of *Romeo and Juliet* and conceived on the grand scale. Texans Schmidt and Jones first wrote *Joy Comes*

---

*The role of the Handyman, originated by Jay Hampton and then played by Laurence Luckinbill and Ty McConnell, was cut in 1961. These three belong to an exclusive club: only they portrayed this character, while the other parts have been played, serially, by armies in New York alone. Librettist Jones was also in the opening cast. He played Henry, under the pseudonym Thomas Bruce.

To Deadhorse about warring Anglo and Mexican ranching families. Then came *West Side Story*. Their show was now extraneous, till fellow University of Texas alumnus Word Baker asked for something for an evening of one-acters at Barnard College in 1959. Schmidt and Jones stripped their gala to its essence—a few characters, a few props, a little space. They called it *The Fantasticks* because that is more or less what *Les Romanesques* means. By chance, off-Broadway thespian Lore Noto saw it, fell in love, and wanted to produce it commercially as a full-length evening.

Unfortunately, Schmidt and Jones had so essentialized their original work that its delicacy and whimsy could not bear expansion. But then, Noto couldn't afford a big show anyway. So there was no expansion. The authors simply made a little more of what they already had. This was: boy loves girl because their fathers told them not to; bored with happiness, boy and girl quarrel, part, and, wiser, reconciliate. There is a compère, El Gallo (a remnant of the original big show), and three kibitzers, The Mute, Henry (a superannuated Shakespearean ham), and Henry's stooge.

The characters are types—another way in which *The Fantasticks* essentializes its material. Not that the show deals in cliché. Its partly-in-verse script is both funny and bizarre and keeps surprising one. But the score serves as a kind of purification of genre, to bring freshness back to the form. Put simply, *The Fantasticks* behaves as if it were The First Musical.

So the Heroine's Wanting Song, "Much More," offers no details of place and time. Its context is itself. Where the heroine of *I Can Get It For You Wholesale* busies us with her breathless list of what matters to her—modern dance, progressive theatre, love—Schmidt and Jones' Luisa dabbles in ageless romantic imagery, such as dancing till dawn and being kissed on the eyes. The scene leading up to the song begins:

LUISA: The moon turns red on my birthday every year and it always will until somebody saves me and takes me back to my palace.

and the cue for her number is a quick prayer to God:

LUISA: Don't let me be normal!

She's every heroine, every young woman who is more than half little girl. Or consider the lovers' duet "Soon It's Gonna Rain": it's very precise in what it says, which is, basically, Nothing can hurt us, including the tests of character coming in Act Two. Any young couple could sing it. The first-act finale, "Happy Ending," is so generic that it doesn't have words, just merry singsong. And the lovers' last, pacifying duet, "They Were You," is Love Songs 101 in its wistfully soaring innocence. But then, the show's most famous number, "Try To Remember," is at once a vague introduction to this particular work and a very specific introduction to any romance at all.

Perhaps the one piece in the whole score that could suit only this particular story is the comic "It Depends On What You Pay," in which El Gallo bargains with the fathers over a faked abduction. Very loosely drawn from a scene in *Les Romanesques*, it emphasizes the word "rape" in a way that makes some uncomfortable nowadays; the authors have lately supplemented the song with a euphemistic alternate.

No wonder this show hasn't closed. It's artful in conception but ingenuous as an experience, as if marvelous people were inventing it as they go along. These were, originally, Jerry Orbach as El Gallo, Kenneth Nelson and Rita Gardner as the kids, and Hugh Thomas and William Larsen as the fathers. A television production brought together Ricardo Montalban, John Davidson and Susan Watson, and Bert Lahr and Stanley Holloway, and stars have taken part on other occasions—John Gavin as El Gallo here and Liza Minnelli as Luisa there. But isn't *The Fantasticks* anti-star—or anti-Broadway, really—in its very being? It's about people one would ordinarily never hear about, folks who will be special only to themselves.

The next Schmidt-Jones title, however, was Big Broadway: a David Merrick show with stars, sets, a twenty-three-piece orchestra, and Agnes de Mille choreography, *110 in the Shade* (1963). Based on N. Richard Nash's 1954 play *The Rainmaker*, it brings Schmidt and Jones to their native Southwest to tell of people who are special to others. We meet File, the local sheriff, much admired by town girls; a crowd-playing con man named Starbuck; and Lizzie, a spinster who, by show's end, has the two frantically proposing to her.

Nash's play offers no more than these three and Lizzie's father and brothers. All Nash had to do in writing *110*'s book was bring in the town and fill out his principals' place in the community. File is the stolid father figure: a good husband. Starbuck is the eternal stranger and show-off: good sex. Lizzie is the victim of her mother's early death, forced to keep house for her family instead of starting one of her own.

Merrick hired Stephen Douglass, Hal Holbrook, and Inga Swenson for the leads, dropping Holbrook for the showier Robert Horton, freed from the nascent *On a Clear Day You Can See Forever* when the Richard Rodgers–Alan Jay Lerner partnership was dissolved. While Douglass and Swenson were natural singers, the heretofore non-musical Horton revealed a surprisingly nimble light baritone. Morever, Swenson's Lizzie was one of the decade's notable singing-acting turns, a unique performance never to be rivaled. With Will Geer, Steve Roland, and Scooter Teague as Lizzie's father and brothers and a very young Lesley (Ann) Warren as Teague's love interest, Snookie (much mentioned but never seen in the original play), Schmidt and Jones had the chance to move from the dainty all the way to robust. So much did all three authors add to *The Rainmaker* that the play has become redundant, like *Green Grow the Lilacs* or *The Matchmaker*. True, New York saw a Roundabout *Rainmaker* in 1999, with Woody Harrelson and Jayne Atkinson. But why go back to the place where all the interesting stuff happens offstage?

The best thing about *110 in the Shade* is that we finally get to take in the entire story, mainly because Schmidt and Jones kept rewriting the score. They were particularly keen on the establishing songs, as if hoping to pour cut passages, subtexts, and variations from Nash's play into three minutes of music. We first see Lizzie just back from a vacation that has only humiliated her longings, and in "Sweetwater" she sadly lays it out for us. It's a lovely song, but this is no way to introduce someone we want to root for. "Love, Don't Turn Away" replaced it—determined, eager, and as pretty as Lizzie thinks she herself isn't: because she is, and it's Starbuck's role to tell her so. His music swaggers—listen to the outlandish strut of the vamp to "Rain Song"—and his lyrics are inflated with inventions instead of facts. Yet he's persuasive. So much so that, for the entire first act, Lizzie is opposed to him, angry at him, exposing him. Because he's going to release her imprisoned femininity, and she knows it and is terrified.

File cannot be too happy, either, not least about Starbuck. The rainmaker doesn't change the weather: he changes people, turning them into what they really are. File wants to be seen as a widower who is content to be single, though he is in fact a wounded divorcé who's afraid to risk being hurt again. "Inside My Head" was the wistful version of his character song, "Why Can't They Leave Me Alone?" the bitter version. Both numbers were cut, finally, in favor of a duet, "A Man and a Woman," a melody simple enough to serve both Lizzie's optimism and File's now resigned and gentle pessimism.

This show has almost as many cut numbers floating around as does *Follies*. "Why Can't They Leave Me Alone?" even has an alternate, on the same melody with a beseeching lyric, "Too Many People Alone (you've got to care)." Yet this was not an epic evening. There were only six sets, and the ensemble had little of de Mille to perform after an emergency cut-down of the running time in Boston. It left not much more than one ballet and an *Oklahoma!*-style two-step for Teague and Warren during their "Little Red Hat." What's big about the piece is its feelings, that Rodgers-and-Hammerstein musical-play throughline that gives the public something to follow, to absorb. One doesn't get that in *High Spirits*.

On the other hand, that throughline does need support from what must prove to be a beloved score. Music can protect a troubled book—*Camelot*'s, for instance. But *110 in the Shade*'s score did not catch on. It's our loss, for it's one of the decade's finest. Ironically, *110*—like *Camelot*—has a *musical* throughline, a three-note motive first heard at curtain rise, D-F#-A (played on the harmonica) in D Major, the outline of a tonic chord. *Camelot* has exactly the same motive—the notes sung on the word "Camelot" in the title song. But *Camelot*'s motive is accented on the first note, while *110*'s is accented on the last.

So they don't ever sound alike—and they work differently as well. *Camelot*'s theme is a fanfare on the idea of a democratic monarchy. The *110* theme is the bad music of too much sun and no water. It's oppression—the oppression, as an objective-correlative, of Lizzie's loneliness. The three notes launch the orchestral prelude to her crestfallen and then terrified soliloquy that closes Act One, "Old Maid," as if uniting her problems with that of the rain-hungry town. But rain can come only after Lizzie's thirst is quenched, when the two men duet in proposal. And this *of course* takes off on the same three motival notes (on Starbuck's "Come with me, [Lizzie]"). Lizzie accepts not the glamorous Starbuck but the

everyday File. And now that she has her man, it can rain. "So long, beautiful!" Starbuck tells her, and a chorister, correctly noting that Starbuck is
more a preacher than anything else, calls out "Hallelujah!"

After the diligent character delineation of the musical play, it is odd to
return to the quixotic tunestacks of musical comedy, where the score is
more likely to close in on situation or novelty than on how people view
the world. How, really, does one write music for *Little Me* (1962), a spoof
that never takes any of its characters or their needs seriously? Neither did
its source, Patrick Dennis' 1961 book of the same title, a burlesque of
movie-star tell-all autobiographies illustrated with campy and erotic photographs. Just the heroine's name tells us that nothing's going to be
sacred: Belle Poitrine, French for "beautiful bosom," or even "nice tits."
From Shantytown to stardom and decline, Belle sleeps and claws her way
to the bottom. In fact, as the narrative ends, we infer that she is just about
to be murdered by her lesbian live-in.

Because so much of Belle's picaresque depended on how the photographs amplified the text with reductive irony, there was no way to musi-
calize the novel in any real sense. Instead, book writer Neil Simon
prepared his own version of the story, showing us how young Belle (Virginia Martin) seeks "wealth and culture and social position" while an
older Belle (Nancy Andrews) dictates the tale to her ghostwriter. Add to
this star comic Sid Caesar playing seven roles—some of them almost
simultaneously in quick-change fun—and breakneck pacing under,
mainly, Bob Fosse, and *Little Me* ends up as a kind of spoof of musicals.
Those inane romances, those dizzying plot twists, those *feelings* amid all
the goofing around. *Little Me* the book has a kind of reality despite the
absurdity of the photographs. *Little Me* the musical has the reality of a
Marx Brothers movie, especially the early Paramounts.

Simon had worked as a writer for Caesar in television, and with his
brother Danny had written most of the sketches for a little-known stage
revue with Pat Carroll and David Burns, *Catch a Star!* (1955). *Little Me's*
musical team, Cy Coleman and Carolyn Leigh, had also got their start in
the 1950s, creating such pop hits as "Witchcraft" and "The Best Is Yet To
Come"; and of course we've already heard their *Wildcat* score. But *Wildcat*
had characters with wishes that only a persuasive ballad could define—
"You've Come Home," the men's chorus "Tall Hope," and the seductively

Latin "One Day We Dance." *Wildcat* even had Lucille Ball's shy and lame younger sister, someone we have no choice but to sympathize with.

Little Me was something else entirely: one of the two funniest musicals of the decade, but not one with chances for the characters to connect with the audience emotionally. For instance, this was the second sixties musical to include a *Titanic* scene. In *The Unsinkable Molly Brown* it was a short one, all in earnest, with Molly forcefully taking charge in the lifeboat downstage while a backdrop depicted the sinking ship alarmingly upended. *Little Me* offered the S.S. *Gigantic*, in an elaborate sequence played aboard the doomed vessel as the set impishly tilted. Caesar, in one of his many reappearances as Belle's childhood love, Noble Eggleston, supervised the launching of the lifeboats:

> NOBLE: Hold it! . . . You! In the yellow dress. (Noble rips off a woman's dress, revealing a man in white uniform.) Aren't you ashamed, Captain?

These gags work in threes, so now comes:

> NOBLE: (pulling off the babushka of a woman in a green polka-dot dress: it's the same man) Captain! I don't want to have to ask you again!

And here's the payoff:

> NOBLE: (screaming at a woman in a green polka-dot dress) All right, what do you say, Captain! (He pulls off the dress. It *is* a woman, very embarrassed.) I'm terribly sorry, madam. The captain wears the same kind of dress.

This is not the atmosphere in which feelings breathe freely. It's gags and spoofs and, ultimately, satire on the American success myth. "Sex and guts made you into a star," Mame hurls at Vera. That's really the caption for a photo of Belle Poitrine. How does that provision the musical material? Coleman and Leigh came up with a sincere Heroine's Wanting Song in "The Other Side of the Tracks," but, later, in "Poor Little Hollywood Star," Virginia Martin had to sing her lament as the audience laughed at the titles of her films: *Dr. Jekyll and Mrs. Hyde*, *The Sweetheart of Gunga*

Din, Ben Her. The show was so little in need of musical refreshment that the second act not only opened without a number—unusual—but went on for ten minutes without offering a new song, almost unthinkable in 1962.

This is odd in that the show has extensive dance spots. But then, dance is abstract enough to function along with the verbal comedy, while the score has to laugh or it will throw the show's rhythms off. There are eight dances in all, from the showpiece "Rich Kids Rag" and Swen Swenson's sexual enticement solo, "I've Got Your Number," to Caesar's faked machine-gun taps in "Boom-Boom" and the strutting-ladies title song, wherein the two Belles duet. So *Little Me* is a musical comedy without the slightest interest in respecting the post-*Oklahoma!* trend toward rationalization. The score does not inhabit the story as, say, *Bye Bye Birdie*'s score does. *Little Me*'s score decorates the story, punctuates it, teases it, and even photographs it, like the illustrations in Dennis' novel.

What the score does not do is explain the story, as *Birdie*'s "An English Teacher" explains Chita Rivera's character. *Little Me* can't even be said to have a gap, as *Birdie* does in failing to put Albert into context musically. *Little Me* has no gaps because *Little Me* has no connections. *Wildcat* has character and situation songs. *Little Me* has *spoofs* of character and situation songs: an "I Love You" filled not with encomiums but class-conscious slurs; or "Goodbye," an operetta burlesque on something no operetta had yet thought to include, a royal death scene with the crowd doing kazatzki steps and wailing. Of course, it's hard to know when Coleman is composing seriously or not, because he is one of those musical wizards. He can do any style, any form, any sound. Is *Little Me*'s "Real Live Girl" a ballad or a takeoff on a ballad?

A third Coleman-Leigh show might have told us more about their attitude, but the team broke up after *Little Me* because Leigh was a lunatic. During the show's Philadelphia tryout, co-director Cy Feuer decided to drop "The Girls of '17," a number that wasn't landing no matter what Fosse did with it. Leigh vigorously disagreed, but the number went out anyway. So did Leigh—onto the street to find a cop. She brought one backstage and demanded that he arrest Feuer; and this was during the performance.

The composer-lyricist Jerry Herman is our next new-to-Broadway-in-the-1960s talent. He is no satirist. He believes in the boy-meets-girl, young-people-having-fun, eleven-o'clock-song concepts that ran musical comedy when he was growing up. One sees him as a kid, dreaming of writing a show for Ethel Merman. Many kids so dreamed; Herman actually got there. At first, though, he was working with such second-liners as Dody Goodman, Nancy Andrews, and Mona Paulee in off-Broadway revues. His Broadway debut score was that for *Milk and Honey* (1961), concerning Americans in Israel both as tourists and émigrés. It's a somewhat serious show, a musical comedy with musical-play characters, operetta voices (Met veterans Robert Weede and Mimi Benzell, and the dancing tenor Tommy Rall), and a score stuffed with feelings. Yiddish theatre favorite Molly Picon played the chief yenta in a group of American widows trolling for husbands, a comic role provisioning the comic numbers that musicals could not do without at this time—the $6/8$ cheer-up march (to become customary Herman art), "Chin Up, Ladies," and a solo, "Hymn to Hymie," addressed to her late husband. Still, the *sound* of the music was partway to operetta, especially in Weede's urgent courting of widow Benzell in "There's No Reason in the World" and "Let's Not Waste a Moment," and in their two waltzes, "Shalom" and "As Simple As That." Had he lived long enough, Sigmund Romberg might not have enjoyed *Little Me*, but he would have appreciated *Milk and Honey*.

True, Herman's music was a bit light for the story's strong feelings. Herman was pure sixties Broadway pop, very conservative in his song structures, conventionally melodious, and eloquently basic in his lyrics. The gossamer images of *The Fantasticks'* "Try To Remember" would never have occurred to Herman; he didn't do atmosphere. He did situation and incidentals; but what he did above all was character. When Tommy Rall (as Weede's son-in-law, a passionate settler of disputed territory) got to dance, he was able to express at once his many several conflicted relationships: to his wife, to his family, to his destiny, to his people. It was a moment of artistry. But when Rall sang to his wife in "I Will Follow You," it was a moment of clarity: boy loves girl even more than boy loves Israel.

Cynics like to say that there's nothing more commercial than a Jewish musical, just as it used to be said that there's nothing more commercial than an Irish musical, for Irish and Jewish audiences have long been New York's most avid theatregoers. However, many Jewish musicals have flopped, some more or less overnight. Moreover, *Milk and Honey* ended, most unconventionally, with Weede and Benzell unable to link up after an evening-long romance. Still married, he saw Benzell off to her plane, promising to try to get his wife to grant him a divorce. Nor did Herman and book writer Don Appell give their public even a shred of hope. I still remember the murmurs of disappointment from women in the house as the curtain fell on an unfinished, but realistic, story. This alone may be why Milk and Honey was the third musical (following Take Me Along and Destry Rides Again) to run for more than a year and fail to pay off.*

No two composer-lyricists could be less alike in the same era than Jerry Herman and Stephen Sondheim. The latter is experimental in his song structures, originally melodious, and psychologically ambiguous in his lyrics. A typical Herman title: "It's Today." A typical Sondheim title: "Sorry-Grateful." Most important, Sondheim, like David Merrick, tends to be the first to do something. Both Herman and Sondheim launched their careers in the 1950s. But while Herman was downtown in revue, Sondheim headed right for The Street with Saturday Night (1955, had it been produced), which went into the trunk on the death of its producer, Lemuel Ayers. Sondheim's second score as composer as well as lyricist, for A Funny Thing Happened on the Way To the Forum (1962), is generally thought of as the first in a line of misunderstood and underrated Sondheim scores. It was: but so was Forum's book, by Burt Shevelove and Larry Gelbart.

"Based on plays of Plautus" is all we're told of their source material, because they had the idea not of rephrasing any particular work of Plautus but of merging what is essentially the Roman version of Greek comedy with American burlesque shtick. In other words, as in its title (the typical "Floogle Street" formulation sitting next to the grandly ancient "forum"), the show would use the disguises, chases, and prankish coincidences of old genre in the language of new genre. In yet other words, the Randy Old Father, the Naïve Son, the Braggart Soldier, the Termagant Wife, the Ridiculously Dutiful Servant, and so on would play in the rhythms and deliveries of twentieth-century American Jewish show-biz humor.

A word, here, about burlesque, which to most minds recalls strippers, "Zip," Ann Corio, Minsky's, and all that hoochie-kooch stuff we meet at

---

*As the first Broadway musical set in Israel, Milk and Honey killed off the second one without even knowing it: David Merrick had scheduled The Blue Star for later that same season. With a book by Joshua Logan and Alfred Palca and a Burton Lane–E. Y. Harburg score, The Blue Star was also to have brought Anne Bancroft to town in her first musical. Milk and Honey's unexpected appearance caused Merrick to cancel The Blue Star. Merrick liked to be the first to do anything, or maybe the twentieth. Never the second.

the end of *Gypsy*. It's an art so debased that Herbie walks out on Rose for exposing her daughter to it.

But that is *late* burlesque. In its heyday, in the late nineteenth and early twentieth centuries, burlesque denoted spoof of literary or theatrical work. Joe Weber and Lew Fields were the acknowledged masters, at around 1900, producing evenings of a single full-length burlesque of the latest hit show, followed by an hour of vaudeville. This, to America, was burlesque at its purest: low comedy and showgirls, yes, but the comedy was clean and the girls kept their clothes on.*

In decline by the 1920s, burlesque eventually sought a new public by edging the girls into erotic territory and dropping the spoof in favor of gags. Many cities banned these shows, forcing their people into lewd Broadway musicals like *Star and Garter* (1942) or *Follow the Girls* (1944) and even into early television. That brings us to comic Phil Silvers, whose Sergeant Bilko made a sitcom of the burlesque style. Silvers even headlined a musical, *Top Banana* (1951), that was an anthology of burlesque tropes. But Silvers proved to be the first of thousands to fail to understand why *Forum*'s script was filled with burlesque gags. "I've been playing this stuff for thirty years," Silvers said, turning down the show as a rehash. No. *Top Banana* was a rehash. Forum was a *revival*.

It almost wasn't anything, as the project bounced from one possible producer to another. Jerome Robbins was to have staged the show, but dropped out when David Merrick took over, out of distaste for Merrick. The authors then bought their script back from Merrick, and Hal Prince became its producer, with George Abbott directing.

Here's another sixties invention, one foreshadowed in the 1950s but rampant in this decade: the tendency for shows to change hands numerous times during the voyage from conception through execution to presentation. In the 1920s, when the musical's Golden Age began, producers commissioned or accepted a show by certain writers and then produced that show. There were few "properties" traveling from one producer to

---

*Those who remember television's *Carol Burnett Show* have seen authentic burlesque, on such an evening as when she presented the famous parody of *Gone With the Wind* along with the usual singing and dancing spots. Add in a pair of "Dutch" (i.e., Jewish) comics and put the girls in tights and you have a 1970s equivalent of a performance at the Weber and Fields Music Hall.

another, or now offered to one writing team and now to another. Every-thing was moving too fast for that. Execution could take but weeks because so many shows were written by the numbers; not long after that, you opened in Worcester, Baltimore, Pittsburgh, anywhere. The United States was theatre country then.

This system held in place through the 1940s. Then, as production costs began to rise, as the great touring road dwindled into a few stands in the biggest cities, as theatre folk increasingly focused on Hollywood, as rock and roll began to push Tin Pan Alley and its Broadway masters to the side, and, especially, as the shows themselves got smarter and thus less easy to toss off, the process slowed down. Producers bought and then resigned options. The availability of this or that star could prove contam-inative. The newly prominent director-choreographer might demand changes in script and score as credential of his prestige; the authors might refuse. (This happened on *Forum*, when Joshua Logan, the second to mis-understand the point of the show, called for revisions that would have denatured it.)

One wonders, sometimes, how much sheer healthy self-esteem it takes for men like Sondheim, Shevelove, and Gelbart to stand by their work and refuse everyone's offer to take them seriously by perverting it. But at least Prince and Abbott seemed to comprehend what was afoot, and Zero Mostel was available to play Pseudolus, top banana of a bunch that even-tually included David Burns (the Randy Old Father), Jack Gilford (the Ridiculously Dutiful Servant), Ruth Kobart (the Termagant Wife), John Carradine (the Unctuous Procurer), Ronald Holgate (the Braggart Sol-dier), and Raymond Walburn (the Senile Dupe).

They had much to play, in the other of the two funniest scripts of the decade, wedded to a score so brilliantly devious that it has been praised as uniquely anti–Rodgers and Hammerstein when it is in fact somewhat in the Rodgers and Hammerstein tradition. *Except*: one, it does without Rodgers and Hammerstein's all-important community chorus (in "The Farmer and the Cowman," "June Is Bustin' Out All Over," "Climb Ev'ry Mountain"); two, it speaks, characterologically, in generalities rather than in Rodgers and Hammerstein specifics ("When we work in the mill . . ."); and, three, it contains one—just one—comic novelty ("Every-body Ought To Have a Maid") right out of the undisciplined 1920s.

The script first. As busy as a carnival and constantly throwing off solutions to problems that of course create new problems, it is true farce. However, classic farce generally goes wild only in the middle third of the evening. Act One is exposition and Act Three resolution. *Forum*, in two acts, starts wild (in all the shenanigans of "Comedy Tonight") and never stops. Yet it is a superbly controlled script, constantly maintaining its throughline (slave Mostel wants his freedom) and its love plot of Naïve Son (Brian Davies) and Virginal Courtesan (Preshy Marker) just enough for us to know that something genuine is happening underneath all the fun.

The fun itself is genuine, because it's made not of miscellaneous jokes but character comedy. For all its laughs, the script resists sample quotation; it is too much a series of modulated progressions to excerpt. What was funny on Mostel couldn't be lent to other characters; Burns' husband and Gilford's servant each pursued unique worldviews of, respectively, resignation and survival; and even the minor roles were consistent in their address. What fit them into a whole was Mostel, the only character who understands everyone else's reality. Thus, unlike those two other cartoons *Little Me* and *How To Succeed*, *Forum* really is about something, a theme traditional to comedy since the days of . . . yes, Plautus: the smart slave outwits any master.

Indeed, Mostel has to, so intense is his need for liberty. We hear it in "Free," one of the score's more inventive numbers, jumping from nervous semi-recitative to fanciful eighth-note bubblings to exaltation in a kind of soaring march: the progression from slavery to independence.* We also hear the authentic sound of romance in "Love, I Hear," the boy's private moment with the audience just as the action begins. Much is made of the irony of the show's main ballad, "Lovely," because it's something of a comedy song, especially when Gilford takes the reprise. But "Love, I Hear," for all its wit ("Today I woke too weak to walk"), is as ingenuous as any Princess Show ballad ever was, because it establishes the concept of

---

*Now It Can Be Told: Natalie Wood was one of the first members of the Sondheim cult, and "Free" started it. In the summer of 1962, I was touring Europe with my family, and we happened to be on the roof of our hotel in Pisa when Wood and her just barely ex-husband, Robert Wagner, were holding an informal party around a phonograph. Wood had brought to Europe the most recent cast albums, of *Forum*, *No Strings*, and *Bravo Giovanni*, and was auditioning them. Wood didn't play LP sides; she played bands, attracted by the mystique of certain titles. When she tried "Free," she was entranced, and delighted the entire roof with an all-evening *Forum* concert.

Boy Needs Girl as surely as "Free" establishes Mostel's reasons for running the insanely intricate plot.

This gives *Forum* a superiority to other total-comedy shows that has been overlooked. It is not a cartoon. It is a cartoon pretending to be a traditional Rodgers-and-Hammerstein-era musical comedy that only pretends to be a cartoon. "Everybody Ought To Have a Maid," with its encore choruses motivated simply by another character's bopping in to join the line, is obviously part of the game. But the rest of the score is character and situation numbers. True, "Pretty Little Picture" is a punctuation number, of no importance to the action and so tricky for non-musicians that revivals have been cutting it. But because *Forum*'s brand of comedy historically has dealt with types rather than individuals, we are too ready to hear a type singing when Sondheim is in fact shading him in a bit for us, in the generation-war duet "Impossible" or the mother's hate-to-love-him "That Dirty Old Man." Again, the lyrics lack the the references to the daily lives and worldview that Rodgers and Hammerstein dote on. Nothing in *Forum* compares to, say, "All Er Nothin' " or "A Puzzlement." Nevertheless, *Forum*'s numbers spring from the thinking that produced, for other examples, "A Cockeyed Optimist" and "Sixteen Going on Seventeen."

Having survived option hell, *Forum* then went into tryout hell. It was a bomb in Washington, D.C., when—in a tale so often told that I ask longtime buffs to skip to the next paragraph—the opening number found the three Proteans (the male ensemble) singing the wistful "Love Is in the Air," prompting the public to expect a light comedy. Sondheim wrote a replacement, the caperingly explanatory "Invocation." But this was too sophisticated for Abbott, so often called the dean of musical comedy and so often discovered sabotaging shows with his tin ear and fear of intellectual content.

Now Jerome Robbins rejoined the show. He got Sondheim to write "Comedy Tonight." Still, *Forum* got off to a slow start in New York, with mostly good notices but slow business till word of mouth sent it into sellout. It played 964 performances, some of them, curiously, with that old Cole Porter stylist Erik Rhodes taking over from Carradine the Unctuous Procurer. Phil Silvers, who played the Procurer in the movie, brought a revival to Broadway in 1972, finally assuming his intended role of Pseudolus. It didn't run, and had similar bad luck in London because Silvers suffered a stroke, but Nathan Lane and then Whoopi Goldberg played Pseudolus in the 1990s for another two-year run.

So the show is a classic—but not the typical Broadway classic revived because people love the songs. Folks still don't get *Forum*'s score, because they don't expect anything melodious in a farce, and what people don't expect they generally manage not to hear. This is the most difficult of the Sondheim scores, then: because it's too easy to take for granted. One knows that *Pacific Overtures* or *Into the Woods* demands concentration; they are not difficult, because one aspires to comprehend them. But when did anyone have to comprehend burlesque?

Anyone Can Whistle (1964), Sondheim's following show, is modern satire, though in another farcical structure. But here the score inhabits the action more boldly. Where *Whistle* mocks the automatic thinking of a conformist society, its score in part mocks the automatic writing of conformist musicals. It's discouraging to realize that dreck such as *Illya Darling* (1967) ran 320 performances while *Whistle*, after the most mixed reviews since *Allegro*, ran a week. Some of the critics even seemed to know that *Whistle* was going to be an Important Flop. In the *Morning Telegraph*, Whitney Bolton warned, "If it is not a success, we sink back into the old formula method and must wait for the breakthrough."

But then, the show was too strange and hard-edged to attract the theatre parties that would reserve *Illya Darling*'s ten-month stand, and neither Sondheim nor book writer and director Arthur Laurents was a ticket seller. Worse, producers Kermit Bloomgarden and Diana Krasny had budgeted the piece too tightly.* It had no room in which to wait out clarifying revisions, no time for word of mouth to circulate.

Whistle had an ugly tryout, mainly because everyone knew that it was a worthy piece that deserved perfecting. "It was a great show for people screaming up and down the aisles," said Angela Lansbury, one of Laurents' villains. She wanted to find some humor in her role, some style; but Laurents wanted only a creep. As a corrupt mayor, Lansbury really should have been something like Kay Thompson in the Fred Astaire–Audrey Hepburn film *Funny Face*, aggressive but elegant. However, Laurents

---

*At $350,000. This was the very least that a good-sized if not elaborate musical could open on. Sixties shows invariably went out of town for tryouts, and those productions not picked up for Philadelphia or Boston subscription series could face crippling losses.

didn't have a friendly piece in mind. His book is as smug and wise-guy as his villains are: are they running the show? His idea of a first-act curtain is to tell the audience, "You are all mad," then present the cast in what appear to be theatre balcony seats, laughing, applauding, reading the program, carrying on. But is the audience really all mad, or is Laurents just an angry jerk blowing smoke?

One admires Whitney Bolton's defense of the piece, because it is brilliantly written. A meanspirited piece of work, yes—but fast, funny, and Sondheim. Laurents gives us a chance to like, at least, the heroine (Lee Remick) and her hero (Harry Guardino). But everything else we like resides in the score. Sondheim needs to tell Laurents about the advantages of ribbing the subject instead of whacking at him; and, in any case, satire is supposed to take its *subjects* apart, not its audience. *Whistle*'s songs criticize with maximum prejudice, but they also know that their targets have if nothing else an attractive vitality—or why are they dangerous?

So the score entertains as it lampoons—in "Me and My Town," a nightclub-diva-and-her-boys number of the kind that Lisa Kirk might have commissioned for a booking at the Persian Room in the 1950s; in the mock-revivalist "Miracle Song," a takeoff on a Frank Loesser takeoff; in "I've Got You To Lean On," a jazzy version of the old "Friendship" genre; and in two cut numbers, "There Won't Be Trumpets" (the "Just Imagine"–"Waitin' For My Dearie"–"I'll Know" heroine's solo, here remade as a war cry) and the quarrel duet "There's Always a Woman." Sondheim gives us in "There Won't Be Trumpets" especially the pleasing irony that the grouching Laurents misses: because trumpets are exactly what we hear when hero Guardino walks on.

It's wonderful to know that *Whistle*'s investors included Irving Berlin, Richard Rodgers, Frank Loesser, and Jule Styne: the Old Talent making sure that the New got heard. Of course Loesser would be there. He was a known champion (and publisher, at Frank Music) of younger writers. So was Jule Styne, one of Broadway's great enthusiasts of music by people other than Jule Styne. Rodgers, too, loved and supported the theatre aside from his own work (and of course *Do I Hear a Waltz?* hadn't happened yet). And Berlin, too! This, truly, is old Broadway playing host, and not to a sure thing or even a likely *succès d'estime*, but to an oddball bazaar of everything Laurents had been stewing about for years. There really is a lot to stew about if one is intelligent and impatiently critical, but that may be this show's enduring problem. What, truly, is it about? How does the cross section of a town, divided into the sane and insane (but which is which?) and run by thieves, reflect the human condition? Why does Remick seduce Guardino in French? Why is it supposed to be so touching that Remick can't whistle (i.e., give of herself emotionally) when she is portrayed as a wow of an emotional dynamo? Sondheim wrote a score beautifully integrated into a mess of a book.

John Kander and Fred Ebb would be the next of our composer-lyricist teams. However, publisher Tommy Valando hadn't yet introduced them when Kander joined his old friends the Goldman brothers to write *A Family Affair* (1962). None of the three, apparently, wanted us to know which of them wrote what. "By James Goldman, John Kander and William Goldman" ran their billing. I guess they're the De Sylva, Brown and Henderson of the 1960s. Their show is a tidy little piece about how the in-laws interject themselves into wedding plans, and though the families are Jewish (one song title is "My Son, the Lawyer"), this is a universal tale. One can almost visualize the girl's uncle (Shelley Berman) and the boy's parents (Eileen Heckart and Morris Carnovsky) duking it out on the *Jerry Springer Show*.

Note the names of three performers not known for singing. Separately or together, they handled eight of the show's sixteen numbers, and they did splendidly. Berman even navigated through a waltz, "(I think it's just) Beautiful." The real singers were the young couple (Larry Kert and Rita Gardner; he calls her "Kid") and the usual Broadway kibitzers (Bibi Osterwald, Gino Conforti, Jack De Lon, and a very young Linda Lavin), who mainly sang a quartet called "Harmony" that celebrated the growing lack of unity in the wedding party. Figaro and Susanna don't suffer worse tribulations, though director Word Baker and set designer David Hays gave the stage an airy, open look, as if for a cute little piece written for a summer tent.

There *was* a cute little bit, in that Boy already Got Girl. Musicals were traditionally about courtship; this one was about the episode we seldom see, Boy *Marries* Girl. Beyond that quirk, *A Family Affair* was a low-powered piece, and ten days before the New York opening, John Kander begged Hal Prince to take over the direction. Prince did. Still, this is a small show, and sixties musicals were big; and sixties musicals were picturesque, but this one is about your cousin Mary's wedding. Remember?

Still, the score is quite capable (a few floppo numbers aside) and at times excellent. One can easily overlook "Every Girl Wants To Get Married," a heart-to-heart between the Girl and her putative sister-in-law, a veteran wife who soothes the Girl's nerves without doing much more than listening. The tune bounces along sweetly, until a fraught middle section leads the Girl to envision an absurd spat—and just then, as the sister comforts her, the bouncy tune sails back in, now dramatic, reassuring, inspiring. It's a wonderful touch, character development in four measures of time. The show's best ballad, "There's a Room in My House," makes virtually the same transition, only now it's the Boy soothing the Girl's anxieties, in a leaping strain that moves into a higher key on each appearance, firming her resolve.

And yet it was the non-singers that got the best out of Kander. Heckart had a keening ballad, "Summer Is Over," and the three elders enjoyed a flagellant's holiday in "I'm Worse Than Anybody," self-pity as cathartic deliverance, so the story can resolve as the kids say "I do."

But the outstanding number is Berman's "Revenge." Hays' wide empty stage produced no more than a couch, a coffee table, and a telephone in front of a large square of wedding lace to suggest Berman's living room at four o'clock of a sleepless night. To a suggestion of Ravel's *Bolero*, Berman plotted to even the score with the meddling Heckart. This man is dangerous: he schemes to tie her down in Africa for an ants' feast, even to cut off her phone line. Berman's vocal featured triumphant chuffles echoed by an unseen women's chorus, and—in a musical-comedy jest so old your great-great-grandmother fell out of her cradle laughing at it—Berman looked around to see who was there. As the number built, Berman decided to preempt Heckart by ordering the wedding cake personally. It's a strange notion to phone a bakery at four in the morning; even more strangely, he encounters an answering machine, some time before they were in general use. The tape is as obdurate as Heckart. First, it hangs up on him. Then it doesn't want to listen. Then it rushes him. So he spits the entire order out in five seconds flat and slams the phone down with a "Go to hell!" as the orchestra explodes with more *faux*-Ravel.

Phone routines were standard kit for comedians in those days, but the moment typifies A *Family Affair*'s charm. For once, it was the incidentals and not the story that provided the entertainment. That's partly because the show has no story. But the accumulation of incidentals—Heckart's spreading of The News by phone, Berman's locker-room disquisition on the advantages of bachelorhood, Carnovsky and Heckart showing off at a barbecue with a hula number—gives the action the gentle bite of real life. It's almost not a Broadway musical: provincial, middle-class, quotidian. It's even set in Chicago.

Along with Kander, A *Family Affair* introduced Hal Prince as a director, leading him to *She Loves Me* and then *Baker Street* in the two years after. However, Prince remained a producer as well, and he tapped Kander and (now) Ebb for *Flora, the Red Menace* (1965), the show that didn't make Liza Minnelli a star.

True, she won the Tony and the beginnings of what was eventually to be a large following. But it's difficult to turn out the total headliner in a show that folds in less than three months after chilly raves touting the nineteen-year-old Minnelli but mostly damning the play. Director and co-author (with Robert Russell) George Abbott hadn't even wanted Minnelli. He saw Eydie Gorme in the part, that of a young Depression-era artist who gets involved with the Communist Party. Gorme, a fine singer, couldn't have acted it well, and was too adept and confident a personality. Flora is uncertain, wild, raw.

In the show's source, Lester Atwell's 1963 novel *Love Is Just Around the Corner*, Flora Meszaros is acerbic and a dedicated Red. The musical gentled her personality, coddled the Party with fond spoof, and pictured Flora generally as unknowing rather than political. "You Are You" is the evening's final song, and also its moral. The ideal American is not part of someone else's movement. The American is an individual.

So the bad guy (Bob Dishy) is a cultist and a joiner and, not incidentally, a Communist. He is also a cheat who more or less swindles Minnelli into Party involvement in "Sign Here." So *Flora* is the rare musical in which we hope that Boy doesn't Get Girl. It was an odd pairing anyway, as Dishy was a no more than passable singer to Minnelli's earful (though he rose to a vivid if precarious high A at the end of "Sign Here"). But then, none in the cast was a singer in any real sense. Mary Louise Wilson played a Communist so fanatic that she is a one-person riot; at a cell meeting, she explored her skills of dedication in "The Flame." Wilson was no Rose-Marie, yet she sustained her high register quite grandly in the choral sections: a vocal intensity mirroring her political intensity. Later, courting cowboy hunk James Cresson, she traded typical thirties jokes in "Knock Knock," and Cresson—even less of a singer than Wilson—joined her harmonically in thirds.

This is one of the musical's most enduring traits. It makes singers of non-singers, shows us how anyone could be a character in a musical because *life* is a musical. That ebullient idealism is why the musical started the twentieth century by gradually conquering the European forms of "light opera." Because it isn't opera. It's light. Better, it's resourceful, protean. There is no equivalent in Singspiel, opérette, or zarzuela to nineteen-year-old Minnelli's jump onto Broadway by playing, more or less, herself. Those arts don't stretch. The American musical, like Walt Whitman, contains multitudes.

Indeed, this musical opens with one: the unemployed of the Great Depression, selling apples and pencils. Despite a lively middle section, the number is . . . well, Depressing. Then *Flora* cuts to Minnelli's high-school graduation, with Minnelli delivering the valedictory. Woodwinds sneak in under her speech, cuing in "Unafraid," the anthem of the first crop of Kander-and-Ebb kids determined to Make It Here. After Minnelli's chorus, the girls take up the song, quietly scared. But the second A introduces some vocal harmony, a sound of structure—of confidence—and the release brings the boys in. By the final A, in a sophisticated vocal arrangement, the kids are truly unafraid; there was a stir in the Alvin Theatre during Minnelli's solo and a storm of applause after the number. Better, the very next scene found Minnelli filling out a job application ("for no job," she ironically joked), backed by three male and three female applicants in "All I Need (Is One Good Break)," the best song Minnelli ever sang in her life. "Soaring" is a word one normally reserves for the kind of singing heard in operetta, but Minnelli's belt soared in this one, and the audience took the house apart.

So she earned her Tony. But *Flora* as a whole failed to catch on. The book never got into anything of interest, frustrating a public that enjoyed the music; and such could-be hits as "Sing Happy" and "Dear Love" never took off. However, Kander and Ebb had definitely established themselves—as musical-comedy stylists; as associates of Hal Prince; as supporters of Minnelli; and as authors with a fascination for those in need. "They take these downtrodden characters," Jerry Herman has said, "and give them dignity." Before Kander and Ebb, the Heroine's Wanting Song was "Somebody, Somewhere." Now it's to be "Theme from New York, New York": as much for success as for love, especially to a frisky vamp as a kind of self-advertisement.

Actually, musical comedy generally gives dignity to the downtrodden. Even back in the late nineteenth century, working-class characters conquering class prejudice or simply a landlord were favored company. One thinks, also, of the many Cinderella heroines of the 1910s and 1920s, of Irene's "Alice Blue Gown" and Sally's "Look For the Silver Lining." Key titles relentlessly recall to us the downtrodden ennobled by the hopes that the musical lavishes on its people—the homeless Astaires in *Lady, Be Good!* (1924), the garment workers putting on their show as *Pins and Needles*, the chorus of *Finian's Rainbow* (1947), the entire company of *A Tree Grows in Brooklyn* (1951), *A Chorus Line* (1975), *Rent* (1996). It's part of the musical's politics, because the sons and daughters of the downtrodden were the creators of the American musical. Who else would have considered a life in the theatre? It was socially disreputable and, for those on the bottom, a hard living. Isn't that why so many performers did blackface routines at some point or other in their careers? Actors were niggers—so they sucked up the insult and dealt with it by sending it back to the audience with a spin of irony.

We've seen the downtrodden aspiring with dignity in this very chapter—so seriously in *110 in the Shade* and, all for a goof, in *Little Me*. Jerry Herman himself got to the downtrodden, most notably later on in *The Grand Tour*'s Jacobowsky, symbol of refugee Jewry, and in Albin, the transvesto who defies Log Cabin Republicans with "I Am What I Am" in *La Cage aux Folles*.

Herman even spares time for the downtrodden in *Mame* (1966) in the character of Agnes Gooch (Jane Connell), though this show is mainly about born winners: a Broadway star (Beatrice Arthur), a rich southern beau (Charles Braswell), a bigoted WASP attorney (Willard Waterman), a pampered nephew (Frankie Michaels; then, grown in Act Two, Jerry Lanning), and, centrally, a bohemian aunt (Angela Lansbury). *Mame* is one of the most basic of shows: pure musical comedy in a tradition uniting song, dance, and somewhat unbelievable plot fun that goes straight back to *Lady, Be Good!*; juicy roles for the lead women while the men are mostly foils; a solid linear-narrative structure that enjoys a state-of-the-art staging team (designers Robert Mackintosh and William and Jean Eckart, choreographer Onna White, director Gene Saks) but doesn't need a super-director or a Concept; and a triumphant transformation of a successful play (and movie) into a successful musical, capitalism's spiciest art. *Mame* was better than successful—a smash. At 1,508 performances, it saw in as Lansbury's replacements the earthily energetic Janis Paige, the coolly patrician Jane Morgan (who couldn't resist an embarrassed hand-over-face gesture after she told off the bigot), and the wintergreen-fresh Ann Miller.

Mame is also the most basic of sixties titles, in a form invented in this decade, which I call the Big Lady Show. This is a star vehicle that doesn't wait for you to be enthralled by the star: it vigorously informs you that the star is enthralling—in writing and direction that make her almost absurdly conspicuous; in, often, an insanely enthusiastic title song hymning her qualities; and even in an elaborately staged curtain call that crescendos ecstatically up to her appearance, more or less inducing, through emotional manipulation, a standing ovation. The curtain call is so generically intrinsic that *Mame*'s published text included it, complete with detailed stage directions, as if it were a number in the score.*

The Big Lady Show lasted into the 1970s, taking in such likely and unlikely divas as Carol Channing, Katharine Hepburn, Lauren Bacall, Liza Minnelli (in *The Act*, as Big Liza, though there was no title song), and even Joel Grey. Of them all, I would nominate Lansbury as the most potential—versatile, glamorous, not a natural-born singer but a wonderful one, and of surprising, perhaps shocking, depth, in *Sweeney Todd*. *Mame*'s producers kept auditioning her over and over; but who would have looked better in Mackintosh's hope chest of couture? The gold pajamas accessorized by a bugle, for her entrance; the silver lamé kimono coat trimmed with monkey fur for her speakeasy dance in "Open a New Win-

---

*Jerry Herman had already done a Big Lady Show two years earlier, in *Hello, Dolly!* I'm saving this title for a later chapter to emphasize how dazzling staging plans began to overwhelm the integrity of composition in the creation of musicals. In other words: how the director became the auteur. This is not the case in *Mame*, a show well written and then well staged.

dow"; the yellow moon gown and matching moon hat for the Moon Number; that southern-belle spoof; an all-white outfit just for the curtain call?

The part might have been commissioned for Lansbury, though it was in fact written for Rosalind Russell. Completely reimagining the Mame of Patrick Dennis' novel when they wrote *Auntie Mame* the play (1956), Jerome Lawrence and Robert E. Lee made *their* Mame less erotic and more loving. They gave her feelings, and so created the matrix for a musical. The most expensive straight play in Broadway history, *Auntie Mame* was "opened up" in a vast, picaresque scene plot and a huge cast of characters. All it needed was the Score, for Lawrence and Lee themselves wrote *Mame*'s book, adhering very closely to the play but for a few expedient snips. Young Patrick's nanny, Norah, and Mame's secretary when she turns autobiographer, Agnes Gooch, were combined into one role. Gooch's drunken sexual breakout with poet Brian O'Bannion was retained, but without Brian. (In the musical, Gooch goes off alone on her rampage.)

This left *Mame* with an abiding flaw. How the Older Patrick turns snob after his liberal upbringing is never explained in play or musical. And in the play, at least, he can object to Agnes' presence as one objects to any problematic stranger. In the musical, however, Agnes is the woman who cared for him before he came to live with Mame. His objection to her now seems extremely callous. If Mame is such a wonderful aunt, how did she create this ungrateful creep? Shouldn't he rather *start* to object and then pull back, humiliated by his own selfishness? Couldn't he even show some compassion, so that we can like him as we liked his younger self? I hope the next revival—it'll be a shoo-in when Melissa Errico is old enough—effects a revision here.

The play moved fast and the musical even faster. Most of the play's best lines are still in place, but some of *Mame* has the character of a comic telegram, as when, in the hunt scene, pounding hooves, snorts, and whinnying are heard offstage while a few grooms nervously back into view. They're trying to saddle what seems to be a bucking bronco:

COUSIN JEFF: Lightnin' Rod! Thought he went mad.
MOTHER BURNSIDE: Did.

PATRICK: My Auntie Mame is riding a mad horse?
MOTHER BURNSIDE: Temporarily.

The first party scene is now a gala character number, "It's Today," which
gave Lansbury a staircase entrance, a ride on a dancing piano, and, a bit
later, a touching reprise, *sola*, when she made her first emotional contact
with Young Patrick. In fact, Herman used music very cleverly in developing *Auntie Mame*, for instance turning the tired old romantic drama that
Mame accidentally ruins into a tired old operetta. Most important, "Open
a New Window" encapsulates Young Patrick's education, in one of Onna
White's most ingenious dances. It's a montage of vignettes, in a gathering
of New York "types" (cop, newsboy, ballerina, organ-grinder, cabbie), in a
cubist art studio, a modern-dance class, a fire-engine ride (stage left to
stage right), then in that speakeasy, in which the patrons go into freeze-
frame as Patrick, at the door, says, "*Mame* sent me!" and in which he and
she tango till the cops raid the joint and everyone rides to jail in a paddy
wagon (stage right to stage left) in a final chorus of Mame's credo and
anthem.

The reason why this character has proved so central to American culture is that she's for freedom. Despite ill-formed progressive instincts, she
has no politics, because she's too busy living to vote. What she has is a
belief in planting and harvesting. She's scattered and willful and even
manipulative: but she's always right, because she's always fair. She judges
people quite harshly: not on what they are, but on how they behave.

That isn't in the novel, by the way. Again, it was Lawrence and Lee,
not Patrick Dennis, who created the Mame we admire. Rosalind Russell
embodied her. Angela Lansbury renovated her.

And Jerry Herman gave her her music. *Mame* is his best score, because
it's full of character. It's not daring in any way, for of our five major songwriters and teams introduced in the 1960s, Herman is the only one who
never experiments. After leaving *Milk and Honey*'s opera singers behind,
he wrote so consistently that numbers from *Dolly!* are stylistically no different from those he wrote twenty years later. They have the odd ability
to function out of context as good mainstream pop while serving very
contextually within the show. "It's Today," "Open a New Window," "My
Best Girl," "Bosom Buddies," "That's How Young I Feel," and "If He

Walked Into My Life" have been sung all over the place and by anyone, with only the occasional skewed line ("Where's that boy with the bugle?") to suggest their specific purpose. Yet this *is* the music of Mame, Vera, Gooch, Patrick—the music of how it feels to live in a state of absolute individuality. To know that "It's Today" was actually written in 1958 for one of Herman's revues (where it began, "There's just no tune as exciting as a show tune . . .") is to learn very little about the number. Not till Mame appears at the top of that stairway for her nightly party, is asked, "What the hell are we celebrating?," and throws off the first excuse that pops into her head did the number have any reason to exist: because now it explains who Mame was Before Patrick. Because it is only After Patrick that this woman realizes that life has more purpose in it than the throwing of parties. So "Open a New Window" *is* the purpose, "My Best Beau" (the second verse of "My Best Girl") is her partner in that purpose, and "If He Walked Into My Life" tells us that Mame has not yet fulfilled her purpose. The latter is the perfect song in the perfect spot, the transition to one last party, during which all the conformist bigots are driven out of the story.

We should mention "The Fox Hunt," a number in a form that Harold Rome favored,* in which as many as five or six melodies are sung separately, then all at once. Rome always used it as sheer music, but Herman makes it dramatic, to contrast the attitudes of people watching Mame riding that mad horse and also to narrate for us the events of the unseen hunt. Cousin Jeff leads off rather neutrally ("Look at her go . . ."), Patrick simply shouts to his aunt to fall off the horse, Cousin Fan and Mother Burnside cram a little dialogue into their section, the chorus girls gloat ("Giddyap, Lightnin' Rod . . ."), then all sing together as the hunt climaxes. The cast fills the stage. Mame has won. She has enchanted all in the cast, the theatre, the world.

This cues in the title song, the last number in Act One (though not quite the finale), and the Big Lady's big moment. Mame does nothing but preen; as well she might, after carrying a show for ninety minutes. Still, there is the feeling that all this Adoration of the Hostess is less contagious

---

*We hear it in *Call Me Mister*'s "Going Home Train," *Fanny*'s "Birthday Song," *Destry Rides Again*'s "Are You Ready, Gyp Watson?," and even in Rome's last show, *Gone With the Wind*, in "Blissful Christmas." There is no such sample, however, in *I Can Get It For You Wholesale*.

than stage-managed, like that last change of costume just for the curtain call. Ethel Merman and Mary Martin never had anything like this in their vehicles. Note that *Jennie*, for all its clotheshorse glamour, did not feel the need for a title song glorifying Martin. The fact that she *was* Mary Martin was its own glory.*

A case of what we might call "titlesongitis" was infecting the musical—these vast productions with their vast star and her vast paean. One every now and then would be fine. But it was becoming a distraction, as when *Sherry!*'s Dolores Gray crashed into the Man Who Came To Dinner's living-room quarters singing "Sherry!" not because she could but because one had to. We even start to worry about the health of the chorus singers, as the sopranos are pushed up ever higher for that last ounce of warped festivity. *The Gay Life*'s women were forced up to six measures of high notes ending on B at the end of "Bring Your Darling Daughter." Yes, it's exciting: so is an afternoon of gladiator combat in the Colosseum. *Mame*'s musical director, Donald Pippin, had his sopranos, on the repeated crying of the heroine's name at the close of "Mame," sitting on B's and A's and crowning them with a sustained C sharp. I hope they got Cunegonde bonus pay.

*Of course, both Martin and Merman played Dolly, title song, Big Lady curtain call, and all the rest of the kit. Still, *Hello, Dolly!* was not, as they put it in the ballet world, "made" on them.

7

EYE ON THE TARGET

FUNNY GIRL

On the night of April 15, 1963, the curtain of the Winter Garden Theatre went up on a backstager on the early life of one of America's great singer-comediennes. With a Jewish mother, an Irish hoofer sidekick, an understanding black maid, and a husband who feels eclipsed by her growing fame, she vows to succeed against the usual odds. Real-life figures peppered the dramatis personae, and defunct genres were revived. The temptation to interpolate songs that the heroine had made famous was resisted in favor of a completely new score. Most of it was given to the young woman playing the title role, a relative unknown with a dazzling singing voice who, rumor warned, might prove to be the next big Broadway star.

Rumor also told of out-of-town troubles: and the critics saw why. To a man they dimissed the show as characterless drivel, and it closed in a week.

The show was *Sophie*, on the rise of Sophie Tucker, the would-be star was Libi Staiger, and it's odd how much the piece has in common with *Funny Girl*: everything in the first paragraph above except the date of the premiere. It's even odder how close *Funny Girl* came to ending up as *Sophie* did. In a way, this chapter is about a big bad flop that now accidentally and now expertly transformed itself into a sellout hit that ran for thirty-nine months in New York and a further year on tour, threw off a giant hit of a movie, and launched the biggest star career in show-biz history.

But, first, how did *Sophie* go so wrong with such similar material? Sophie Tucker was every bit as interesting a star as Fanny Brice, complete with anthem ("Some of These Days," a jazzy challenge to Brice's mourn-

ful "My Man"), memorializing film appearances, and a Name that rang
with meaning even after her death. Like Brice, Tucker had content, as a
feminist performer who played top to her men and shopped for new
before the old ones wore out. She ran through many of the forms of show
biz when it was the Great American Thing—minstrel blackface, vaudeville, burlesque, the *Follies*, the London visit, radio, Hollywood, a Cole
Porter book musical, and finally nightclubs.

One problem was *Sophie's* inexperienced crew: producers out of
nowhere offering a book by Phillip Pruneau and a score by Steve Allen,
with direction by Gene Frankel, replaced by Jack Sydow. Only Allen's
name is of note, at that mainly for hosting a television talk show. In fact,
Allen was also a successful pop songwriter in the 1950s.

But that's what Allen wrote for *Sophie*—pop songs, not a theatre score.
There are no character numbers, no situation numbers. No *story*. Where
is Sophie and her world and the distinctly melting-pot ethnicity of the
stage as she knew it, when all the producers were Jewish, all the musicians
were Italian, and all the lawyers were Irish? Sophie's "onstage" numbers
are badly turned, with nothing even approximating a Tucker specialty.
Another of Tucker's anthems was "I'm the Last of the Red Hot Mamas," a
boastfully self-deprecating strut, goofing on herself even as she vaunts her
grandeur. But Allen's runoff, "Red Hot Mama," is a piece of nothing.
Worse, he mistook the burlesque of Sophie's day for the stag show that it
had devolved into by the 1930s. No, Tucker's burlesque, as I've explained,
was family fare. Yet "Queen of the Burlesque Wheel"* found the chorus
girls in elaborately old-fashioned underthings and feathered hats, assuring
us that "She can shake like the Quake of Nineteen-oh-six," as if Sophie
were stripping. Nowhere in American show biz was there anything like
that at this time.

Tucker herself had laid down, in *Some Of These Days* (1945), what her
early life was like. It is a rich and wonderful book, full of backstage atmosphere—exactly what *Sophie* lacked. Didn't anyone read the book? Yes:

*Wheels were touring circuits, established generically and geographically, in which stock
companies would move from town to town, always returning to the same theatres. There
were wheels in various parts of the country for minstrel companies, for companies rotating
Shakespeare, Restoration classics, and American warhorses, for musical troupes, and so
on. For example, the young Laurette Taylor of *Jennie* worked the Northwestern Melodrama Wheel. The rise of film and the concomitant "going over" of legit houses to cinema
stopped the wheels turning in the 1920s.

because one incident, in which a black maid named Mollie explains to Sophie that every troupe has one "Patsy" who is sneered at but who eventually winds up a star, got into the show as "Patsy," a cheer-up duet. Rosetta LeNoire played the maid, Berta Gersten played Mama, Eddie Roll played the Irish hoofer, and various others played agent William Morris, manager Marcus Loew, director Julian Mitchell, and diva Nora Bayes, who vigorously attains cliché by demanding that Sophie's attention-getting song set in *The Follies of 1909* be cut. Okay, it actually occurred—but it came off in the show not as biography but as Hackneyed Backstage Volcano Eruption: "Either *she* goes or *I* don't sing!" Worse yet was the obvious ploy of characterizing Sophie as lacking confidence in her looks simply to add what in her day was called "heart interest" to the saga. What, the big lug likes her? "I didn't think he'd give me a second look!" They dialogue, and it's promising, so: "Please God, don't let him give me a second look!"

That was Art Lund as the guy and Libi Staiger as Sophie, the latter a coming star stopped by having to carry a bomb show. It was a big one, unmissable; Sophie herself attended the premiere and graciously clapped like heck at the end. Well, she was a performer, and she knew what performers go through. It isn't their fault if their starring vehicle is a stupid mess. But they get blamed for it just the same.

Barbra Streisand was going to be blamed for *Funny Girl*, and she knew it. The Boston tryout was a disaster. At least her singing was going over well, and she could hardly be called miscast. But she was not yet twenty-two, and relatively inexperienced. Her featured role in *I Can Get It For You Wholesale*, less a character than a series of vocals with one "personality" number, had not prepared her to play Fanny Brice. As written by Isobel Lennart and revised by an unbilled John Patrick, the character is moody and unpredictable, as likely to resent what she needs as to chase after it. A good director could help her center the scenes, build the character. But the original director, Jerome Robbins, backed out at around the time that co-producer David Merrick did, leaving Merrick's ex-partner, Ray Stark, with Bob Fosse. Well, that would work—only Fosse walked when Stark, a Broadway tyro, questioned his ability.*

---

*Stark made the mistake of asking this question of Merrick, who gleefully reported it to Fosse. Merrick often played people against each other, claiming it honed them for the battle of Making a Hit. Actually, he just enjoyed playing people against each other.

Stark ended up with Garson Kanin, who couldn't have been wronger. A good writer, Kanin had the habit of directing his own scripts, in a tradition that goes back to the nineteenth century, when there was no such profession as "director" and either playwrights or producers (usually the star, heading his own troupe as the "actor-manager") did the honors. Kanin might never have strayed into the musical but for having written the novel that *Do Re Mi* was based on. Naturally, Kanin wrote the show's script; thus, naturally, he directed it. So now he was a director of musicals.

But it was Kanin's idea that a director's main work lay in, one, perfect casting, and, two, letting the actors know when they were *too*. That is: too grand, too nuanced, too intense, too understated. He had had little or no experience with someone like Streisand, who was not yet into the part enough to be anything. She didn't need to be told what not to do. She needed to be told what to do.

Nor was Kanin equipped to fit together the complex machinery of a big sixties musical, with its supporting roles, its balance of strictly vocal with mainly danced numbers, its all-important first ten minutes, its strange way of falling totally apart if just one scene went awry. As the *Funny Girl* company played to somnolent and even walk-out houses in tryout, Ray Stark must have been wondering what *Funny Girl* would have been like if Anne Bancroft—the next to be considered after Mary Martin said no— had played Fanny. She was no singer, but she certainly wouldn't have had trouble validating Fanny Brice in the dialogue.

However, Bancroft didn't like *Funny Girl*'s lyricist, Bob Merrill. Or that's what Merrill said. Composer Jule Styne had wanted Streisand from the first; what composer wouldn't? With a combination of the typical Stynean enthusiasm for a performer he admired and the also typical Stynean expertise, he and Merrill planned a score beyond Bancroft, beyond even Mary Martin. One of the first songs they wrote was "Don't Rain On My Parade." Can you imagine Martin sounding right in that? Another of the first songs was "I'm the Greatest Star." Jule Styne asks you, Bob Merrill asks you, and I ask you, Who but Streisand?

Styne and Merrill wrote an astonishing number of songs for *Funny Girl*. Not because, like Schmidt and Jones on *110 in the Shade*, they wanted to explore the material, but because at that point in *Funny Girl*'s history nobody knew what the show was. To Frances (Mrs. Ray) Stark, it was an adoring memorial to her mother. To Styne and Merrill, it was a backstager with a sad romance tucked in. To costume designer Irene Sharaff, it was another of those period things with the big hats and the demented shoes.* To choreographer Carol Haney, it was an extra heavy job, because, given Kanin's lack of experience, she would have to stage much of the show herself. To Streisand, it was a ticket to Hollywood.

And to Isobel Lennart, it was two very different shows married to each other, like that jumble of comedy and tragedy that they put on in Richard Strauss' opera *Ariadne auf Naxos*. *Funny Girl* has two throughlines. Or even: *Funny Girl* comprises two genres. One is a "Yes, I *will!*" backstager, which unfortunately peters out near the end of Act One. The other is the romance, which keeps getting bogged down in the marital soap opera that takes up all of Act Two. Loosely binding the two is the subtextual matter implied in the show's title: the heroine fears that when she isn't joking around, men will think her funny-looking.

Even the bungling *Sophie* knew what it was: a suspenseful *can she? will she?* backstager with love songs. But *Sophie* didn't have the personality such a show needs. Just to compare "I'm the Greatest Star" with the similar spot in *Sophie*, "I'll Show Them All," is to see one major difference between hit and flop: content. Sophie's Wanting Song is anybody's Wanting Song. Worse, it nears its climax with a clause—"I'll make them crawl"—made to rhyme with the title (and final) line. Why would Sophie Tucker want anyone crawling? On the contrary, her book charms through its lack of arrogance. Styne and Merrill don't go wrong trying to fill out a rhyme scheme; nor do they lack for themes. "I'm the Greatest Star" is plaintive, demanding, mercurial. It is exactly the note—or, rather, the series of notes—struck by the person who, grown more confident, will sing the plaintive, demanding, mercurial "Don't Rain On My Parade."

From the start, Styne and Merrill knew what the show was: but they were the only ones. They even understood Nick Arnstein, little more than an engaging shadow in the script (partly because the real Arnstein was still alive and litigious). For Nick, Styne and Merrill wrote a fine

---

*One seldom-told tale finds Sharaff showing her first designs for Streisand's costumes to Streisand herself. Sharaff was one of the most successful of her kind and Streisand a neophyte, yet each design that Streisand rejected she carefully tore up. Sharaff's sketches were artwork, but Streisand felt that if there's a chance for someone to screw up, someone will screw up, and she was taking no chances. Even then, she knew.

character number in the swinging Styne mode, "A Temporary Arrangement (is the only permanent thing in life)," another of the show's many cut numbers.

"People" would have been cut, too, if Garson Kanin had had his way. Oddly, the music was not going over with audiences. But then, Streisand didn't know how to play the scene leading up to it, the first chorus, the following underscored dialogue, and the second chorus. Fanny is alone with Nick on the night of her triumph in the *Follies*, and she in effect blurts out what is on her mind. It's a sixties version of "Deep in My Heart, Dear" or "Make Believe": impulsive love talk, but now to be heard in a cynical age. This is a tricky scene and Streisand was flubbing it, so confusing the audience that they couldn't enjoy the song. Kanin didn't have a clue, used as he was to seasoned veterans enacting characters of his own invention. Luckily, Streisand had engaged her former acting coach, Allan Miller, behind Kanin's back, and Miller showed her how to play it. First, she's a kid, generalizing about big ideas on a Lower East Side stoop overlooked by all her mother's friends. Uncertain, she sings to the audience. But, listening to herself, she starts to believe her own notions. She's a woman now, and, on the line "Lovers are very special people" she suddenly looked right at Nick, and the number was landing big-time.

Of course it was: how does one flop with one of the biggest song hits of the decade? Why did "Camelot," to pick one other instance, play so beautifully that even the show's detractors conceded it? Because Moss Hart knew what the show was; he also knew what a musical is, and it most definitely isn't merely, one, casting and, two, critique of overplaying. Jerome Robbins also knew what a musical is, and when Ray Stark got Robbins to edit the production, during the Philadelphia leg of its lengthy tryout, it rose from a disaster to a flawed composition that was playing very, very well. When Stark decided to postpone the New York opening and spend a few more weeks cleaning house in Philadelphia, *Funny Girl* had to leave the first-choice Forrest Theatre for the long-disdained Erlanger, a big old barn way beyond what is called Center City. Yet *Funny Girl* sold out. Word was spreading.

Robbins made one general and three very precise changes that seemed to shift all the show's emphases. He couldn't fix the problem of the two different shows playing together; that is intrinsic and will never go away.

But he did notice that, after Miller's coaching, what worked was Streisand. So everything else had to play around and to her. That was the general change. Though Streisand and Sydney Chaplin had equal billing above the title, *Funny Girl* became strictly her show. Kay Medford as Mama, Danny Meehan as the Irish hoofer, and Jean Stapleton as a neighborhood kibitzer were sound support, as, indeed, was Chaplin in what was left of Nick's role.

The first of the precise changes came near the end of Act One, in a seduction scene to Nick's solo, "You Are Woman." A serious number, it gave Streisand nothing to play except "indications" of various kinds, and the scene was failing. Robbins seized on the song's ticktock accompaniment, asking Styne and Merrill to write Streisand a verse of her own to that staccato scan. Both men were facile creators—Merrill could write you the second chorus of a ballad during five minutes of backstage hammering—and the expanded "You Are Woman" became a highlight of the evening.

Of course, it was now Streisand's comic scene, with background vocal by Chaplin. Similarly, Haney's spectacular "Cornet Man" dance had to be shredded to nothing, for it was too good for what followed it and also pulled the audience out of the story for some exhibition-level choreography. But "Cornet Man" is not a *Follies* number: it's a bit of five-and-dime vaudeville. Besides, its purpose is to establish young Fanny in her first show-biz break. A big number at this point is simply wrong for the story, even if cutting it back robbed dancer Buzz Miller of his solo spot. Miller had been one of the two boys doing "Steam Heat" in the original *Pajama Game* with Haney, so a bit of history was ruined here, especially for Haney and Miller.

But then, the *Funny Girl* saga was never about them, or Kanin, or Ray Stark and David Merrick, or Mary Martin and Anne Bancroft, or Eydie Gorme (whom Stark was holding in readiness, just in case), or Allyn Ann McLerie (whose featured part was written out in Boston), or even Kaye Ballard, who would have played Fanny if the show had gone up in the 1950s, when Ballard auditioned with an LP of Brice specialties. No, *Funny Girl* was about the explosion of Barbra Streisand upon Broadway, this time not as an intriguing piece of an ensemble show but as the show itself. What *Funny Girl* would have been like if Bob Fosse had gone

ahead in the first place is a fascinating but worthless question—worthless
because we'll never know but fascinating because the limitlessly inventive Fosse might have brought forth something extremely unusual in
form.

Funny Girl is not unusual. It is one of the most usual of all sixties musicals: in its production, with the "wagons" of scenery rolled on and off, the
traveler curtain, the backdrops, the stationary sidepieces; in the medley
overture; in the action-advancing dialogue between verses of songs; in
the long Act One and shorter Act Two; in the dancing leased out in
breaks in vocal numbers and bits here and there but no full-out ballet.
After all, by now that was so . . . well, so *Oklahoma!*.

Then why was this show so hard to put together? *Funny Girl*'s tryout
hell can fairly be called legendary, with eruptions of geschrei so intense
that many felt it would close not so much because of defects as because
everyone in it was going to the hospital with a coronary. Kanin retained
his director's billing, with Robbins cited after "Production Supervised by."
But the hell lasted literally up to the last minute, when Norman Krasna
was flown in for further book tinkering till Robbins got his third precise
change, a "button" on the romantic throughline in the last scene between
Fanny and Nick:

> NICK: What did I ever do for you, darling? What did I ever give you that
>   you couldn't have gotten for yourself?
> FANNY: A blue marble egg. No one would ever have given me that but
>   you. And you made me feel sort of—beautiful, y'know?
> NICK: You're not sort of beautiful. You *are* beautiful.

They rehearsed the final version of the scene as the audience was filing in
on opening night, March 26, 1964.

After all that trouble, however, the show is one of those taken-for-
granted hits. It is enjoyed, but not admired—not even for its score, which
I call one of the great ones. It was Styne and Merrill, I repeat, who figured
out who *Funny Girl*'s heroine was; many of the best lines in the script were
written in response to what the songs told about Fanny's belief system.
Along with performance numbers, Nick numbers, Allyn Ann McLerie
and Danny Meehan numbers, were two key Fanny numbers, "Absent

Minded Me" and a title song.* There's even a Fanny Leitmotiv, a pair of consecutive falling thirds set to the words "Nicky Arnstein" and as sharp an invention as *Gypsy's* "I had a dream" theme.

So *Funny Girl* is a rich score, more than just a set of songs. Interestingly, there is no suggestion of the period (the 1910s) in the music. The onstage ensemble numbers—"Cornet Man," "His Love Makes Me Beautiful," and "Rat-Tat-Tat-Tat"—are modern versions of the kind of songs Fanny Brice might have sung, even if Ziegfeld would never have put anyone but a showgirl in a showgirl's part (in "Beautiful"). Everything in *Funny Girl* is modern. There are some waltzes, generally a nostalgic usage in the 1960s; and "Sadie, Sadie" has a slightly classic lilt, as if it were one of those records that Fanny claims to play all day. Ralph Burns' orchestrations are especially up-to-date, filling the pit with hot band and plenty of brass solos. Overture buffs invariably cite the one to *Gypsy* as their favorite, but *Funny Girl's* rivals it for unity (in the "Nicky Arnstein" motive's binding appearances) and overall excitement—note the ecstatic piano glissando in the release of "Don't Rain On My Parade."

"Parade" and "People" are the hit tunes, but the classiest number is "The Music That Makes Me Dance," Styne's densest harmonic structure ever and Merrill still writing the show that *Funny Girl* always should have been in "I'm better on stage than at intermission." As "I Want To Be Seen With You" looks toward "People," the two numbers in effect creating throughline number one (the romance), "The Music That Makes Me Dance," though a love song, looks back to "I'm the Greatest Star," resolving throughline number two (the backstager). The score *is* the show. "Music" pulled off a sneaky *coup de théâtre*, too, for it began with Streisand in an overcoat, singing the verse in a spotlight. As the orchestra played the slowly rising chords leading into the refrain, an offstage voice announced, "Ladies and gentlemen, Florenz Ziegfeld presents the one and only Fanny Brice!" and Streisand came forward, now magically out of the coat, in regal *Follies* couture. (The offstage voice was another piece of mistaken history, for Ziegfeld never "announced" performers; his public

---

*Streisand recorded "Absent Minded Me" on her *People* album and released a single of "Funny Girl" that has never been reissued—not even on her four-CD set with rare archive material. The "Funny Girl" heard in the film, though by Styne and Merrill, is a different composition.

followed the listings in the program. Even to those who didn't, Fanny Brice needed—as they say—no introduction.)

Let me not only praise one more number but show you why I think the score is easy to undervalue. This is the opening, "If a Girl Isn't Pretty." It comes after Streisand's entrance, a bold one that had never been tried before: the star walks onto an empty stage at the very start of the show. Well, not quite empty. A piece on a wagon gives us her dressing room. "Hello, gorgeous," she says, into her makeup mirror. Well, that's one throughline.

We're in a flashback frame—another of the many emendations during the tryout that saved the show. The understanding black maid asks why Fanny is staring so into her mirror. What does she see? "A lot of years," says Fanny, twice. Just then, at stage right, a wagon rolls on with Mama's poker circle, depositing them inches away from Fanny, who is still staring straight ahead. They sing their card game, Fanny talks to the maid—no, to the poker ladies: "You were wrong, Mrs. Strakosh!"

Jean Stapleton calmly answers her from the past. Medford speaks, Fanny replies. It's a dialogue with her youth, with her fears of not being . . . talented? Attractive?

"If a Girl Isn't Pretty" takes off, the present-day Fanny vanishes, and suddenly the story has begun, in that "Cornet Man" vaudeville house. Fanny is fired, and now Danny Meehan takes up the song. "That map of yours just ain't no valentine," he explains—Bob Merrill at his best, real talk in music. As the scene changes, the number continues, everyone taking up the chorus to show us how universally doubted Fanny is.

And right there—"I'm a bagel on a plate full of onion rolls!"—Fanny stops Meehan and all of show biz with her Wanting Song, "I'm the Greatest Star." She stops the show. She makes *Funny Girl* a hit. She goes on to be Barbra, as Harold Rome, Jule Styne, and Bob Merrill look on, proud as daddies.

But try leaving a phone message and see if she returns it. When Streisand is finished taking from you what she needs, she is finished with you. And, boy, could she not wait to be finished with *Funny Girl* and on to her movie career. The performance one hears on the *Funny Girl* cast album—all told, the greatest eleven song spots by one singer in cast-album history—was not generally, or perhaps ever, heard in the Winter

Garden Theatre. Streisand often walked through her part, experimented, fiddled, mocked. Can one separate her from the show? Her new stardom was the show, a great hit but not a great piece. Nevertheless, after Streisand left it, Mimi Hines (with her husband, Phil Ford, in Meehan's role) and Johnny Desmond kept it running for another eighteen months. The final tally was 1,348 performances, with a further thirteen months of national tour with Marilyn Michaels, Anthony George, and Lillian Roth.

So the show is more than just Streisand. Yet it is uniquely unrevivable, especially as Streisand keeps appearing in the generally faithful film version. We will have to pass into a fresh era before this show is seen on Broadway again. As Kaye Ballard once told a friend, "Timing is everything."

8

WHEN MESSIAH COMES

THE SUPER-DIRECTOR

When one entered the Imperial Theatre for *Carnival!* (1961), the curtain was already up, on a field in southern Europe guarded by trees so thin that they looked like stick figures. Onto the empty stage came Pierre Olaf with an accordion, which he began to play. A few others came out—a dwarf blowing trumpet, roustabouts, circus talent—and soon all were engaged in hauling in the wagons and throwing up the tent.

Then the entire troupe came into view, as the manager (Henry Lascoe) exhorted the Incomparable Rosalie (our Fanny Brice wannabe Kaye Ballard) to lead the company in their theme song, "Direct From Vienna." More of the carnival was revealed—harem girls, a trained dog—in an air of picturesque excitement. What musical before this one had begun with the curtain up? When had an opening number taken off with such bizarre naturalism? Who had ever seen the cast, and not stagehands, build the set? It was all so unusual that one wondered if this was director Gower Champion's response to Bob Merrill's words and music or if the staging concept came first, the composition folding itself into the production. Does that make the director a co-author? In this decade, he became one.

Carnival!, officially billed as "based on material by Helen Deutsch," was drawn generally from fiction by Paul Gallico but mainly from Deutsch's script for the MGM film *Lili*, which introduced "Hi-Lili, Hi-Lo." *Carnival!* was a David Merrick project, with a book by Michael Stewart and a surprisingly large score from Merrill, counting twenty-six vocal or dance numbers. The raw material was ideal for what Champion had in mind, just unusual enough to look *really* unusual once he staged it.

There's the colorful carnival background, the eccentric carnival people. There's a touch of Europe, a little seedy here, a little elegant there. The leads include an angry guy (Jerry Orbach) in love with an almost retarded young woman (Anna Maria Alberghetti), and four puppets, her best friends. They actually save her from suicide. She adores them and hates the angry guy—but he works them. He *is* the puppets. He's her love.

It's a fine story, but did it need a super-director *conceiving* it? As a composition, *Carnival!* is one of the very best of the sixties musicals that is not an acknowledged classic. Stewart's book is solid and nuanced, and Merrill's work is superb, bursting with character numbers, even for the puppets. The underrated Merrill had an admirable knack for bringing out characters' daffy sides in his lyrics; it's one reason why Streisand was able to make so much of her *Funny Girl* songs. Similarly, Alberghetti's whimsically nutty Lili is beautifully developed, not only in the simpleminded "Mira" but in the effervescent "Beautiful Candy," wherein she expresses joy in "The sun today will be scrambled for my soufflé."

So couldn't *Carnival!* have been staged by one of the less ambitious directors of the day? Did it need Champion's emphasis on real circus effects—an aerialist, a magic act in which a man in the audience is beckoned onto the stage to have his shirt torn off him from under his jacket? Did it need Champion's bringing so many of his actors on and off through the auditorium? This is not to mention his obsession with eliminating the blackout during changes of scene—because, in this show, there weren't any. That field we saw as we entered the theatre was a unit set.

Actually, all musicals needed the smarter directors, because musicals were more complexly derived now. The dancing had become specialized, greatly varying from story to story; the scores were dramatic entities; the roles were acting challenges; the physical technology of stagecraft was in mid-revolution. The breakthrough title may well have been *Carousel*, the first major work that needed fastidious but also comprehensive superintending. Its director, Rouben Mamoulian, was musically gifted, and its choreographer, Agnes de Mille, had thespian wisdom. De Mille combined the two appointments as director-choreographer of *Allegro*, inaugurating this new age, and, yes, *Carnival!* needed Champion. I can't think of another guide it could have had and still run 719 performances. All of Champion's most typical shows are carnivals, a series of acts leaping up into view one after the other in a big open space with not a lot said but a great deal of fun had. They're cotton-candy musicals.

Here, however, relatively early in Champion's career as director-chore-ographer, the book is substantial and the characters more than candy. Anna Maria Alberghetti, the show's sole above-the-title name, was a child-prodigy soprano who grew into early womanhood losing all her phenomenal top notes while somehow suggesting that she could yet stun La Scala at will. (Julie Andrews was another such.) Alberghetti still maintained a sturdy high B flat, and *Carnival!* exploited it, but what really stood out was her insanely terrible diction.

Still, English wasn't Alberghetti's native language, and she did give wonderful life to this strange role of the child-woman who truly doesn't know that her best friends are her worst enemy: Jerry Orbach. His Paul offered something that the musical had not yet known, a bitter hero. Not an anti-hero, but a damaged personality unable to integrate his essential goodness with a scarring war experience. Lili's key character number is "Mira," about her hometown, a safe place. His key character number is "Everybody Likes You," sung to Carrot Top, the nicest of the puppets. Of course everybody likes him: he isn't real and there is no safe place.

Or take their vocal solos. Her showpiece is "Beautiful Candy," not for any coloratura singing but for the sunny nature of her sound. Barely twenty-five when *Carnival!* opened, Alberghetti had the timbre of a teen, even a child, perfect for a heroine whose confidants are hand puppets. His vocal showpiece is "Her Face," a passionate wish to *have* a sunny nature, so that he may deserve the captivating Lili.

But her most dramatic number is "I Hate Him," and his is this same "Her Face," now sung in counterpoint to it, as Merrill reaches the near limits of opera. This the musical was increasingly doing throughout the decade, even in a musical play masquerading as a Merrick-Champion musical-comedy staging treat.

The power of the songs is astonishing. There's one near-floppo entry, "Sword, Rose and Cape," the establishing piece for magician Marco the Magnificent (James Mitchell). It doesn't really establish anything; it's an excuse for Mitchell and the roustabouts to dance. However, I can praise no more surely than to point out "Humming," a comedy duet for Ballard and Lascoe (about Marco: her only theme). In any other show, it would have been a throwaway, a ditty on how Mitchell always hums after cheating on Ballard, and it would have been cut in Philadelphia. Here, it's what one might call a "show turn," a rabbit-out-of-the-hat number that dazzles not because of its melody (that would be the "Hi-Lili, Hi-Lo" replacement, "Love Makes the World Go Round") or its staging (that would be "Yes, My Heart," for Lili and the roustabouts, which you *know* is going to explode into dance but which turns out to be too excited to do so). No, "Humming" dazzles because it's so correct for these characters at this moment that you'll never be able to enjoy it properly again. It's a story number, a theatre experience, performers, set, and costumes under the lights. It's that moment come to life.

If it takes Bob Merrill to write it, it takes Gower Champion to realize how important no one in the audience will ever realize it is. It defines Ballard, it gives Lascoe something to do besides threaten to fire everybody, and it gives us a break from that unit set by opening up one of the camp wagons for a scène à deux. There's plenty of comedy scattered about this rather dark show, as when the diva puppet recalls singing "high M above L." (Her best role was "the madam, in *Butterfly*.") Still, "Humming" is *Carnival!*'s only out-and-out comic number, a sign of how much musical comedy was veering into musical play.

The super-director didn't have to effect his "conceiving" around the utterly unencountered in order to surprise and delight. Co-directing with Abe Burrows, Bob Fosse (with choreographer Hugh Lambert) made of *How To Succeed in Business Without Really Trying* (1961) a Sunday color comic strip filled with running gags, zanies striding into panel to play shtick, even colored-in line drawings for the sets. True, with Frank Loesser doing the score and Burrows the book,* the show was in no great need of super-directing.

Or was the public becoming so accustomed to the high-tech dazzle of the de Mille–Robbins generation of directing choreographers that few shows could get by with the dependable but sparkless pros who had been

---

*Jack Weinstock and Willie Gilbert were also credited, as it was they who had first adapted Shepherd Mead's satiric book of 1952, as a straight play. But it was so "understood" on The Street that Burrows was the author of the musical's script that the usually clueless Pulitzer committee, awarding *How To Succeed* their drama prize, cited Burrows and Loesser only.

staging musicals since, say, the time of *Lady, Be Good!* and *Anything Goes?*

How To Succeed is a relatively tight little piece for a big show, It takes place entirely within (also, briefly, outside on an upper floor of) a Park Avenue office building. There, the hero (Robert Morse, the only actor in history with a likable smirk) describes a meteoric arc under the guidance of a voice-over version of, presumably, Shepherd Mead. Morse made a gala entrance, as the first of the cast to be seen, lowered from the flies as a window washer to sing the near-to-title song, "How To." As he reached the song's end, he unstrapped himself, stepped onto the street, and, as the building wall rose, found himself in the lobby of the World Wide Wickets Company. Inc. Now comes the other star entrance: in the confusion of a scene filled with rushing people, Morse collided with someone, and the two of them crashed to the floor in a perfectly balanced setting as everyone else backed away and looked aghast. To the right, Morse. To the left, Rudy Vallee, as the CEO. What followed moved so quickly that, before the scene was over, we had met Morse's love object (Bonnie Scott), her sidekick (Claudette Sutherland), his nemesis, Vallee's nephew (Charles Nelson Reilly), and a sample executive (Paul Reed)—and Scott had already kicked the romance into gear with "Happy To Keep His Dinner Warm."

The romance, so very central to most musicals, is window dressing here. *How To Succeed* is one of those musical *comedies* that were to be overwhelmed in the coming years by the musical play, even by serious musical comedies. Like *Little Me* and *Forum, How To Succeed* knows that boy must get girl but that the overall fun is more important. Here, that fun is satire on office culture, a laugh at television, and, as in every show, jokes about marriage:

> THE BOSS: How will I spend those lonely nights?
> HIS GIRL FRIEND: You could stay home.
> THE BOSS: I can't stay home. I'm a married man.

Or just look at the names—J. B. Biggley as the boss, Bud Frump as the slimy villain, executives Bratt, Twimble, Gatch, and Tackaberry, heroine Rosemary and sidekick Smitty, temptress Hedy (Virginia Martin, our *Little Me* heroine), and, as the boss' dreaded secretary, the deceptively harmless-sounding Miss Jones. (True, the hero is J. Pierrepont Finch, an ambiguous christening, but that's from Mead's book.) Even the huge company itself is busy making "wickets"—in other words, nothing.*

In yet other words, this show has no content. Rather, it has perceptions. "Coffee Break" found Fosse's dancers making ballet out of caffeine hunger as if they were drug addicts, all to Loesser's musical version of withdrawal. "A Secretary Is Not a Toy" deals with surprising prescience about one of the most trendy problems of the millenial era, sexual harassment on the job. But then, Loesser enjoyed inventing musical numbers—not adding to an established genre but starting off a genre fresh. Why not invent social torts as well? *How To Succeed*'s score teems with one-of-a-kind numbers—"Been a Long Day," the trio in which Claudette Sutherland more or less reads Morse and Scott's thought balloons for us; "The Company Way," a ruthless look at corporate etiquette; and the hit tune, a ballad sung by Morse to himself in the executive men's washroom (as kazoos in the orchestra simulate electric razors in the late-afternoon pre-meeting shave), "I Believe in You."

Loesser dropped in a few pastiche numbers—the college fight song, the tearjerker, and the revivalist rave-up in "Grand Old Ivy," "Love From a Heart of Gold," and "The Brotherhood of Man." These create a musical equivalent to what Burrows and Fosse were doing in script and choreography: jazzing around. The Pulitzer people may have believed they had discovered a work of sharp social commentary, but *How To Succeed* is really more a gagfest in suits: the show's unique look and style fooled everyone into thinking that it made a statement of some kind. *Little Me* is crazier and *Forum* has a better score; but they got straight-on stagings in typical early-sixties manner. They were not fashioned, twisted, *produced*.

No Strings (1962), on the other hand, was written for unique production. Richard Rodgers' first show after Oscar Hammerstein's death, *No Strings* redeemed experiments made in their *Allegro* (1947). The first concept show, *Allegro* introduced into the musical such avant-garde techniques as an omniscient, commentative chorus, the inclusion in certain scenes of characters who are not meant to be physically present in real

---

*Actually, a wicket is a small opening—the little metal hoops one shoots for in croquet, for instance, or a box-office window, which usage is specifically cited in the first chorus of *The Girl in Pink Tights*, Sigmund Romberg's last show. Still, it was Mead's joke, surely, that "world wide" industrial firms aren't built on such humdrum products as croquet hoops.

time (including characters who have died), and the suggestion of locale rather than its realistic presentation. *No Strings* followed the love story of two Americans in France, he a novelist and she a fashion model, and the entire show was planned to look like an issue of *Vogue* come to life. Scenes took place in pools of high-key lighting surrounded by darkness. An army of lamps oversaw the action, sometimes moving closer to it as if to clarify a photographer's shoot. Places were established by odd assemblies—café chairs, racks of things, a curtain. Gorgeous women assumed tortured poses, or served as a chorus that never sang or spoke. They were, literally, models—and, to top it off, some of the orchestra men wandered in and out of the action while playing their reed or brass solos. There were, of course, no strings: the title is a pun.

Its other meaning, developed in the title song, is that love, not marriage, is the true bond, for David (Richard Kiley) and Barbara (Diahann Carroll) are "modern" in their thinking. Indeed, they carry on an interracial romance without ever referring to it. The love plot is vexed, rather, by her ambitions for him, a writer of talent who has somehow lost his commitment. Having risen from Harlem to being an icon of Parisian glamour, Carroll knows nothing but commitment, and is appalled at Kiley's love of living high on someone else's money. As Samuel Taylor's script explains, "You've heard of 'tennis bums' . . . and 'ski bums'. . . . Well, this one is a 'Europe bum.' "

For a musical of 1962 to feature an interracial liaison was not unheard of. *Show Boat* (1927) has one, *Beggar's Holiday* (1946) offers a triangle involving a white man with women both black and white, and *Kwamina* had occupied the 54th Street Theatre six months before *No Strings* did. What was special here was the worldly European acceptance of Barbara and David as a couple. Not a single line of the text dealt with race till the show's last few minutes, when the couple plan to leave Europe and return to Kiley's native Maine:

BARBARA: But I would like to take all of my beautiful Paris dresses!
    May I?
DAVID: (smiling) You won't have much use for 'em there.
BARBARA: (gaily) Oh, I can wear them to the Saturday-night dances!
    (A moment) Don't they have Saturday-night dances?
DAVID: (quietly) Yes, quite often.

They're only now realizing what a charmed dream they have been living in: soigné, "divine," where beauty and talent are in control, not social tradition:

> DAVID: Look, Barbara, it's not going to be easy, we both know that—
> BARBARA: (brightly) Of course we know it! We're neither one of us fools. It won't be like Paris! . . . I'll read, and I'll sew. I might even join the ladies' sewing circle. (And then) No.

Taylor was a good writer, but while he was always an author of "comedies" (such as *The Happy Time*, *Sabrina Fair*, and, with Cornelia Otis Skinner, *The Pleasure of His Company*), he didn't have much of a sense of humor. These are enjoyable but seldom *funny* plays, and *No Strings* is actually rather serious. ("I do wish somebody had thought of some jokes," said John Chapman in the *Daily News*.) Writing his own lyrics, Rodgers injected some humor into the action,* and also a certain je ne sais quoi, for as a poet Rodgers is telling but quirky. His love songs are pure, but his character numbers have their surprises.

The music suggests a return to the musical-comedy Rodgers of the 1920s and '30s. "Loads of Love," "Be My Host," and "Eager Beaver" swing like Jule Styne, and the Gallic bilingual charm song "La-la-la" impishly jump-starts its refrain on one of those famous Rodgers "wrong" notes, the seventh degree of the scale. Again, the amorous numbers are more serenely composed, though "Nobody Told Me" contains slithery, rising chromatic patterns, and "The Sweetest Sounds" also relies on a dissonance, this time a stinging augmented fourth right on the "sweet" of the title line—preparing us, in this opening number, for the stinging sweetness of David and Barbara's affair.

This is an unhappy show: the lovers part. What made *No Strings* a hit was not the discouraging story but the truly weird staging, by Joe Layton. It was Layton who toyed with those strolling musicians and arrestingly

---

*Rodgers had written lyrics by chance during his days with Lorenz Hart, usually during rehearsals or tryouts when a new song was needed and the gadabout Hart could not be found. Though Rodgers never wrote another solo stage score—it made him feel lonely—he did write both words and music for the *State Fair* remake and a television adaptation of *Androcles and the Lion*. In both cases, the lyrics sing competently but lack the twisty sophistication of *No Strings*.

lifeless models to create atmosphere while unifying the episodic action. Let Kiley go into "How Sad (to be a woman)," and the models started freaking about behind him, and suddenly Kiley was reviving that old standby number of the joker and les girls, so ancient a trope that no historian can plot its origin. A comedy number, "Love Makes the World Go (square)," found smart-aleck editrix Polly Rowles and Texas heiress Bernice Massi getting irritated by the trombonist's whinnying "laughs" and stealing his slide, playing comic crossovers with it while the instrumentalist sternly followed them, waving a warning finger.

This gaming with "reality" is one of the concept show's identifying qualities. The audience doesn't have to believe in a musical's naturalism, but surely the characters do. When they betray their knowledge that they're performers—free, for example, to flirt with the orchestra personnel, who really "shouldn't" be onstage in the first place—they explode the work's naturalism.

But then, *No Strings* itself was exploding naturalism by teaming white and black; or, even, by dressing its marquee with "Music and Lyrics by Richard Rodgers." It was a shock to a Broadway enjoying the fifth decade of the American musical's (and Richard Rodgers') Golden Age and taking a great deal for granted.

It took Joe Layton for granted, certainly. Because he never established the high-maestro choreographer's credentials in the way that de Mille, Robbins, Kidd, and Fosse did *before* they became directors, Layton was the man nobody knows. True, Gower Champion also burst into directing without an *Oklahoma!* or *Finian's Rainbow* in his résumé: but Champion, uniquely, made his fame first as a dancer.

What better marks the beauty of how *No Strings* behaved than the framing of the show with "The Sweetest Sounds," a Wanting Song? At the opening, it is a solo—first for her, then for him, in separate pools of light. A flautist charms her; a clarinetist supports him. The characters are not aware of each other yet, and cross the stage passing without seeing. At the show's end, the piece is a duet, though still a Wanting Song, for love will not work for them. Again, they pass as they cross the stage, again without seeing, all too terribly aware of each other this time, yet still showing nothing. On that, the curtain fell.

One problem that producer Rodgers suffered on this show was getting stuck in that backwater on Fifty-fourth Street. He had arranged to open at the Mark Hellinger, where *My Fair Lady* was winding down its six-and-a-half-year run. But when the "Last Weeks" notice went up in *Fair Lady*'s ads, it inspired a sub-population of lazies and schmudls who had not yet seen the Show of the Century and now besieged the box office. Rodgers had to scramble for an alternate booking, though after six months he was able to move *No Strings* down to the Broadhurst for another eleven months' run. A hit, no question. But a London mounting with Art Lund and Beverly Todd did so-so business, there could hardly have been a film, and revivals were scarce. Barbara McNair and Stuart Damon tried it in a summer tour in 1969, and Equity Library Theatre gave Mary Louise and Robert Tananis a shot at it in 1972.

Then it vanished, perhaps because unique stagings are suitable only for classics, such as our next two shows, both of 1964. In fact, at this writing, they are never revived in major venues except in some replica of the original production. Is this necessary?

But then, if one allows the director to join the collaborative team, to bring a show back without his work seems a little like leaving out the book or the songs. Certainly, no one has yet thought of a way to take the Jerome Robbins out of *Fiddler on the Roof*; and no one wants to try *Hello, Dolly!* without Gower Champion's staging, by far the most brilliant of his career.

These are good shows to compare, because they are very unalike in nature. *Dolly!* is a musical comedy with a story of universal appeal, one of those show-biz sure things following a hit play and its hit movie version.* *Fiddler* is a musical play, and a most parochial one—or so everyone assumed. "Tell me, do they understand this show in America?" *Fiddler*'s Tokyo producer asked its book writer, Joseph Stein. "It's so Japanese!"

Both shows were led by stars. But *Fiddler*'s Tevye heads an ensemble, while Dolly does a star turn. Then, too, though the opening Tevye, Zero Mostel, was a comic first and everything else after, the role really wants a singing actor, while the ideal Dolly is the ideal entertainer, a fabulous

---

***Dolly!* claims highly textured origins, as its immediate source, Thornton Wilder's 1955 comedy *The Matchmaker*, was a revision of Wilder's *The Merchant of Yonkers*, which failed, in 1938, because star Jane Cowl didn't cotton to the director, genius Max Reinhardt. So Reinhardt simply staged around Cowl, leaving her as a kind of Mammy Yokum at a fashion show. *The Merchant of Yonkers* was itself a reworking of an Austrian play reworked from an English original. To further knot the history, Wilder spiced *The Matchmaker* with a few bits drawn from Molière.

freak. The great Dollys have been great stars—Carol Channing, Pearl Bailey, Mary Martin, Martha Raye, Ethel Merman, Barbra Streisand.

Comparing scores separates the two shows further. We've met *Dolly!*'s Jerry Herman in musical play (*Milk and Honey*) and *Fiddler*'s Jerry Bock and Sheldon Harnick in musical comedy (*Tenderloin* and *She Loves Me*). Here, they switch roles. Herman revels in his tunesmith's ease and lyricist's devilry, as when he scoops plot into "Put On Your Sunday Clothes," bustling even as Dolly does from one story line to the next ("Ermengarde, stop sniveling," she sings; "don't cry on the valises") till the stage fills with folks riding into town for the Day of Their Lives.

For their part, Bock and Harnick are constructing a score, one made of numbers that interlock thematically and characterologically. Also, where *Dolly!*'s sound is contemporary Broadway, *Fiddler* now and then utilizes the strangely Eastern cast of Jewish music. The songs veer from standard Broadway ("Matchmaker, Matchmaker") to partly ethnic ("If I Were a Rich Man" or the cut title number, which remains in the show as the Fiddler's motif).

The two books? Michael Stewart's, for *Dolly!*, is one of the drollest ever, though—as with everything in this work—we take it in through the filter of Champion's steering. By now, there are familiar lines—"The well-known half-a-millionaire"; "You stamped, Mr. Vandergelder?"; "Eat out"; "Chocolate-covered peanuts. Unshelled"; "You go your way and I'll go mine." Yet we recall them in the context of how Champion wanted them played. Even the "peanuts" joke—Vandergelder's courtship gift to the milliner Irene Molloy—is forever locked into its payoff, when an infuriated Vandergelder stalks out of Irene's shop. All on stage wait motionless. Pause. Vandergelder reappears, reenters the shop, walks toward us—and I recall some of the audience murmuring, "He's going to take the candy back." Yep. He did, the others still motionless. It's a classic libretto staged in classic manner by a director who never did like a book unless it consisted of two or three jokes heading toward a song cue, over and over till the curtain calls.

Fiddler's book is a play accommodating song and dance. There is no feeling that, as soon as a number ends, director Robbins wants to speed us to the next number. *Fiddler* is a folk play whose implications are made explicit in Robbins' dancing, while *Dolly!* is the most vivacious of all the Champion carnivals. Finally triumphing over the blackout and the stage wait, Champion changed *Dolly!*'s sets before our eyes. Designer Oliver Smith, at the apex of a long career that rivals those of Jo Mielziner and Boris Aronson, gave Champion a combination of lithograph-like backdrops and extremely mobile three-dimensional pieces (including a train), and of course there was that runway along the outer edge of the orchestra pit. This is what pure fun looks like. Champion even made a tease of the set changes, for instance letting the milliner and her assistant themselves seem to push the façade of the hat shop around to reveal its interior. (The real work, naturally, was done by unseen stagehands, who also slipped in a row of closets to complete the picture.)

Conversely, Robbins could not play games with fourth-wall reality. But then, *Fiddler*'s wide-open look resisted the notion of walls, as if presenting the center of the modest expanse of Anatevka village. Robbins' designer, this same Boris Aronson, borrowed from Chagall, thus fantasizing the show's reality; a revolving stage kept *Fiddler* moving as smoothly as *Dolly!* Champion wanted us watching his set changes; Aronson seemed almost to move a camera from one part of the village to another. This is what a culture looks like.

Dolly! is a Big Lady Show; Champion wanted Nanette Fabray. She would have been terrific, but she isn't a freak, and that might have dwarfed the show, made it too reasonable. Musical comedies of this kind aren't reasonable. *The Gay Life* and *She Loves Me* are reasonable. *Dolly!* is bizarre, a David Merrick–Gower Champion creation that was going to run seven years, racking up 2,844 performances: big hit, big *fun*, big *weird*. Not Just Carol Channing but a bevy of dizzy dames in succession keep the show gala and spry. One can't stale in this part: it's too crazy. What other musical gives the star a chance to eat her way through a roast chicken while the entire show comes more or less to a standstill, watching?

Obviously, there can be nothing like this among Tevyes. Though Danny Kaye, Tom Bosley, Danny Thomas, and Alan King were all under review for the part—suggesting a headliner slot—Zero Mostel's replacements were mostly has-beens, unknowns, or Jan Peerce. Different Dollys create different shows, but the Tevyes all played the same piece and never made one miss the original star. And *Fiddler* outlasted *Dolly!* by almost exactly a year.

The two very long runs, now common but astonishing at the time, attest to the validity of the director-choreographer. But why did choreographers start directing in the first place?

Because they already *were* directing. Staging all the numbers, they were naturally staging the book scenes that led up to them, and were thus directors in all but title. We've seen how the director-choreographer appeared in the 1940s and became somewhat acculturated in the 1950s. On the edge of the decade at hand, in 1959, Bob Fosse pulled off a Tony-grabbing sensation in *Redhead*, a show that was ordinary in its composition *but not in its staging*. That was the breakthrough, because after that, choreographers could be not only directors but God. After all, even the magisterial Robbins could not Make, in any real sense, *West Side Story*, two years before *Redhead*. Because *West Side Story* was written on the utmost level of quality. Its authors Made it. But Fosse it was who Made *Redhead*, and now, in the 1960s, all choreographers want to direct. And all the producers are begging them to. Everyone wants a *Redhead*.

One odd thing is that none of these promoted choreographers ever lost his interest in dance. The usual four-week rehearsal period passes by so fleetly—with always, *always* things to be done that could not be got to in time—that one would think the dancing might suffer. Never. But then, Robbins demanded eight weeks of rehearsals for *Fiddler*. And Champion's *Dolly!* dances mark his best work—so sassy yet, when we want it thus, so charming, so just for the sweetness of it.

"Dancing" (the number, that is) could be dropped, couldn't it? The story doesn't need it. But Champion knows that after all the clowning and the character songs, the wit and substance of the show, we all need breathing space. We need charm. So "Dancing" sneaks into the plot by artifice, just so the set can glide away to give the dancing corps its chance.

Champion breaks them into soloists, small groups, full corps flying across the runway. The principals take part here and there, telling us a bit more about themselves. And, in general, the number solidifies the growing self-confidence we have to see in the two store clerks (Charles Nelson Reilly, Jerry Dodge) going out on the town with the two milliners (Eileen Brennan, Sondra Lee).

The purpose of this dance, really, is dancing itself. It doesn't need a reason. But it has one. "Five minutes," Dolly promises, "and I'll have you dancing in the streets." And that is exactly what occurs, in musical comedy's long-held belief that when characters learn to dance (i.e., learn how to express love) they learn how to like themselves. One might, in a way, define the American musical as the theatre in which people learn how to dance.

More famous than "Dancing" is the restaurant sequence. This starts with "The Waiters' Gallop," conducted as if a symphony by the haughty headwaiter and broken into by book scenes. This leads up to the title song, another of those obsessive salutes to the star. At least this one isn't a full-company kowtow. It's more like Dolly's solo with adoring responses from the twelve waiters, then a dance as they glide along with their arms out, teetering now up, now down, in a duck-waddle step.

This is of course a classic sixties number, one of the biggest of hit tunes* and the reason why Champion had to have that runway: to bring the sheer joy of the moment closer to the audience. To top himself. To make the biggest showstopper of all time.

Yet, at the time of the New York premiere, the restaurant sequence did not end there. What could follow "Hello, Dolly!"? Nevertheless, after an extremely funny dinner scene between Dolly and Vandergelder (David Burns), in which she virtually rapes him with words ("It's no use arguing. I've made up your mind. Here, let me cut your wings . . ."), Champion attempted one final number. *Hello, Dolly!* has four couples, for besides Dolly and Vandergelder, and the clerks and the milliners, there are Vandergelder's niece and her swain (Alice Playten, Igors Gavon). All eight are in the restaurant; the last two, in fact, are part of the floor show.

Here's where Champion may have miscalculated, in a Nymph Num-

---

*Mack David sued Herman over a resemblance between "Hello, Dolly!" and David's 1948 hit "Sunflower," and Herman had to settle handsomely. Further, Bob Merrill worked with Herman on "Motherhood" and "Elegance." However, Herman himself wrote "Before the Parade Passes By," despite occasional reports to the contrary. The use of interpolations was routine in the early twentieth century, but was very rare by the 1940s and utterly finished in the 1950s (despite the rumor that Frank Loesser and not Meredith Willson wrote *The Music Man*'s "My White Knight"). What is curious about the reinstitution of the interpolation, in such sixties shows as *Dolly!*, *Ben Franklin in Paris* (two, by Jerry Herman), *Baker Street* (four, by Bock and Harnick), and *Her First Roman* (three, by Bock and Harnick), is the absence of credit for the ringers. Their work is actually passed off as someone else's. This was never true in earlier decades. One exception to this new usage is *Tovarich*'s program, which credited the guest authors of "You'll Make an Elegant Butler (I'll Make an Elegant Maid)": Joan Javits and Philip Springer.

ber, "Come and Be My Butterfly." Gavon sang the refrain, and Playten was one of the nymphs, drawing an enraged Vandergelder onto the stage and into confusion with the nymphs and their spacious costumes. (There were some great lines here for that deadpan curmudgeon David Burns: "Out of my way, I got no time for foliage!," and "Watch those feelers, Miss.") The number slowed Act Two at a crucial moment, with two further numbers and a lot of plot action yet to come. Perhaps *Dolly!*'s chaotic Detroit tryout left Champion too busy to freeze the show properly—especially when Merrick himself arrived and Champion drove off into the Michigan scenery, not to return till Merrick departed. (This, after a few stubborn days, he did.) In any case, *Dolly!* opened in New York with the "Butterfly" number, though almost nobody saw it. Champion cut it immediately after the premiere, leaving RCA Victor stuck with a photograph of it on the cast album.

The *Fiddler* dances are not as famous as those in *Dolly!*, though everyone remembers the "Wedding Dance" of men balancing bottles on their heads. Rather, the famous Robbins dances are from *On the Town* (even if no one has seen them in their original form in over half a century), *High Button Shoes*, and particularly *West Side Story*, though *The King and I*'s "The Small House of Uncle Thomas" must be the most familiar single Robbins ballet. What Robbins gave to *Fiddler* was not dances but a feeling that runs through the staging from its opening to its very end. "What is this show about?" he kept asking, and someone would reply, "It's about the marriages of Tevye's daughters."

Well, that's what *happens*. But that's not what it's about. Finally, someone said, "It's about the passing of a way of life." *Yes!* So Robbins had Bock and Harnick write "Tradition," by common consent one of the greatest of all opening numbers.

At first, it's a title *picture*: Tevye, in front of his house, looking up at a violinist in folk dress, sawing away. Fiddler on the Roof. Tevye does a bit of explaining, then gets to what Verdi called the "parola scenica"—the key word that, properly set to music, encapsulates an emotion, an event, or even an entire show. Tradition. And out come Anatevka's residents, papa, mama, son, or daughter. There is no one else in the place, save the matchmaker, the beggar, the rabbi, and a few Christians. Anyone who has seen this show will surely recall this moment, when the ensemble

comes out from behind Tevye's house, hand in hand, in Robbins' styl-
ization of something between dancing and being, beaming because
they've been living these particular lives for so many years that nobody
asks *why?*

Naturally, the question is going to come up for the next three hours or
so, as if challenging the source of this music, the Fiddler. As if trying to
identify him. For this strange character never speaks, and is clearly not an
actual Anatevkan in the census way of things. It's a small role; yet the
Fiddler *is* the show. *He's* what it's about—though we don't learn that till
the final four or five seconds (which I'll get to presently).

If the musical play tends to the unconventional, musical comedy—
even a singular example—uses conventions creatively. So, while *Fiddler*
has no overture, *Dolly!* should sport one, but an unexpected one—staged,
perhaps, like *Donnybrook!*'s, or employing mixed-media embellishment,
like *Bye Bye Birdie*'s. No. *Dolly!* has no overture.* To a syncopated, almost
ragtime-like vamp, the curtain rises as the chorus, frozen in elegant poses,
hails the talented Dolly and a streetcar rolls on at stage right. *Dolly!*
fooled us: no overture, but a good old opening chorus of the kind that had
been virtually retired. Another convention inheres in this most famous of
all star entrances: the streetcar riders, all engrossed in newspapers, drop
them one by one till Dolly! drops hers last of all. To applause that she
would get if my Aunt Agnes were playing the part, Dolly comes forward
in orange topped by a bird's-nest hat and armed with a heavy purple bag
filled with business cards suitable for, apparently, any opportunity: "Social
Introductions." "Surgical Corsets Reboned." And, as we know, "Instruc-
tions in La Danse."

A snappy exposition ensues. Of course: all expositions were snappy in
a Champion show. This leads into the first full-out number, "I Put My
Hand In," cutely structured in that its verse ("I have always been a
woman . . .") serves also as the B strain of the chorus. Champion will of

---

*For some reason—I suspect at David Merrick's urging—*Dolly!*'s cast album adopted an
orchestral version of the title number, terming it an "overture," and many another *Dolly!*
reading has copied it. The published score printed a conventional medley overture,
though noting that it wasn't used. (It may have been an out-of-town casualty.) Yet a second medley overture was recorded—though still not used—for the second Broadway
recording, with the all-black cast headed by Pearl Bailey. This *Dolly!*, which took over the
St. James in November 1967, presented the reinvesting of an entire show in the middle of
its run without a break in performance, a unique event.

course not allow Dolly simply to stand and deliver, so individuals of the ensemble illustrate Dolly's test cases as she sings.

So now we know what she is. What does she want? A period back-drop of Grand Central Terminal comes down, and Dolly, making the show's first use of the runway, addresses her dead husband. She wants a rich marriage, and she'd like a sign from him that he approves of her snaring Vandergelder. This may seem like a bagatelle with which to adorn the denouement, but it is in fact a unifying device. It is less about marriage than about Dolly's having to get back into the high life in which she flourishes. The show's throughline lies not in the disposition of the four couples, but in the arc that rises through "Before the Parade Passes By" (the resolve), leaps onto "Hello, Dolly!" (the celebration), and climaxes in "So Long, Dearie" (the liberation: though, in the end, she settles for him after all). One reason why *Dolly!* was foundering in Detroit was that the lack of "Parade" obscured the throughline, making Dolly more an accessory than a protagonist. This isn't just her show. It's her story.

Comparing the *Dolly!* and *Fiddler* scores, we remark immediately on the superior popularity of the former. Though *Fiddler* did field a hit tune in "Matchmaker, Matchmaker," and though "Sunrise, Sunset" has become a perennial at weddings, writers fail to appreciate Bock and Har-nick's artistry in finding the voice of Anatevka. True, this is one classic musical that has a beloved staging more than a beloved score. Perhaps the songs serve Stein's book so well that it absorbs them, limits their popular-ity out of context. "Matchmaker, Matchmaker," remember, is known only for its extractable chorus, quite without the important middle section ("Hodel, oh Hodel . . .") that enlarges the social perspective from the daughters' point of view.

One song stands out especially, because it is the essential *Fiddler* num-ber yet was cut during tryouts: "When Messiah Comes." A solo for the rabbi at the moment when the villagers learn that they must all leave their homes within three days, it more or less sums up the history of the Anatevkans as a people, from Abraham to Tevye. Yet it's a comic song, and this is not a comic subject. Rather than lose what serves as a brother to "Tradition"—the latter is cultural, the former spiritual—the authors reassigned the piece to Tevye. He is, after all, a comic figure. Still, audi-ences were cool. Like *Candide*'s "Dear Boy," "When Messiah Comes" is a sharp number that will never go over and must be cut. At least Stein found a way to encapsulate it in a simple exchange:

MENDEL: Rabbi, we've been waiting for the Messiah all our lives. Wouldn't this be a good time for him to come?
RABBI: We'll have to wait for him someplace else. Meanwhile, let's start packing.

Another standout number is, to my mind, one of the greatest syntheses of the dramatic arts ever attempted—plot, score, design, and staging all wrestling with something intangible that only theatre at its most poetic can pin down. This is The Dream, or, as it is unassumingly titled, "The Tailor, Motel Kamzoil." Technically, it is Tevye's invention to convince his wife to allow their eldest daughter to marry the man she loves rather than the one they betrothed her to. But what we see is an extravagant display of village folkways, on how religion, social mores, and economics are coordinated. The number is a character study, too, for it shows how resourceful Tevye is, using not one but two ghosts to challenge the nuptials. One is his wife's grandmother. Disturbed, Tevye's wife asks how she looked. "For a woman who is dead thirty years," he replies, "she looked very good." She's spry as well: at each mention of the chosen bridegroom, she leaps ten feet into the air.

The other ghost is the bridegroom's dead wife, Fruma-Sarah, a twirly giant who draws dream into nightmare. Note how she recalls her eminence as a village worthy: in control of clothing, pearls . . . and keys. It is one of Sheldon Harnick's great formulations. One visualizes a house broken into areas defined by class: the servants, certain guests, certain Other Guests, the private rooms. It is Anatevka itself, perhaps, and who carries the keys? Not the rabbi, nor the rich men: their wives.

The very look of the number was extraordinary, from the first coup de théâtre—as Tevye, in bed with his wife, began to recount his dream, he mentioned musicians, and, in time to musical captioning, three such calmly rose behind the headboard. Again, it was not choreography per se that made this show Robbins' masterpiece, but numbers like this one, in which we encounter a miniature world in how it behaves and what it thinks.

Comparing *Fiddler*'s finale with *Dolly!*'s, the latter turns up pure Big Lady. There isn't even a curtain fall after the plot action is concluded. The big choral reprises set in, the ensemble struts and poses, the players take their applause, and the whole structure rises so inexorably to Dolly's apparance to Her Song that the audience rises in salute as if they, too, have been directed by Gower Champion.

Believe it or not, the musicals with Mary Martin, Eddie Cantor, Ethel Merman, and Bert Lahr never got standing ovations. American show biz was then in its glory, and even the biggest talents were taken for granted, for there was so much talent around. Look at the scores from the 1950s, even *My Fair Lady*—the music for the curtain calls lasts less than a minute. There's no time for an ovation. No *need*.

It was the 1960s and shows such as *Hello, Dolly!* and *Mame* that created the audience-participation finale. *Fiddler*'s bows, too, are laid out in high style, as the characters glide in on the revolve till they fill the stage in a line, this parting at the center to reveal Tevye. It's the perfect coda, but it's little more than a shrug when set against *Dolly!*'s applause-athon.

No, *Fiddler on the Roof* ends where the story ends, before the clapping, in another of Robbins' visual coups. On the emptied stage, the people we have come to know look at one another, then march off in different directions, in Anatevka's personal diaspora. Tevye and his family are the last to go. As they start off, the Fiddler magically appears from behind Tevye's wagon. The stage is empty because, when the show began, Tevye's house was Anatevka, and now the village is over. Its life is over. But the Fiddler joins Teyve on his journey, because the Fiddler is Tradition, something portable that Tevye can take along till Messiah comes. So now we, too, know what the show is about. As the Fiddler plays his theme for Tevye, the curtain comes down.

The Broadway Tevyes were, after Mostel, Group Theatre veteran Luther Adler, Herschel Bernardi, Harry Goz, Jerry Jarrett, Paul Lipson, and, yes, opera tenor Jan Peerce. Maria Karnilova opened as Golde, and Bette Midler took over as daughter Tzeitel during the mid-1960s. One actor in the show in its eighth and final year told me that, before each performance, the cast would gather onstage in a kind of communal meditation (which may explain the Moscow Art Theatre pacing of the piece in its last months). Another actor, who played Lazar Wolf on tour, told me he hated the show. "All those dreary people!" he said. "The *clothes!*" No, he was straight. But he longed for *The Music Man*, even *Lady, Be Good!*. He wasn't happy with the darkness—the reality, the density of sociological honesty, the new range of subject matter—that was seeping into the musical.

He liked the glamour, and that was *Hello, Dolly!*. The Dollys were, after Channing, Ginger Rogers, Martha Raye, Betty Grable, Bibi Osterwald (generally the understudy, though she briefly held the St. James on her own just before Pearl Bailey's company came in), and Phyllis Diller. Then Ethel Merman agreed to do the role that was in fact conceived for her, adding in two numbers that Herman had originally written as Merman numbers—"World, Take Me Back" and "Love, Look in My Window." Along with Merman came her *Call Me Madam* juvenile, Russell Nype, not a comic (as Charles Nelson Reilly had been) but more a mature young man in quietly great need, just what the role can use. Cab Calloway had played Pearl Bailey's Vandergelder with an ageless impishness that wronged the character but charmed the public (and got him bigger billing than David Burns had got). Merman's Vandergelder, the Australian Jack Goode, played it as an oily has-been matinée idol. He was a real test of how many different directions these roles can take.

Dolly!'s tours took in Mary Martin, the avid Channing, Eve Arden, and Dorothy Lamour. Martin took it to London's Drury Lane, succeeded by Dora Bryan; and of course Barbra Streisand did the 1969 film, with Walter Matthau. Streisand's youth destroyed the concept of Dolly's coming out of retirement, but no one else has sung this music as well. Streisand's "Before the Parade Passes By" may be one of her greatest single tapings ever. As this was the age of super-movie-musicals, Louis Armstrong guested in the title number; similarly, in the 1971 *Fiddler* film, with the London Tevye, Topol, Isaac Stern guested on the soundtrack as the "voice" of the Fiddler.

Big shows, international successes. When *Dolly!* closed, it was the longest-running musical in Broadway history. But when *Fiddler* closed, it was the longest-running Broadway attraction *of any kind*, beating out *Life With Father*'s famous 3,224 performances by two weeks. It cannot be coincidence that both musicals were not only excellent compositions but excellent stagings, because stagemeisters were taking over. But if all shows—and an accustomed public—want them in charge, what happens to the shows that can't attract them? For there are always fewer genius directors than there are shows going into rehearsal. Careful—or you'll end up with Garson Kanin directing yours.

9

HEARTS GROW HARD ON A WINDY STREET

CABARET

This is the essential sixties musical. It could not have happened before the 1960s and would have been unnecessary after; and the decade is inconceivable without it. How to approach it?

One could call it another of those dark shows, the encore piece for Hal Prince and the team of Kander and Ebb after *Flora, the Red Menace* but now in thirties Germany instead of Depression America and with ruthless Nazis instead of comic Communists.

One could note that it was originally to have been *Goodbye To Berlin*, by Sandy Wilson, author of *The Boy Friend*. However, Wilson's producer, David Black, lost his option on Christopher Isherwood's stories and John Van Druten's play based on them, *I Am a Camera* (1951). Wilson had finished the script and much of the score, but Prince took over the option, commissioning Joe Masteroff as book writer. The two felt that Wilson's music missed the warped three-penny Berlin that they needed to hear.

One could propose the rise of the concept musical in the theorem [*Allegro* + *Love Life* → *Cabaret*]. In other words, the musical's strict sense of realistic linear narrative is first challenged in the 1940s, for *Allegro* is non-realistic and *Love Life* (1948) is non-linear, and both shows were written with unique staging plans built into them.

One could, adapting an old definition of jazz, say that the concept musical is so slippery in its form that it is indefinable: but you know one when you see one.

One could give a little whistle on the new importance of the director in the shaping of composition. Prince is a producer-director and not a director-choreographer; Ronald Field was *Cabaret*'s dance master. But

Prince was in on the writing of the show from the start, as editor and inspirer. (Of course, if the director knows what the show is better than the authors do, this is a good thing. But what happens when the director is a jerk with a buttinsky complex?)

More grandly, one could see *Cabaret* as the show that launched a new era. When does "Rodgers and Hammerstein" end? Their influence is endless in the broad sense. More specifically, though, the final cluster of works rather wholly in their style occurs in the early 1960s. *Greenwillow*, *Jennie*, *110 in the Shade*, *Fiddler on the Roof*, and *Ben Franklin in Paris* are the last of the Rodgers and Hammerstein musical plays. Yet there is one other that outranks them all because of its universally popular score, an absolute in Rodgers and Hammerstein creativity. *Oklahoma!*, *Carousel*, *South Pacific*, *The King and I*, and *The Sound of Music* each have it: and so does *Camelot*.

Camelot, then, is the show that ends Rodgersandhammersteinshchina: the time of their rule. Six years pass. Then comes *Cabaret* (1966), and the new age begins.

Ironically, the show's provenance is modest. Isherwood published two volumes of stories about Berlin, *Mr. Norris Changes Trains* and *Goodbye To Berlin*. Van Druten's play hones in on a bitty piece of them, all in a single set, his action built around Sally Bowles, a cabaret singer. It's a star part. Van Druten originally called his play after her, and he gave the role to Julie Harris, fresh from her tour de force in Carson McCullers' *The Member of the Wedding*. There is also Sally's live-in boy friend, actually called "Christopher Isherwood" (as he is in the stories); the gruff landlady, Fräulein Schneider; and two of Isherwood's language students, Fritz Wendel and Natalia Landauer.

That anyone saw a musical in this, much less the kaleidoscopic musical-within-a-musical that *Cabaret* became, is a wonder. But then, *Cabaret* at first followed a straight-on narrative beginning with a group of songs depicting the Berlin atmosphere from a variety of viewpoints. One was sung by a Chinese girl. One was "Herman the German," possibly a mockup of the real-life Claire Waldoff's twenties specialty "Hermann Hesst Er," which was generally thought to be a spoof of Hermann Göring. And one song was "Willkommen."

At some point, this prologue of songs was broken up and the numbers distributed between book scenes, at first randomly and then, as the possibilities became apparent, with relevance to the action. Songs were discarded, to be replaced by more germane songs. Meanwhile, the adaptation of Van Druten had opened up to take in more of Berlin and more of its people. The landlady was now no anti-Semitic grouch but worldly and tolerant. She had a beau, with a fruit store. The male lead became an American, Clifford Bradshaw. Another of Fräulein Schneider's tenants, Fräulein Kost, was a prostitute, and the last new principal, outside of the cabaret, was Ernst Ludwig, a Nazi.

Thus, two shows were being written at the same time: the musical that was opening up *I Am a Camera*, and the musical that was opening up *that* musical with onstage cabaret numbers. Commentative numbers—"Two Ladies," on the pleasures of the liberated ménage; "The Money Song," on the advantages of reckless opportunism; "If You Could See Her," on Nazi social politics; "Cabaret," on not voting when democrats oppose communazis in elections.

Ingeniously, these numbers use exaggeration and grotesquerie to uncover the hidden extremism in what the story's characters are doing. They tell their own exaggerations, present their own grotesquerie, but in secret. They raise money for the Nazis because, well, money is so handy. They accept racial stereotypes because, well, doesn't everyone else?

So the cabaret numbers cut jaggedly into the story while remaining outside it. Yet the two performing arenas are bound at one brief but extremely telling moment early in the show, after the second book scene. Having arrived in Berlin and rented a room, Cliff settles down to work. Suddenly, a girl appears. She isn't "there," of course. She represents the excitement of a new place—a new world, really. Singing a few lines of the "Telephone Song," she beckons to Cliff from the Kit Kat Klub, making the first connection between the cabaret and the plot. Cliff dashes off for a night on the town, and the Emcee appears, to introduce the next act.

Note: not the next *scene*. *Cabaret*, like *Love Life*, is a junction of two different formats, the one a revue and the other a musical play. And *Cabaret*, like *Allegro*, is "fourth wall" naturalism except when it isn't. Most oddly, *Cabaret* comprises not only two genres but two worlds. The Kit Kat Klub is more than a series of numbers, more than a "stage." Like Cliff, we *go* there, to find an entity at once real and metaphorical, a fantasy, a warning. But if the cabaret "is" Germany in the perilous early 1930s, when Weimar democracy was crumbling and the Nazis were steadily on the rise,

what then is the rest of the show, with its landlady and grocer, its prostitute and Nazi, its Cliff and Sally? Where are they supposed to be?

Sally is the link between the two worlds, the character most real and
most phantom: the only one at home in both places. Or is she? Cliff is so
real that he must leave the story altogether at the end—that is, not just
conclude his tale but exit it. Sally, however, closes off her part in the story
by singing "Cabaret": as if locking out reality to thrive in the lovely evil of
the "other" world.

Clearly, this is rich work. The idea is unique, the book masterly, and
the score one of the all-time top ones. A musical-comedy sound is perva-
sive (but for "What Would You Do?" and, perhaps, "Why Should I Wake
Up?"). But how could a musical play contain the weaselly Emcee and the
spots for such naughty pieces as "Don't Tell Mama"? Nor could a musical
play capture Sally's infectious appeal with the period swing of "Perfectly
Marvelous," a musical scene in which we actually hear the process by
which Cliff falls under her spell by taking up her refrain.

There is vivacity here above all, then; but worry as well. "Tomorrow
Belongs To Me" is sinfully pretty, though Nazi anthems were in fact generally marches, not wistful pastorales. "Meeskite" (which would correctly
have been spelled "Mieskeit") is harmless as a composition but, as staged,
treated the audience to one Nazi's seething hatred. "The Money Song" is
dangerously hedonistic, a showgirl number whose take-a-peek glee
obscures the lyrics' sociopathic worldview. "If You Could See Her" is so
smartly ironic that some of the public misunderstood its intention, especially the final line's allusion to Nazi racial typing: "She wouldn't look
Jewish at all." Rather than offend audiences uselessly, the authors effected
a clever substitution with an allusion to "Meeskite" that says the same
thing less crudely. In a way, the *Cabaret* score is musical-play music by
other means.

However, choreographer Ronald Field was strictly a musical-comedy
specialist (though he stepped into ballet for the *On the Town* revival in
1971). This was Field's first major Broadway show, after the insignificant
Nowhere To Go But Up (1962) and *Café Crown* (1964). Those two lasted
a combined total of 12 performances, so few saw Field's work. He put
everything he had into *Cabaret*, and it showed. "Willkommen," an opening to rank with "The Carousel Waltz," "Runyonland," "We're Alive,"
"Tradition," "The Advantages of Floating in the Middle of the Sea,"

Titanic's medley of opening numbers, "Ragtime," and very little else, is too familiar to us today. We can't be shocked. But it was shocking in 1966. As for *Carnival!*, the curtain was up. The stage was bare but for a giant mirror that reflected the audience. When the show began, the drummer gave us a roll and a cymbal crash, and, to the first of the great Kander and Ebb vamps that characterize a song even more than the melody does, Joel Grey seemed to materialize rather than enter. His white-painted face and dirty smile were a disturbing puzzle. Did he believe his own spiel? Was he part of the entertainment or of some enormous lie? Was he the lie itself? "And now it's time to meet the cabaret girls!" he crowed, as a gaggle of terrors stalked in—or, rather, downstage from out of the darkness. Were they supposed to be so untantalizing? Isn't the musical's oldest Essential the captivating chorus line? Still, the boys, dressed as waiters in red jackets, were presentable, and, as the number continued, the dancing reassured with the combinations one expects of classic show-biz choreography. At one point, the ensemble huddled together, stepping as a tight unit, turning their heads now left, now right. This was hardly cliché Broadway: but it *was* Broadway.

However, then the train compartment appeared, and a book scene introduced the Cliff, Bert Convy, and the Nazi, Edward Winter. The juxtaposition of the delightful yet somewhat mystifying "Willkommen" and this bit of plot exposition pursued the deliberately uneasy marriage of *Cabaret*'s "two shows," the story and the revue. The idea, one presumes, was to confound audience expectations. After almost half a century of Golden Age, the public could anticipate being entertained and even surprised. But not startled. *Cabaret* reclaimed the theatre's oldest Essential, going back to the Greeks: to challenge the public, make it rethink its first principles.

True, once one got used to the cabaret "intrusions," the show was not so unnerving. Field's "Telephone Song" staging featured one couple that danced a lazy tango in lip-lock, an inventive touch; and his engagement-party dance gave Lotte Lenya a memorable fox-trot with a small fleet of sailors. But the finale was a shock—"Willkommen" again, only now in cacophony and with the principals quoting their own lines in limbo, the cabaret now presenting real people in its acts and the two worlds at last brought together.

Sally was Jill Haworth, an English girl known for film work. Lotte

Lenya and Jack Gilford were the landlady and her grocer, and Peg Murray played Fräulein Kost. After Julie Harris' Sally in *I Am a Camera*, one might have anticipated a headliner, but *Cabaret*'s Sally is no longer a star role. She isn't even the protagonist any more: Cliff is. At that, this ensemble lineup was unbalanced a bit by the prominence of Gilford, a straight actor who also did musicals (such as *Forum*; and, a few years hence, the *No, No, Nanette* revival), and of Lenya, the very voice of Weimar Germany as Kurt Weill's widow and primary stylist. Moreover, the casting did produce a star in the Emcee, Joel Grey.

The critics didn't get the show. A few responded to the sheer theatricality of the event, but the ones with intellectual pretensions were thrown by the paradoxes, the seriousness of the spree. A unique work is seldom understood when new. Critics prefer an important work to be the ninth or tenth of its line, not the first, when they don't yet know how to react. A few of them bashed Haworth, one of the best Sallys I've seen; even Prince ended in resenting her, though if she was that bad, why wasn't she fired? They tried altering her coloring, as if that would nourish her portrayal. In Boston, Haworth was little-lost-girl blond, dressed in prom-dress white, till Prince put her into a black wig and garish bugle-beaded skirts in reds and greens. A friend of the production told Prince that it didn't look right, and Prince replied, "It's the only way I can get her to play it."

At 1,165 performances, *Cabaret* was obviously too big a hit right from the start to wait for a post-Broadway life. Interestingly, the simultaneous national tour's Schneider (Signe Hasso), grocer Schultz (Leo Fuchs), and Sally (Melissa Hart) now had over-the-title billing. On Broadway, no one did. Even Lotte Lenya was somewhat undervalued in the middle of seven names, reminding us how difficult it is to establish a pecking order for this show's characters. Judi Dench (Sally) and Lila Kedrova (Schneider) were the stated stars of the London staging, in 1968, but they had established themselves previously. When Joel Grey reassumed his part for a 1987 Broadway revival (again directed by Prince), he was the sole player with star billing.

Jerome Robbins, catching a last run-through before the Boston tryout, threw a terror into Ron Field by suggesting that Prince cut all the dancing except in the cabaret numbers. But if the characters in the story show can sing, why can't they also dance? Still, Bob Fosse took the same view, albeit more consistently. In his 1972 film adaptation, there is no song or dance except where such would occur in real time—on the Kit Kat stage, heard on a phonograph, or at a group sing. The screenplay, by Jay Allen and Hugh Wheeler, hews more closely to *I Am a Camera*—Fritz and Natalia are back—and Fosse ordered new songs from Kander and Ebb to beef up the cabaret scenes. "Mein Herr," "Maybe This Time," and a completely new "Money Song" joined the show's tunestack at this time. Fosse also staged "Willkommen" to present not just the Emcee and chorus but the club acts, which include a midget ventriloquist with giant dummy, a contortionist, and Liza Minnelli.

It's just a moment, but a crucial one, because Fosse built up Sally as a figure of importance *in the cabaret*, as if he, at least, understood how the dramatis personae parse. Sally isn't just the link between the cabaret and the plot action. If the grinning Emcee personifies the growth of evil in Weimar's helpless republic, Sally is the Emcee's "familiar." She serves as not only his star but his confederate, an active participant in "The Money Song" (onstage, it was his number, with the girls) and someone who seems most alive when performing: for him. Around Michael York (in the Cliff role, now named Brian), she is a third-rate talent in a dive. But in the cabaret she is inspired, as if she had made a Faustian pact with the Emcee.

Fosse's film occupies an important place in the history of *Cabaret*. Most Hollywood versions of Broadway have been either unfaithful (and thus not helpful in understanding what a show *is*) or very faithful, and thus merely replicas (helpful in animating history, but not influential). *Cabaret* the movie is neither. It respects the stage show's intentions while entirely revising its material. It was much seen and became, for a while, the *Cabaret* that most people, even theatregoers, knew.

It immediately affected stage revivals in three ways. First, everybody now knows who the leads are—Sally and, especially, the Emcee. Many European revivals revolve around some television star or dancer as the Emcee, as when ballerino Wayne Sleep headed the cast in England in 1986 in a staging by director-choreographer Gillian Lynne. Second, the songs written for the movie have become part of the official score, displacing numbers heard on Broadway in 1966. Third, the boldly erotic atmosphere that Fosse exploited has been infecting productions for a generation. Lynne's was typical, with plenty of transvestism (the cabaret "girls" counted a few men) and decadence of various kinds. This finally led us to that ineluctable transformation that must come to many post-Rodgers-and-Hammerstein classics—*Cabaret: The Reassessment*.

It came to New York from England in 1998, choreographed by Rob Marshall and directed by Marshall and Sam Mendes. It is by now customary in the Reassessment phase of a show's life for the director to take an ungrateful whack at his predecessors, for youth with respect is youth without hip. The original, Mendes said, was no more than "the embryo of a dangerous show that was wrapped in conventional Broadway wrapping."

Luckily, Mendes is a better director than historian. *Cabaret*'s authors have not denounced his version—Masteroff even wanted to reword Mendes' revision of the original book. And there is considerable revision. Revivals of the 1980s and 1990s are routinely rewritten, but these are usually refinements—*The Music Man*'s borrowing lines from the film script, or the subtle nagging of *Kiss Me, Kate* with pointlessly new ways of saying the same thing that the original lines said, along with the recharacterization of a minor player and the addition of one song.

Mendes' *Cabaret* is no refining. There are wholly new scenes, important new lines in old scenes, and the dropping of four Broadway* numbers in favor of three from the movie and "I Don't Care Much," originally cut in Boston but often heard in revivals. The actual number of rewritten lines is not as large as one might suppose, but the *effect* is revolutionary, bringing out things latent in or absent from the original, particularly the erotic. Then, too, Mendes' staging itself, in Robert Brill's "cabaret" set, most strongly differentiates his drugagonzo Nazisexo inferno from anything one saw in 1966. Cliff is bisexual, for instance, and even Ernst, an absolute Nazi in the old *Cabaret*, is now homosexual, as if from the Ernst Röhm wing of the party.

Nothing is stinted, suggested, or offstage. To an audience forced to sit at tables and denied their programs till evening's end, this *Cabaret* turns the bifurcated entertainment of 1966 into a lurid dream of one thing

---

*Obviously, Mendes would replace the original "Money Song" with its louche movie alternate, as Mendes' *Cabaret* is generally a dark musical comedy turned into a dark musical, period. Similarly, he would drop the "Telephone Song." But Mendes also eliminated two important character numbers, "Why Should I Wake Up?" and "Meeskite," while retaining, also from the movie, "Maybe This Time," a pop tune akin to Kander and Ebb's "My Coloring Book." In musical style and lyrics, "Maybe This Time" has nothing to do with *Cabaret*. "Lady Peaceful"—does that sound like Sally Bowles' articulation of her self-image in the 1930s? It's wrong for the character and wrong for the era.

only. In this production, life really is a cabaret, because the cabaret now *contains* all the life one sees: hetero, homo, upright and downtown, old and young, Nazi and apolitical. The stage numbers seem even more commentative than before, as when Cliff rebuffs an old boy friend and Sally then goes into the "drop-dead letter" number, "Mein Herr," on a gigantic high chair; or when one of the Two Ladies is a man. The Emcee, in drag, sings "I Don't Care Much" into a microphone as we watch Sally cinematically abandoning Cliff for her former liaison at the Klub. Even the Pineapple Number, "It Couldn't Please Me More," became literally a Pineapple Number, with fruit lowered from the ceiling and three girls doing a tiny Ziegfeldian Pineapple-Number dance on the upper level.

The costumes alone were an announcement of intention, with the girls in S&M fetish outfits and the boys shirtless in evening dress. Still, the production's most arresting aspect was musical. Except for the conductor, a pianist, a drummer, a bass, and one trumpet, the entire orchestra was formed out of the acting pool. This was no stunt, but real music making. Michele Pawk, the Fräulein Kost, accompanied her own launching of the first-act finale of "Tomorrow Belongs To Me" on the accordion, and the ensemble played the entr'acte, perched on the upper level in the middle of Brill's crooked picture frame lined with lightbulbs. And, boy, did they swing.

The cast was somewhat more consistent than many a *Cabaret* troupe, as befits Mendes' integrated conception. Most noted were the Emcee and the Sally, Alan Cumming and Natasha Richardson; both won the top performer Tonys. Cumming was everyone's idol, but Richardson was underappreciated here and there by those who want more (or less) voice from Sally, and who failed to see that Richardson got this difficult character down first and then let the voice complement the portrayal. She is the best Sally since Judi Dench, and sang the most intense "Cabaret" ever heard, suggesting that the very center of the show was collapsing under the weight of both personal and social pressures: that Weimar democracy must fall just as Sally falls. All sensible people leave (like Cliff). And the Emcee, who had personified or maybe just tolerated but also ignored Nazi evil—Mendes makes his role ambiguous—ended in the production's greatest break with 1966. In a last "shot," as the cabaret dissolved into a dead white space, the Emcee became the ultimate victim, in the striped pajamas of the Nazi murder camp.

Mary Louise Wilson and Ron Rifkin were the Schneider and Schultz, enjoying top billing with Richardson and Cumming, as this musical continues to use poster credits to discover who is essential and who assists. Strangely, John Benjamin Hickey, the Cliff, was below the title. Are we losing sight of this character, or is it simply that, denied his only solo number, he's virtually back in *I Am a Camera*? Denis O'Hare enjoyed Mendes' radical reinstruction of Ernst, almost a different person now. In 1966, Edward Winter was cold and confident; the new Ernst is a wheedling, seductive figure, so trembly when he tries a surprise kiss on Cliff, then so hurt (Winter was dismissive) when Cliff fails to sympathize with Nazi anti-Semitism.

Altogether, Mendes' *Cabaret* had New York agog, not least because the pseudo-nightclub venue could not seat as many as the Broadhurst (and then the larger Imperial, in one of the few times that a show incurred the now all-but-prohibitive union expense of moving) in 1966. Everyone wanted to check in with an opinion on how Mendes had altered the original, and a certain amount of false history was issued. This was not the most extreme Broadway revision of a show—that would be the 1973 Debbie Reynolds *Irene*. Nor did this *Cabaret* change the spirit of the original more than, for example, the 1946 *Show Boat* did.

But this was, interestingly, a revival of an American classic that originated in England and with two Brits in what are, for the moment, the main roles. This yields a pleasant transition to the next chapter, which wonders why the English influence on the Broadway musical, currently at its most intense, was at best dormant in the 1960s.

10

All Caught Up in Her Oo-la-la

The English Musical

Parochial and twee is how only some people perceived the English musical in the postwar years. True, its reliance on tradition while the American musical was undergoing its *Oklahoma!–Street Scene–Candide*
transformation is telling. It says much that, in the 1950s, most of our hits
went over there and only two of theirs, *The Boy Friend* and *Salad Days*,
came here. Twee those two certainly were, especially *Salad Days*, with its
magic piano that makes people dance.

However, Broadway knew nothing of the *other* styles in the British
musical—works of social realism; slyly sensual adaptations of Fielding and
Vanbrugh in pastiche rhythm from madrigal to tango; views of the London underworld, by turns romantic in *The Crooked Mile* (1959) and zany
in *Fings Ain't Wot They Used T'Be* (1960). American show music had been
traveling the globe since the 1920s, but even theatregoing Americans
couldn't name the masters of West End music, the Monty Normans and
David Henekers. One heard nothing of such unusual scores as those of
Expresso Bongo (1958), a satire on the pop-music world in Britain; of
Make Me an Offer (1959), on life in a flea market and almost entirely
made of character songs; of *Belle* (1961), in which the infamous Dr. Crip-
pen murder case was presented as an evening of irreverent music hall; or
of *Maggie May* (1964), about the tragic love between a prostitute and a
union organizer in Liverpool, which so entranced Judy Garland that she
recorded four of the songs. True, these are parochial—but so are such
West End hits as *Guys and Dolls* and *Bye Bye Birdie*.

Quite suddenly, in the 1960s, the Brits began to pitch camp along The
Street. The breakthrough might have been *Valmouth* (1958), Sandy Wil-

son's adaptation of Ronald Firbank's unbelievably minty novel. (Sample character name: Lieutenant Whorwood.) *Valmouth* came here in 1960, presented off-Broadway, but in a replica of its West End staging, by Vida Hope in Tony Walton's sets. Apparently a look at the doings of some lusty hags at a spa but more truly an explosion of subversive gay humor, *Valmouth* has been nominated by more than a few as the best of all English musicals. Certainly, it finds *The Boy Friend*'s author in a wicked frame of mind yet as melodious as ever. The ladies in New York included Anne Francine, Constance Carpenter, Elly Stone, and, in her original role as an Indian masseuse, Bertice Reading. It was an impressive cast for off-Broadway, but this show is just too daring for its good, and it closed in two weeks.

More likely, then, the breakthrough would be *Stop the World—I Want To Get Off* (1961). Written by its star, Anthony Newley, and Leslie Bricusse, this parable of Littlechap and his life and loves ran fourteen months in London and then packed up its unit set, its costumes and orchestrations, and all four of its principals (there was otherwise only a small girls' chorus) and ran even longer in New York, starting in 1962. The show absolutely enchanted its American producer, David Merrick, because it cost only $75,000 to mount. Merrick dreamed of an epoch of Anthony Newley shows in unit sets with a small girls' chorus.

At least this one did finally give New Yorkers an authentic taste of the British musical. Not as *Boy Friend* charmer or *Valmouth* over-the-top brilliance, but a good, solid piece of what the English were doing on *their* Broadway when striking new poses. Detractors called it *"Stop the Show—I Want To Get Out."* Perhaps they found Newley's white-faced, high-waisted-suspender-pants-over-black-top clown look a little trying, his piercing vocal delivery unpleasant, the circus setting a short-cut symbolism, and the lack of plot enervating. Still, the show had a raw, weird presence entirely its own. It was so idiomatically English that it had to come over as it was, untranslated. Bricusse and Newley (billed in that order) produced three long-term song hits, "What Kind of Fool Am I?," "Once in a Lifetime," and the gospel rave-up "Gonna Build a Mountain." But the score's charm lay in such less obvious winners as the Russian lullaby "Meilinki Meilchick," the colorful "Nag! Nag! Nag!," and four versions of a single number, "Typically English." These were sung by Anna Quayle, playing the women in Littlechap's life in a shapeless smock with a fluffy white collar: his wife, Evie; a Soviet functionary in "Glorious Russian" (with the chorus interpolating snatches of "The Volga Boatman"); a German maid in the Nazi march "Typische Deutsche"; and finally a breathy Marilyn Monroe copy in "All American."

Stop the World offered more showmanship than substance, perhaps. When Newley and Bricusse tried the format again in *The Roar of the Greasepaint—The Smell of the Crowd*, England wasn't interested, and the show folded during its tryout. But David Merrick was interested. After all, it was another unit set with a few leads and a (slightly larger) girls' chorus. Merrick brought *Greasepaint* to New York in 1965 and got half a year's run out of it, while Newley scored another trio of hits, "A Wonderful Day Like Today," "Who Can I Turn To? (When Nobody Needs Me)," and the bitingly ironic "The Joker." Still, with Newley as Cocky and Cyril Ritchard as Sir (it's class war), and with such other roles as The Kid (Sally Smith) and The Negro (Gilbert Price), *Greasepaint* really was just another *Stop the World* circus fable with everyone in rags.

Meanwhile, in 1964, Merrick (with Gerry Raffles) had again brought over an English musical, *Oh What a Lovely War*. Or was it a musical? Or, even, who wrote it? Long before *A Chorus Line*, here was a piece "invented" in improvisations, shaped by a director (Joan Littlewood), and set into text by a writer (Charles Chilton). A product of Littlewood's Theatre Workshop, an aficionado's ensemble working out of an old playhouse in East London, *Oh What a Lovely War* used antique songs to punctuate and remark upon a kaleidoscopic view of World War I from every conceivable viewpoint. As if this weren't odd enough, the cast worked in the commedia dell'arte costumes favored by English revue troupes of the period. The threnody "Roses of Picardy" and the hopeful "Till the Boys Come Home" (generally known as "Keep the Home Fires Burning") stood next to marches, pop tunes, "Silent Night" (in German), and so on: a wild gallimaufry, as much agitprop as art. Strangely, for such a theatrical creation, it made a splendid movie. The New York run was four months— not bad for such a hard-edged work. But Merrick had troubled to retain not only the original staging, but many of the original cast. I wonder if the Pierrot costumes doomed it. Without the historical context for them, Americans were simply bewildered by the look of the piece.

So that, too, was not the breakthrough. But it was David Merrick who made it, at that in a twee and parochial work that has been going around the world for decades. This was *Oliver!*, Lionel Bart's adaptation of Dickens. At first only a lyricist (on *Lock Up Your Daughters*), then strictly a songwriter (on *Fings Ain't Wot They Used T'Be*), Bart was *Oliver!*'s sole author and, in his quiet way, the man who renegotiated the reputation of the English musical.

Many legends attach themselves to this work—that only a handful of seats had been sold when it had its London premiere (after a stupendously nasty critical drubbing out of town) on June 30, 1960; that Dame Edna Everage was in the original cast; that Sean Kenny's elaborate wooden constructivist set, which completely changed form for each scene, could be operated by one stagehand pressing buttons; that Bart objected to the casting of Georgia Brown as Nancy simply because they had known each other as kids; that Merrick sent the show on an American pre-Broadway tour so prolonged that he'd make money even if it bombed in New York; that Bart later foolishly sold his copyright to outside agents, losing a fortune and ending up more or less homeless; and that producer Cameron Mackintosh, presenting a sumptuous revival at London's Palladium in 1994, felt honor-bound to pay Bart a percentage that he wasn't legally entitled to.

Legends! Legends! And apparently they're all true. One key fact to note—American tourists seeing England in the 1950s never cited a specific musical show as a cultural must-see. There were various Shakespeare stagings; or something with Olivier, Gielgud, Richardson; even Agatha Christie's *The Mousetrap*, as a lark. No American went to English musicals . . . until *Oliver!*. Throughout its six-and-a-half-year run, this was the theatre piece one had to take in.

The show held New York for a bit less than two years in 1963 and 1964, and it has never become the classic here that it is over there. Still, *Oliver!* made a tremendous impact for the ease in which it boiled a short but complex novel into workable size, all the while hurling a set of music-hall numbers over the footlights in a bizarrely inappropriate modernistic set. There was something wonderful—but also really strange—in watching the Artful Dodger take Oliver under his wing in a knees-up chorus called "Consider Yourself" while Kenny's dovetailed platforms and stairs kept turning into different places. It was like a children's show put on by radical experimentalists. It was Piscator's idea of a musical, Artaud's. It was as if theatre history had decided to jump from Drury Lane melodrama to space-age hologram theatre, skipping Nazimova, Brecht, and Gower Champion entirely.

I can't imagine what theatregoers were thinking at those first London performances. These were greeted with ovations; but word had it that *everyone* had begged producer Donald Albery to close the show in Wimbledon. Dickens buffs might have been startled to find no program listing for Monks, Rose and Harry Maylie, and other characters so salient in the novel's unmasking of Oliver's identity. Bart was more interested in Oliver's adventures than in his genealogy.

Anyone at all, however, might have been startled by the show's opening twenty minutes. There was no overture. After a bit of quaint fanfare,* the curtain rose on the first of Kenny's crazy wooden places, in this case the workhouse. To anxious altered chords, an underling opened a gate as orphan boys filed in to take their places at table. A vamp punctuated by woodblock strokes led to "Food, Glorious Food" while the audience was wondering which one was Oliver. Slyly, though the orchestra kept anticipating his three-note theme, Oliver was but one of several boys with short vocal solos. Not till he Asked For More did we discover our protagonist. The title song immediately followed, and, as Kenny's pieces pirouetted into someplace else, the beadle Bumble and the workhouse beldame Corney held tête-à-tête in "I Shall Scream." Again immediately, Bumble took Oliver off to apprenticeship with an undertaker in the minor-key "Boy For Sale," a wailing street cry of a solo.

Indeed, Edna Everage, billed as Barry Humphries, played in *Oliver!* (in New York as well as London), as the undertaker. He proved to be so intriguingly Dickensian that Bart wrote "That's Your Funeral" especially for him. It's a piece of comic guignol, set by orchestrator Eric Rogers to the bald beat of a mourning drum. Bumble abruptly turned and walked off stage during it—and that odd little action typifies the absurdly unpredictable nature of this show. Songs pile upon one another, then a book scene will exhale a cloud of expository detail, then that junk heap of a set

---

*For the previously mentioned 1994 Mackintosh revival, our old friend Sam Mendes, ever revisionist, devised a prologue to a dramatic new rendering of this music. A storm fit for *Macbeth* or *King Lear* howled as we witnessed the death of Old Sally, which plays a significant part in the eventual redemption of Oliver. It's also a neat way to bemuse the jaded theatregoer who thinks he knows every show by heart, at the same time completely mystifying anyone who hasn't read the novel within, say, the last three weeks.

turns into something with a bridge, then characters we take as essential vanish for two hours or never return at all, then we get a load of impenetrable English comedy, then somebody is brutally murdered as we watch.

What is most pleasing about *Oliver!* is that it really is based on *Oliver Twist*. Bart found music to match what Dickens created, in Nancy, Fagin, Bill Sikes. He made the beadle an eerie high tenor (anticipating the beadle in Sondheim's *Sweeney Todd*), the Widow Corney a music-hall comic, the Artful Dodger a kid star in a talent contest on Saturday afternoon at the local Empire.

Bart was no craftsman, but rather a genius who got there from nowhere and started inventing. *Oliver!* is primitive. The orchestrations are dinky, and there is little choral harmony and no choreography. Well . . . no choreographer credited. Director Peter Coe apparently wanted no dances, only informal hoofing during the vocals—a sloppy kick line in "It's a Fine Life," a mock gavotte in "I'd Do Anything." Oddly, the untutored Bart contrived an almost operatic quartet in the reprise of "It's a Fine Life," a slash-and-burn plot number.

Bart also wrote not one but two quodlibets, in "Be Back Soon" and "Oom-Pah-Pah." They abut across an intermission, for "Be Back Soon" sees Fagin's crew off to mischief that closes Act One with Oliver's arrest, and "Oom-Pah-Pah" opens Act Two with Shakespearean intensity of suspense. We want to learn what happened to Oliver. But Bart gives us Nancy in a pub delivering another of those music-hall specials. Then—once again in this musical that respects no rules for the writing of musicals—Bill Sikes, the principal villain, makes his first appearance, one hundred minutes into the running time. Instantly, he goes into his crude establishing number, "My Name." And, moments after that, Nancy gets her torch song, "As Long As He Needs Me." It's amazing how much sheer stop-and-sing this work contains, when one considers that it also has more plot than *Li'l Abner* and *Les Misérables* combined.

Some feel that Bart sweetened Dickens. He didn't. At the center of *Oliver Twist* is the remark that there are bad people on the good side and good on the bad, and Bart illustrates this. The righteous Bumble and Corney are bad; the criminal Nancy is good. True, Bart gentled Fagin, even ennobled him by giving him the last scene in the action proper: stumbling off alone and without hope as the curtain falls. (Dickens leaves him facing the gallows.)

What was the influence of *Oliver!* on Broadway? It had no imitation, and Bart himself went on to other kinds of musicals. No, *Oliver!*'s influence lay in the American acculturation of the English musical. *Half a Sixpence* (1963), twee and parochial, could now successfully dare Broadway in 1965 when, before *Oliver!*, it would have stayed home. An adaptation of H. G. Wells' 1905 novel *Kipps*, *Sixpence* was a vehicle for the rock-and-roller-turned-variety-star Tommy Steele. Kipps is a nobody who inherits a legacy, moves among the nobs, then loses his position but regains his girl. That's English art: class peace.

Granted, for the first time since the early 1900s, a London hit was heavily revised specifically for Broadway. Five of David Heneker's songs were dropped and one added, Edmund Balin's choreography was replaced by Onna White's more high-powered numbers, and even the director, John Dexter, was superseded by Gene Saks. There was a feeling that, even in the original sets and costumes and with the original star (and one supporting player, James Grout), *Half a Sixpence* was being Americanized. Not in its idiom, but in its performing style. Some commuting theatregoers found the Broadway *Sixpence* more exciting; others thought it less charming. The *London Evening News* had praised the work's "reserve and delicacy," but, in New York, Walter Kerr spoke of "a fast number made of so many banjo strokes that you think the participants will surely have one."

Still, the show was a hit, partly because of its disarmingly sweet score but mostly because of Tommy Steele, easily the most likable person ever to have rocked. Thrumming that banjo, improvisationally retrieving a dancer's dropped hat during a hectic number (night after night: the business was staged), and nicely embodying Wells' naïvely earnest store clerk, Steele was that rare Broadway thing, a full-fledged star that few had heard of, let alone experienced. He was not a Novelty Star—music was his business. Of eleven numbers, he shared or led eight and dominated the dancing in an awesomely energetic performance. One can't imagine anyone's taking on such a challenge twice in a lifetime, though Steele had played the piece for nineteen months in London first.

Did *Half a Sixpence*'s score have any effect on Broadway? There is an enviable ingenuousness in the title song, a soft-shoe romance; a quietly confident showstopper in "If the Rain's Got To Fall"; a choral waltz in "The Old Military Canal" that is risibly pretty, as if it knew it didn't really belong in the show but knew also that this sort of thing is usually done at this point in an English musical; and a comic patter number at breakneck speed citing celebrities of the past in "Flash, Bang, Wallop!" These are all genres typifying the West End style, but Americans have used them, too. Perhaps, by the 1960s, some *English* musicals were under the *American* influence, blurring the formal differences.

Shows from other European countries, however, were very different from ours; and suddenly they were coming over. In 1964, the Folies Bergère paid a visit with a company headed by singer Patachou, showgirl Liliane Montevecchi, the indispensable Trotter Brothers, the authentic huge staircase down which les girls would parade, and of course the can-can. Like it or not, it was authentic, and it lasted half a year at the Broadway. But 1964 also revealed an Austrian production of Johann Strauss' *Wiener Blut* (Vienna Blood) at the Lunt-Fontanne that the critics excoriated as cheap and clumsy.

A far worthier attraction, though a quick failure, was *Rugantino* (1964). A perennial in Italy (where it has enjoyed three cast recordings, besides one made for New York), this show truly lives in another world from Broadway. Its plot mixes sex and politics in a romantic way (an American show would mix them in a satiric way), and its anti-hero is finally beheaded. One actually hears the blade fall in the music. Pietro Garinei and Sandro Giovannini were the reigning word masters of the Italian musical, and with composer Armando Trovaioli they created their masterpiece in this work. At once carefree and gloomy, *Rugantino* is nearly as different from other Italian musicals as it is from the Broadway style. Even the principals defy type. The women are buxom know-it-alls, the roguish hero a skinny runaround, the villain comic and obese.

Set in Rome in 1830, *Rugantino* exploits the antique in décor; but the music is modern, a bit on the pop side yet Italian pop, of a foreign make. The entire Italian company, headed by Ornella Vanoni, Bice Valori, Nino Manfredi (the titular hero), and Aldo Fabrizi (his nemesis, the municipal executioner), was taken to New York. But what about the language problem? Alfred Drake, bilingual because of Italian parentage, translated the libretto, and Edward Eager, an occasional lyricist of obscure Broadway flops, supplied the lyrics. Their English was then projected before the audience in an anticipation of opera surtitles. The show's American co-producer and fanatic inamorato Alexander Cohen superintended a tremendous technical effort to work out the logistics of the titles, so it is sad to report that *Rugantino* did not catch on and closed in four weeks. One curious footnote: amid all the Italian names of the poster stood that of Broadway's own Dania Krupska, suggesting to some that *Rugantino's* choreography had been beefed up, like that of *Half a Sixpence*. On the contrary, Krupska had staged the dances for the original production.

In the end, all this European matter came and went without remark. Nor can we discern any influence in visits from Englishmen Michael Flanders and Donald Swann in their programs (1959, 1966) of comic songs sung and introduced by Flanders and accompanied by Swann; from *Beyond the Fringe* (1962) and its satiric quartet of Alan Bennett, Jonathan Miller, Peter Cook, and Dudley Moore; in *La Plume de Ma Tante's* sequel, *La Grosse Valise* (1965); or the South African revue *Wait a Minim!* (1966).

In fact, when Broadway tackled subjects that might well have benefited from allusions to or whole adoptions of the English style in the musical, Broadway did no more than import English performers. (This was easily done then; today, Equity would throw pies at you.) Take *Walking Happy* (1966), an adaptation of Harold Brighouse's 1915 play *Hobson's Choice*. A specialist in the language and manners of Manchester and its environs, Brighouse would seem an unlikely source for an American show, especially as a vehicle for Mary Martin. But Martin said no, as she was continually doing at this time. The role suited her: a spinster, chafing under the rule of a tyrannical father, who sets out to become the business and love partner of her father's irreplaceable but spineless employee. The business is "boots," as the English term our "shoes," and the play is a classic case of a good story with rich characters ready to open up in song and dance.

As an English musical, right? With, say, Cyril Ornadel and Leslie Bricusse doing the score for father Wilfrid Brambell, daughter Vivienne Martin, and expert bootmaker Kenneth Williams. Peter Coe might direct it; but Sean Kenny can't design every English musical, so let's give this one to Loudon Sainthill, even if the North Country is a bit gray for his preening pastels.

No. *Walking Happy* starred Norman Wisdom, Louise Troy, and George Rose, with a score by James Van Heusen and Sammy Cahn and choreography by Danny Daniels and direction by co-producer Cy Feuer. This is an American show with two English actors and a tiny bit of English atmosphere in the script, such as the North's characteristic use of noun without article ("And leave you two in charge of shop?") and the expression "By gum!"

In fact, *Walking Happy* is a thoroughly American mid-sixties musical comedy in every way. It bears a trace of what it might have been like as a Mary Martin vehicle in that, while Wisdom was the star, Troy ran the plot, pushing and conniving and bargaining. ("It's in the blood!" groaned a tradesman, noting how like her skinflint father she is at making a deal.) During the tryout, Van Heusen and Cahn tried to soften her by moving her determined Wanting Song, "I'll Make a Man of the Man," from early in Act One to early in Act Two. They replaced it with the tender "Where Was I?," but that song is too light for what is left of the bustling, Dolly-like figure that Martin was to have played. Worse, "Where Was I?" is idle flutter, while "I'll Make a Man of the Man" is a clenched-fist ballad, jumping off of a discord to defy father, society, all. In Act Two, it was lost, almost a throwaway.

But then, *Walking Happy* was supposed to be Norman Wisdom's vehicle, built around his trademark sadness and shrugs. Like all great comics, Wisdom had a unique persona. It is related to Eddie Cantor's in its milquetoast demeanor—but Cantor was bullied by tough guys. Wisdom is bullied by capitalism. This being an American show, he eventually takes control of the available business and even finds himself in love with the domineering Troy. It's a happy piece, as the title tells. But it was not a hit.

Maybe the opening was the problem. We've discussed many wonderful first scenes in this book. Now let's discuss a terrible one. The curtain rises on a man-filled pub, and a book scene provides rather a lot of exposition: George Rose has three daughters, but he's a control freak who will keep the eldest (Troy) unmarried and working for himself: "A valuable piece of property, that one, and I don't part easy with value."

Oh, the snake. But hold, A temperance fanatic enters. As his two sons are in love with Rose's younger daughters we sense plot construction. But, no, the fanatic wants to lead us all into a Temperance Number, "Think of Something Else," a dead song walking. What could be worse, by 1966, than one of those old-fashioned, slow-starting first scenes? In the year, may I remind us, of "It's Today" and "Willkommen." Don't flop shows always start with a flop number like "Think of Something Else"?

At least, once that scene is over, the score picks up. It's not a sharp score. Except for "You're Right, You're Right," there are no real plot numbers. It's all charm songs and charm dances: "Use Your Noggin'," "How D'Ya Talk To a Girl?," "Such a Sociable Sort," "Clog Dance," "Box Dance." Oddly, this show that begins so poorly has that rare thing in musical comedy, a solid second act. It has, even, a wonderful title number, which choreographer Daniels built into a showstopper. It was basically just a self-repeating parade of dancers, while Wisdom kept passing through, trucking furniture to his new boot shop, always hapless yet smiling. It was a literalization of the show's title, the title song coming true. Another of those very stylish big dance numbers put on by experts, it worked very, very well. There was never anything this expert in an English musical.

Clearly, sixties Broadway might host the foreign show but not learn from it. Broadway was teacher. *Darling of the Day* (1968) could boast a virtually all-British set of leads in a highly English period piece from an Arnold Bennett novel. It could even coax from composer Jule Styne and lyricist E. Y. Harburg more than a touch of romance in its score. Nevertheless, it was wholly Broadway in style. *Walking Happy* eked out 161 performances, but *Darling of the Day* got raves from Clive Barnes, John Chapman, and Richard Watts Jr.—a grand sweep of the *Times*, the *News*, and the *Post*. That must be why it closed in a month.

Actually, Barnes missed *Darling of the Day*'s opening night to cover a dance event, postponing his appreciation and leaving a second-stringer to become notorious for damning a show whose acolytes call it the *My Fair Lady* of flop musicals. Barnes had also held up the first night of *The Happy Time* a week earlier; he was late getting back from a speaking engagement. These and one or two other contretemps led to important history: critics were now to be invited to final previews rather than the premiere, which gave them time to absorb a show and organize their thoughts.

Obviously, this didn't help *Darling of the Day*. It went through a more than typically disorienting series of book writers and directors before and during rehearsals and tryouts, when it was briefly known as *Married Alive!* This is an allusion to its source of 1908, Bennett's *Buried Alive*. Monty Woolley and Gracie Fields played in the more famous of two talkie versions, *Holy Matrimony*: he as the genius painter who yearns for anonymity and she as a village widow. When his valet drops dead, the painter fakes his own death and assumes the valet's identity. But it seems that the valet had been Corresponding. You know—through one of those discreet marriage bureaus? And so the two meet.

It's a dandy tale, because the painter goes on painting. So, when his work surfaces, the art world realizes that their late genius is still available and tries to reclaim him with all the glory and ceremony that he loathes. That's a much better subplot than the timeworn second couple that used to keep us occupied while the leads were resting up in their dressing rooms. But how to find a singing equivalent for a genius painter?

Some blame *Darling of the Day*'s failure on Vincent Price. He did lack charm, no doubt; but he played the role quite well and even held his own in eight numbers. This can't have been easy opposite Patricia Routledge, one of the great singers of the English stage and a marvelous performer of very wide range. Tantalizingly pert in "It's Enough To Make a Lady Fall in Love," airily waltzing in "Let's See What Happens," and simply stopping the show in "Not on Your Nellie," Routledge was a comic soprano and a dancing actress, one of those rare entertainers commanding not only concentration but unpredictability. "The most spectacular, most scrumptious, most embraceable musical comedy debut since Beatrice Lillie and Gertrude Lawrence," said Walter Kerr. Wouldn't you have bought tickets?

Some blame the show's failure on the score. It's the kind that buffs treasure, but it hasn't one potential hit. "Putney on the Thames," a real Styne swinger, was dropped before the opening, perhaps because it didn't jibe with the rest of the music. The score was defined by art dealer Peter Woodthorpe ripping his way through "He's a Genius" in Henry Higgins Sprechstimme, or by Price daintily and exuberantly explaining the art of the landscape to the chorus in "I've Got a Rainbow Working For Me," or by the caroling "What Makes a Marriage Merry?," or by Price and Routledge looking forward to a romantic old age in "Sunset Tree." It's halfway back to operetta, and this was not a time that admired the style.

Some might want to blame the fact that no book writer was credited in the program; but how many notice those things? Maybe it was Vincent Price's beard. Maybe it was the coming and going of so many of the creative staff, which left the piece incomplete, slowly paced and plainly staged. It had the makings of a hit, but it needed a strong director. It needed a director, period.

One wonders how *Darling of the Day* would have gone over in London in this same package. Shows sometimes succeeded there in stagings that Broadway would have derided—*Canterbury Tales* (1968), for instance, not exactly amateur night but an imperfect composition indifferently produced. Broadway saw it in 1969, in a somewhat different mounting and an entirely different cast, though with plenty of Brits, including Martyn Green, George Rose, and Hermione Baddeley. In London, *Canterbury Tales* lasted 2,082 performances; in New York, 121.

Clearly, the English musical's age of reascendency has not yet begun. However, only three and a half years after *Darling of the Day* closed, *Jesus Christ Superstar* opened.

HAVE YOU GOT CHARM?

THE OFF-BROADWAY MUSICAL

Only in the 1960s. Earlier, there weren't enough musicals on off-Broadway to speak of; after, they were more often than not Broadway shows in all but their playing venue (like *Grease*, or *The Best Little Whorehouse in Texas* before they moved onto The Street), or offbeat but uptown slick (like *Little Shop of Horrors*), or alternatives to Broadway but of a completely different kind from what the term "off-Broadway musical" originally denoted.

This term refers to a certain thing of a certain time, roughly between *The Fantasticks* in 1960 and *Promenade* in 1969. A number of forms favoring the small physical scale of the theatres, or addressing a public assumed to be uninterested in the "bourgeois" Broadway style, flourished at this time particularly.

It all started, of course, with Marc Blitzstein's English translation of *The Threepenny Opera* at the Theatre de Lys (now the Lucille Lortel) in 1954. With an interesting cast that included Charlotte Rae, Beatrice Arthur, Jo Sullivan, and, most historically, Lotte Lenya, the production instantly became a town topic: because Kurt Weill's music had been somewhat in limbo following his death, in 1950; because Weill's widow, Lenya, was entering her great new "life is my cabaret" phase and adding a sort of cackling gravity to the event; because this staging displayed amazing staying power. A prior booking at the de Lys caused *Threepenny* to close after three months. But word of mouth continued to spread, and no less an authority than Brooks Atkinson kept demanding a return.

After fifteen months, there was one: and this time the piece ran for more than six years. Dolly Haas, Nancy Andrews, Jane Connell, Edward

Asner, Estelle Parsons, Jerry Orbach, and even tourist Georgia Brown are among those who spelled the original company, all helping to suggest that a small stage in a functional auditorium rather than a Broadway *boîte* might be the correct environment for a work out of the mainstream. After all, these were the years when *Damn Yankees*, *My Fair Lady*, and *The Music Man* defined what Americans meant by "a musical."

Note that *The Threepenny Opera* was a revival. It had been done on Broadway first, in 1933, and flopped after receiving intensely scornful reviews. Then a Broadway hit of 1954, *The Boy Friend*, was revived, in 1958. Like *The Threepenny Opera*, this was a work of pastiche. There the resemblance ends, for the *Opera* is a Brechtian disinterment of old work for wily political purposes and the other is the purest nostalgic entertainment. They are the two most opposite musicals in history.

Meanwhile, Jerome Kern's *Leave It To Jane* came back, in 1959. Like *The Boy Friend* a two-year success, it helped solidify the first of the sixties off-Broadway genres, the small-scale revival of the full-scale show.

True, *Threepenny*, *The Boy Friend*, and *Jane* are in fact medium-sized. The first was conceived (in 1928) for an antique house in Berlin seating fewer than eight hundred. *The Boy Friend* grew out of a sketch in a thespian club's revue night, never had a chorus, and played its entire five-year London run to piano accompaniment. And *Jane*, though it was originally produced (in 1917) at the Longacre, held to Princess Theatre regulations as an intimate piece.

Still, revivals after these three largely drew on Big Broadway—Cole Porter and the Gershwins, with the scripts fiddled and the scores diddled. *Gay Divorce* and *Oh, Kay!* reappeared in 1960 and *Anything Goes* in 1962, the last in a revision that became the standard performing version till the 1987 Lincoln Center production. Generally, the cast and techies were culled from the ranks of those who hadn't made it yet. Many would do so—it was his choreography for *Anything Goes* that sent Ron Field up to Broadway; and his Reno Sweeney, Eileen Rodgers, had, exceptionally, distinguished herself on The Street in *Fiorello!* and *Tenderloin*.

Gay Divorce is probably the least impressive of the three revivals. A 25-performance flop at the Cherry Lane, it had Frank Aletter in Fred Astaire's role and Judy Johnson opposite him. The sole name of note in the cast was that of Beatrice Arthur, in Luella Gear's old role and singing the acidic "Mister and Missus Fitch." This actually *is* from *Gay Divorce*, but half of the score was gathered by director Gus Schirmer Jr. from the rest of Porter's stage and film catalogue. At least Schirmer kept to what was then more-or-less unheard Porter. Over at the Orpheum, *Anything Goes* included "Friendship" and "It's De-lovely," old news even then. Irritatingly, the two have dogged the show ever since.

Rodgers and Hart came off better, with faithful resuscitations of *The Boys From Syracuse* in 1963 and *By Jupiter* in 1967, both at Theatre Four and directed by Christopher Hewett. *Boys* was so successful that the production was expanded to fit London's Drury Lane later that year, and both shows were sung without a single missing or added number. (*By Jupiter* even restored "Wait Till You See Her," cut in 1942.) A *Best Foot Forward* in 1963 introduced Liza Minnelli, just turned seventeen, in this most youthful of shows; and, as the visiting movie star, Paula Wayne was replaced by Veronica Lake. Landmark political shows returned, *The Cradle Will Rock* in 1964 and *Pins and Needles* in 1968; and two classic black shows, *Cabin in the Sky* in 1964 and *House of Flowers* in 1968, gave younger theatregoers a chance to sample cult favorites. True, without the Balanchine staging and Ethel Waters, Todd Duncan, and Rex Ingram of the former; and without the latter's spectacular visuals and Pearl Bailey, Diahann Carroll, and Juanita Hall—what was one sampling, exactly?

Perhaps the off-Broadway musical's greater invention was the Offbeat Little Show. This tradition stems from *The Fantasticks*; that work's spiraling international success must have inspired many a writer to whom The Street's great doors remained barred. One was John Jennings, the sole author of *Riverwind* (1962), a look at interpersonal relations at an Indiana summer-cabin spot. This show boasted a second-league Broadway-caliber cast. Lawrence Brooks had been Broadway's Grieg in *Song of Norway*; he and his wife (Elizabeth Parrish) are returning to Riverwind to try to respark the flame of their love. Brooks Morton and Lovelady Powell were later in big-time Broadway bombs; Powell's didn't even get to New York. They played a bohemian couple, shockingly (for the time) unwed. Widow Helon Blount ran the camp; her employee Martin J. Cassidy had a crush on Blount's daughter, Dawn Nickerson.

That, off-Broadway-style, was the entire cast. *Riverwind* is a reverie about love: how to get into it, how to stay in it, what it's for. Intimate? It's downright confessional, with such an appealing score that an English firm, Decca Records, taped it (with orchestrations created for the disc) at a time when few *American* companies bothered with off-Broadway. The bohemians' comic "American Family Plan" (an anticipation of Stephen Sondheim's "banned" lyric for "We're Gonna Be All Right" in *Do I Hear a Waltz?*) was used as a linking device, but then so was the wistful title song. This is a rich score, as contemporary as it is nostalgic, jazzing and waltzing and finally, in Blount's "Sew the Buttons On," creating a unique picture of a woman who comprehends life by not thinking about it. Another of Jennings' irresistible waltzes, this odd number blends pure melody with lyrics of resignation. Nickerson keeps pressing her mother for nuances of sorrow, but Blount replies in music that refuses to feel bad: or perhaps just doesn't know how to.

Decca also brought out *Ballad For Bimshire* (1963), again expanding the modest theatre pit. This was very necessary if the music was to tell properly. *Bimshire* is a black show, on life in Barbados, and its action is really an excuse for the songs, by Irving Burgie. Known professionally as Lord Burgess, he enjoyed a successful pop career but adapted easily to the needs of the story score. The music has two realities, one as a showcase for the Caribbean sound and the other as theatre—as in, say, heroine Christine Spencer's powerful ballad "Deep in My Heart," or her duet with Frederick O'Neal, "Have You Got Charm?," in which drums chatter away as if dishing the two singers. Jimmy Randolph's "Silver Earring" is sly—is it a takeoff on a pop hit or planning to be one? The pop influence was especially felt in the lyrics, which constantly indulge in false rhymes; still, the music is infectiously rhythmic. It was not enough to keep the show running, but then off-Broadway played to a public that saw musicals as the ultimate in mainstream, and so avoided them.

Ironically, the black musical was largely limited to off-Broadway at a time when Broadway casts were becoming more integrated. A few fifties shows set in New York used one or two black choristers, and this practice was amplified in the 1960s. More important, black choristers were hired for shows with inappropriate settings, in color-blind casting. There was, for example, a black male dancer in the *Funny Girl* line, though he showed up in ensemble scenes (*Follies* numbers, the second-act party in Fanny's house) that more authentically would have been all-white.

One of the most successful of all off-Broadway musicals was *You're a Good Man, Charlie Brown* (1967), which spun off six American touring companies while playing 1,597 performances at the Theatre 80 St. Marks.

Oddly, the show began as a song cycle, on LP, in one of the first "concept albums" to become a theatre piece. Orson Bean, Barbara Minkus, Bill Hinnant, and the composer-lyricist, Clark Gesner, sang the numbers; and when Gesner wrote a book to connect the songs (under the pseudonym John Gordon), Hinnant alone stayed on, as Snoopy. His brother Skip played Schroeder, Gary Burghoff (later Radar in M*A*S*H, on both screens) was Charlie Brown, Bob Balaban was Linus, and the two girls were grouchy Reva Rose and amiable Karen Johnson.

Though the LP had had an orchestra, the show made do with off-Broadway's trusty piano-and-drums combo, and director Joseph Hardy had the most minimal of sets to work with, four or five wooden "shapes" for the cast to sit or stand on while faithfully reflecting Charles M. Schulz's *Peanuts* originals. Lucy courted the heedless Schroeder as he played Beethoven's "Moonlight" Sonata and told Charlie Brown of her plans to become queen; Linus had his blanket and Charlie Brown his impedient kite; Lucy gave Charlie Brown psychological analysis; Snoopy fought the Red Baron and rhapsodized over his filled food dish; and so on. The book is a trifle, an excuse for a record album to be staged; but the score is good at getting down Schulz's voices. Best of all is the free-form musical scene "Book Report," in which the kids characteristically prepare homework on *Peter Rabbit*. Lucy connives, counting out the words till she reaches the assignment's quota while saying very little over and over in different phrasings. Charlie Brown procrastinates. Linus is lovably pedantic:

LINUS: In this report, I plan to discuss the sociological implications of family pressures so great as to drive an otherwise moral rabbit to perform acts of thievery which he consciously knew were against the law. I also hope to explore the personality of Mr. McGregor in his conflicting roles as farmer and humanitarian . . .

There is one false note, when Snoopy sings "I think they're swell" about the kids. He doesn't. From beginning to end in the strip, Snoopy cared nothing about the kids. Indeed, it was the dog's identifying feature, aside from his more famous role-playing. Unlike the children, who have to deal with school, social mores, and various traumas, Snoopy was an absolutely free soul, a dog without affections.

We have seen very little of the decade's ideological issues seep into the musical so far. But 1967 did produce the highly political *Now Is the Time For All Good Men*. Like *Riverwind*, this show is set in Indiana, but in a busy place of township loyalties, gun-toting bigots posing as "patriots," and grown-ups-versus-kids. The atmosphere foretokens that of the film *Footloose*, though in this case the protagonist is not a kid but a grown-up, an idealistic English teacher. David Cryer had the role, and his wife, Gretchen, wrote the book and lyrics, to Nancy Ford's music. Gretchen also took a lead (as "Sally Niven," in order not to appear grabby).

Why was this show not done on Broadway? There is nothing inherently small about it; the tuneful score completely outstrips the tinkly quality of so many off-Broadway pieces. Word Baker staged it, at the Theatre de Lys, and though it lasted three and a half months and got a cast album, it never caught on as a sixties statement. It might well have, for while a bit of mystery anent the teacher's military service directly connects him to the Vietnam War, the notion of a freethinking teacher up against hidebound traditions is timeless and thus always relevant. "Keep 'Em Busy," a chorus of schoolteachers bent on giving the kids no time to think—the opposite of what "education" means—typifies the show's trim outlining of social tensions. Bouncy and friendly, the music *almost* hides what these mean little people are like. Best of all is the treatment of the gym teacher, who closed down the dramatic society: "They made a mess of *Charley's Aunt* all over my gym floor!" This man is the work's villain; he actually fires his shotgun at Cryer, luckily missing. In the end, Cryer must move on to another town. But *Now Is the Time* is as idealistic as he is, and the gym teacher's son tells Cryer that he will become a teacher, too. What he means is: a democrat, like you.

An alternate way of going political was simply to reflect the times, since sixties culture was so revolutionary. In January 1968, two different versions of Shakespeare's *Twelfth Night* opened ten days apart. The more faithful version, *Love and Let Love*, closed in two weeks. *Your Own Thing* ran for 937 performances, largely on an impishly trendy blend of Elizabethan verse and modern slang, of rock, half-rock, and not rock, of Shakespeare's games with gender fitted to sixties youth culture's unisex hair and clothing styles.

Unlike *Love and Let Love, Your Own Thing* dropped Malvolio and the comics to concentrate on the lovers. They were backed by a rock trio called The Apocalypse and constantly challenged or guided by projections of the famous (John Wayne, W. C. Fields, God) making observations. Olivia (Marian Mercer) owns a discotheque; Orsino, renamed Orson (Tom Ligon), agents for The Apocalypse (originally a quartet: Disease got drafted); and Viola (Leland Palmer) and Sebastian (Rusty Thacker) are singers. Throughout, book writer and director Donald Driver and songwriters Danny Apolinar (who also guitared in The Apocalypse) and Hal Hester combined Shakespeare's plot, themes, and lines with the contemporary:

SEBASTIAN: And though 'tis wonder that enwraps me thus,
　　Yet 'tis not madness. What a groovy lady.

Truth to tell, if this was the counterculture, it was easy to love: charming players, fast pace, Shakespeare without tears. It was even rock without tears, for those who feared the injection of airwave pop into theatre scores. As with *Hair*, another counterculture downtown show (before it moved to Broadway), the music was nifty and the lyrics, even those not by Shakespeare, were smart. There was even a New Dance Sensation, "Hunca Munca," which dissects the nightlife in cabarets in a single line: "crashing bores with eyes aglaze."

None of these original shows was truly "alternative theatre" in the way that so much of off-Broadway's non-musical stage was: the small collectives with various artistic missions, the experimental works, the dangerous European writers like Jean Genet. There was nothing experimental about *Ballad For Bimshire*, *Now Is the Time For All Good Men*, or *Your Own Thing*. But one off-Broadway title really was too avant-garde for Broadway, *Promenade* (1969), which opened the Promenade Theatre on upper Broadway.

Maria Irene Fornes wrote the book and lyrics and Al Carmines the music for a tale of two escaped convicts who more or less tour modern society in a series of encounters with eccentric people. With scenery (mainly bicycle wheels on poles) by Rouben Ter-Arutunian, costumes by Willa Kim, lighting by Jules Fisher, and orchestrations by Eddie Sauter, this was no thrift-shop trifle. Principals Ty McConnell and Gilbert Price (the convicts), Alice Playten, and Shannon Bolin had played leads on Broadway; and Madeline Kahn and George S. Irving were in it, too. In fact, *Promenade* really was a Broadway-sized entry that was genuinely offbeat in a confidently creative way. But wasn't *West Side Story*? *Fiddler on the Roof*?

Yes: but they weren't crazy. *Promenade* is crazy, like your favorite uncle who never married and would pass pungent remarks at the Thanksgiving table. Much of the fun stems from Fornes' making apparently harmless statements, inverting them, then drawing non sequitur conclusions. The actual titles of the songs don't sound weird—"Unrequited Love," "The Cigarette Song," "Chicken Is He," "Capricious and Fickle," "The Clothes Make the Man"—but their thought processes are. Carmines' music is enjoyable, yet he seems to be floating helplessly on the waves of Fornes' poetry, as if her lyrics were composing the music. He does it ably, perhaps because he had done it with Gertrude Stein's lyrics in *In Circles*, also off-Broadway, just two years earlier.

If *The Fantasticks* promulgated the one-of-a-kind show, *Little Mary Sunshine* inspired a brace of genre spoofs, all campy and sophomoric and, unlike *Little Mary*, targeting Hollywood. *O Say Can You See!* (1962) took a poke at forties wartime films, *We're Civilized?* (1962) at South Seas adventure, *Curley McDimple* (1967) at Shirley Temple Depression-tonic features. Only the last ran—for twenty-seven months—but it shows far more the spoof format's weaknesses than its strengths.

After all, these are literally *imitation* shows, often only feebly clever, throwing in every gag that occurs to the authors in hopes that at least some of them will go over. *Little Mary Sunshine* has consistency and an excellent sense of invention while it imitates. Its successors can be amazingly uneven. *Curley McDimple*'s villain, Miss Hamilton, obsessed with dragging little Curley off to the orphanage, is obviously modeled on *The Wizard of Oz*'s wicked witch, Margaret Hamilton. But other characters are just young or just there, with no clear generical mandate. Of course, there's a Bill Robinson, to dance with Curley on the usual bit of stairway, and such songs as "Dancing in the Rain" and "At the Playland Jamboree" are Shirley Temple tintypes. But dream sequences seem less echoes of old-movie tropes than attempts to pad out a thin evening. There are zany moments, as when Curley has a Snow White dream and the other six actors shuffle around on their knees with fake little shoes dangling, the seventh dwarf a cardboard dummy. But there are many less piquant moments. Even the best of these shows are revue sketches that go on too long. The strength of *Little Mary Sunshine* lay in its story and characters, embodiments of genre but also diverting on their own.

We're Civilized? was unusual in having an exceptional amount of dance, unusual because of the small stages that off-Broadway provided almost as a rule. At least the choreography (and much of the actual dancing) was by Bhaskar, who had finally got over the failure of *Christine*. Karen Black and Robert Fitch were among those present, and the show did stay open (just) long enough for Bhaskar's fans to make return visits. But the Ray Haney–Alfred Aiken score is now not even a memory: nothing vanishes as thoroughly as a flop *off*-Broadway musical.

O Say Can You See! flopped twice, for a revision, called *Buy Bonds, Buster* (1972), failed to reprieve the piece. That's unfortunate, for this one has a nice score. The Bill Conklin–Bob Miller–Jack Holmes songs summon up the worldview of a place and time in brand-new numbers, not only pastiche salutes. "Doughnuts For Defense" is something never tried in wartime film, the lament of an amateur baker who then proceeds to *sing* the unappreciated family recipe in toto. "Just the Way You Are" is the familiar "You're worthless yet I love you" duet, here distinguished by brilliantly dippy lyrics that no forties lyricist would have thought of. "The Dogface Jive" finds a redneck sergeant drilling his recruits with surprising tenderness. Then, underscored dialogue sets in for a little of the usual bullying:

SERGEANT: All right, you men, I want you to repeat after me: I'm a creampuff.

PRIVATES: You're a creampuff.

SERGEANT: No, maybe you didn't understand me right. Now, for your benefaction, I'll say it again: I'm a creampuff.

PRIVATES: We know.

There were also pure pastiche numbers: "Canteen Serenade," "Chico-Chico Chico-Layo Tico-Tico Pay-Pa-Payo Buena Vista de Banana-by-the-Sea," and the usual camp takeoff on a show-biz diva Doing Her Number, "Veronica Takes Over." Still, the overall effect was not of something old but of something new in the old style.

Yet the only work to rival *Little Mary Sunshine*'s success (eventually to outdo it in staying power) was something old, *Dames At Sea* (1968). This one revives the Warner Bros. thirties backstagers, with Ruby Keeler, Dick Powell, Joan Blondell, and Busby Berkeley's epic numbers, more special effects than dancing. The joke is that *Dames At Sea* does it with a cast of six, to two pianos and percussion.

George Haimsohn and Robin Miller wrote the book and lyrics, Jim Wise composed, and Neal Kenyon found the way to stage the tiny monster. *Dames At Sea* is directly comparable to *Curley McDimple* generically, with the mixture of good and poor jokes, the evocation of bygone forms without enlightening spin, the sheer raising of the dead. Take Dick's entrance. The starving Ruby faints just as he arrives. Catching her, he breaks right into a list song, "It's You." That's funny—but the lyrics try to rhyme "Jean Harlow" with "Greta Garbo" and "Richard Arlen" with "Spanky McFarland."

Meanwhile, the usual nasty diva for whom Ruby will eventually have to go on, Mona, has her "The Man I Love" rip-off, made of a repeating melody over a descending bass line, the ballad's Esperanto in the 1920s and 1930s. This is "That Mister Man Of Mine," a reasonably good example of the form. So, by now, we're aware that *Dames At Sea* stands between *Little Mary Sunshine* and *Curley McDimple*: not as unfailingly creative as the former but more intelligent than the latter. If nothing else, *Dames At Sea* was the show that put Bernadette Peters over (as Ruby) as the next available Broadway ingenue. This led her directly to Giulietta Masina's role of Gelsomina in the hapless *La Strada* (1969) but eventually to the defining Hildy in the Ron Field revival of *On the Town* in 1971.

One odd thing is that the miniature *Dames* works well as a big show. A television version in 1971 made it a spectacle. With Ann-Margret as Ruby, Harvey Evans as Dick, Anne Meara as Joan, and Dick Shawn as The Captain, this was uptown casting. And Ann Miller played Mona, a part that might well have been modeled on her. Not on characters she played. On *her*. "Wall Street," originally a solo, became a production number, with a full complement of boys and girls backing Miller in a tap festival framed by hanging ticker-tape ribbons; and "Star Tar," rivaled Eleanor Powell's battleship finale of *Born To Dance*. *Curley McDimple* couldn't be enlarged. The whole thing takes place in little more than a closet, anyway. And while *Little Mary Sunshine* might well absorb a full-

THE DECADE IN PICTURES

A PHOTO ESSAY

CURTAIN GOING UP!

Actually, *Hello Dolly's* first-act curtain is about to come down, on "Before the Parade Passes By," at one of Carol Channing's many tour dates. The extra-large stage has forced the company to spread out, losing the cramped, stuffing-the-thoroughfare feel of Gower Champion's New York parade.

Photos by Friedman-Abeles. Photos reprinted by permission of the Billy Rose Theatre Collection, The New York Public Library for the Performing Arts, Astor, Lenox and Tilden Foundations.

Boy Gets Girl remained mandatory in the 1960s, with a few exceptions. Barbara Cook and Walter Chiari go "Rain in Spain" in *The Gay Life*'s "Who Can? You Can!"

Then Boy (Richard Kiley) does not Get Girl (Diahann Carroll) in *No Strings*. The mixed-race romance of this show cues in the growing sixties realism.

And what are we to make of *Mame*'s Angela Lansbury and Beatrice Arthur, in "Bosom Buddies"? Mame has her Beau and nephew Patrick, but her platonic romance with actress Vera Charles (Arthur) may well be *Mame*'s most enjoyable throughline. Note the liquor, which flows so freely that revivals should consider interpolating the "Drinking Song" from *The Student Prince*.

Dance was as strategic as ever. In this photo, we bring you Forbidden Broadway circa 1960, in a ballet cut from *Camelot*, "The Enchanted Forest."

Lansbury, in fox-hunt black, gives us another look at *Mame*, in the title number.

The Star Entrance remained good showmanship. Now Lansbury's in *Dear World*, coming up through an open manhole in a shot taken during tryouts. Immediately around her are juggler Ted Agress, café waiter Michael Kermoyan (who played a different role on Broadway), ingenue Pamela Hall, and tiresome mime Miguel Godreau.

Because he was the sole director of only three musicals, Moss Hart fails to make the short list of innovators. Still, in *My Fair Lady* and *Camelot*, he developed the musical integrated not only in composition but in staging. Everything is in one style—décor, dancing, the way the actors move across the stage: all matched. Here, Julie Andrews leads the ensemble in "The Lusty Month of May," a rare production number in which the big dance *precedes* the vocal. Thus, Hart (and choreographer Hanya Holm) can establish Arthur's court kinetically before Alan Jay Lerner rings in his Ironies.

Even conventional musical comedy adapted to the new power of the director. *The Gay Life*, with Loring Smith, Walter Chiari, Jules Munshin, Barbara Cook, and Lu Leonard at center, never quite conjoined the stylized Viennese elegance with the Broadway fun.

But *Tenderloin* anticipated the abstract spaces of the concept show. Here, pastor Maurice Evans reads the Bible in his study while all New York devours his scandal, together in one "place."

Another sixties invention is the Big Lady Show. Here's more of *Mame*, as Angela Lansbury models the biggest wardrobe in Broadway history. For "It's Today," she's in pajamas.

There were no Big Man Shows, but the musical's gay subtext—so encoded in, say, Cole Porter's lyrics—became overt in the 1960s, paving the road to *Falsettoland* and *Kiss of the Spider Woman*. Here, devastating redhead James Corbett alarms Travis Hudson in *New Faces of 1962*. Leonard Sillman, who was in show biz as far back as the national tour of *Lady, Be Good!* (in Fred Astaire's role) in 1926 when still a teenager, started producing the *New Faces* shows in 1934 and waited over twenty-five years to dare this stunt. The musical had had beefcake moments before, but never one so deliciously gratuitous.

If *Camelot* concludes the previous era, of the Rodgers and Hammerstein "musical play," *Cabaret* initiates the next era. Ironically, *Cabaret* drew partly on energies released by the most Rodgers and Hammersteinian musical play of all, *Allegro*. But *Cabaret* also looked toward the Sondheim-Prince masterworks of the 1970s.

This show contains everything. First, *Cabaret* has Fabulous Opening Number.

Second, *Cabaret* has yet more Forbidden Broadway, as we reveal Jill Haworth's kewpie doll look in Boston. Here she offers an engagement gift to Lotte Lenya and Jack Gilford.

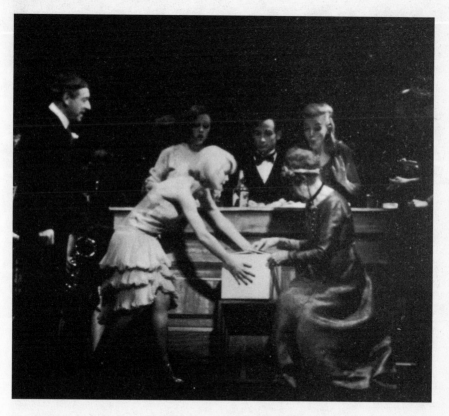

Photo by L. Arnold Weissberger, courtesy of Jay Harris.

Cabaret has violence, when Bert Convy smashes Nazi George Reinholt (who succeeded Edward Winter as Ernst).

And *Cabaret* has cabaret, with Haworth now in the dark wig and loose-lady satin that Hal Prince imposed on her. (Who's that cute gypsy trying to sneak costar placement into our shot?)

Last, we offer the immortal Lenya in rehearsal. This adorable beldam sang in only three American book shows, once every ten years. Moreover, she really made her name as Kurt Weill's widow and as a movie grotesque. Yet she remains one of the twentieth century's great musical personalities. She *is* cabaret.

sized chorus and elaborate décor, it would then seem like just another old show instead of a loony dream of long ago.

Clearly, there were differences between the Broadway and off-Broadway styles of musical besides the obvious one of cost. By the mid-1960s, a good-sized uptown show ran about $500,000. There were no good-sized off-Broadway musicals; but a typical offering ran to about $15,000.

So costs were very low; so were profits. One couldn't make a living as an off-Broadway actor. But more than a few people found themselves trapped in the little forms for reasons that are not readily explainable. Bernadette Peters, we know, climbed out easily. But Elmarie Wendel, a gifted singing comic, never seemed able to break free of her *Little Mary Sunshine–O Say!* haunt, and others found themselves comparably typed.

Another off-Broadway quality was the "small" quality of the score. Part of this was the small accompaniment; but more of this was the limited compositional style. Some scores sound like the shows written by and for college students, with simplistic harmony and obvious lyric hooks. This was especially true not only of the pastiche shows but of our fourth off-Broadway genre, the Adaptation of an Ancient Play.

Once again, there is a founding title, *Ernest in Love* (1960), from Oscar Wilde's *The Importance of Being Earnest*. Generally, the sources were much older: Goldsmith's *She Stoops To Conquer* for *O Marry Me!* (1961), Sheridan's *The Rivals* for *All in Love* (1961), Molière for *'Toinette* (1961) and *The Amorous Flea* (1964), Thomas Dekker for *Shoemaker's Holiday* (1967). James M. Barrie and Ashley Dukes got a look in, too. But the most typical shows seemed happiest in wigs and tights.

Ernest in Love is one of many settings of Wilde's "trivial comedy for serious people." *Oh, Ernest!* (1927) played Broadway; every ten years or so after World War II brought some new adaptation for summer stock; and a German version, *Mein Freund Bunbury*, debuted in Berlin in 1964. *Bunbury* includes a full-sized chorus, updates the action to the 1920s, makes of Jack and Cecily soldiers in the Salvation Army, and offers such songs as "Piccadilly," "Die Upper Ten," and "Ein Bisschen Horror und ein Bisschen Sex." In short: a transformation in the truest sense.

Ernest in Love is slavish. Its tunestack reassures any Wilde buff: Lady Bracknell's "A Handbag Is Not a Proper Mother," Chasuble's "Metaphorically Speaking," Jack and Algernon's "The Muffin Song," all right off the

Victorian page. Lee Pockriss and Anne Croswell, with *Tovarich* yet in their destiny, were the authors. They did an effective job of making music while strictly construing Wilde. But is that necessary?

Similarly, Jacques Urbont and Bruce Geller respected *The Rivals* so well that they actually created a number for Mrs. Malaprop (Mimi Randolph), "A More Than Ordinary Glorious Vocabulary." Alas, they also created one for Bob Acres (Dom DeLuise) in "Odds," a comedy song so stupid that even George S. Irving would have refused to do it.

Another faithful adaptation of a nineteenth-century play—yet far more creative in its fidelity than *Ernest in Love*—was *The Streets of New York* (1963). There was a hint of the silliness of the genre spoofs in this work's tone, making it almost a crossover piece. The source, Dion Boucicault's 1857 melodrama *The Sidewalks of New York*,* does not of course offer the musical genres, plot hooks, and dialogue clichés one finds ready to wear in twenties musical comedy or Busby Berkeley backstagers. Still, Barry Alan Grael and his composer, Richard B. Chodosh, leer amusingly at *their* genre's contrivances as surely as *The Boy Friend* and *Dames At Sea* do at theirs.

So, for example, Boucicault's pure-good-versus-pure-evil landscapes, bizarre coincidences, instant moral conversions, synoptically confessional asides, great jumps in chronology, cries of "Villain," and touches of obsolete daily life (as in the viewing of stereopticon slides) are not only preserved but lampooned. Here's a taste of *The Streets of New York*'s first minute. The bad guy tosses exposition like confetti to the angry roar of a crowd outside:

> BLOODGOOD: Listen to that mob, clamoring for their deposits. How did they get wind of the fact that my bank is failing? Somebody talked! How do they expect me to cover? They're *forcing* me to take what's left and run! Luckily I came to the bank today ready to travel. If only I can keep them out of here. They'll have my head. I hope those oak doors from that German cathedral are as strong as they look.

---

*An adaptation of a French piece, Edouard Brisebarre and Eugène Nus' *Les Pauvres de Paris*, Boucicault's play was also called *The Poor of New York*, closer to the original French title. Confusingly, the British version of Boucicault's script was billed as *The Streets of London*, and revivals of the American version sometimes called themselves *The Streets of New York*. Like *Twelfth Night*, the work became two off-Broadway musicals in the 1960s, the other being *The Banker's Daughter* (1962).

It's as if Boucicault has given Grael and Chodosh so much plot to develop that they will simply cram it all in, seeking not unity but antique camp.

Call the show faithful in a devious way. The score matches the script, reveling in character pieces for implausible characters or piling on the quodlibets, syncopations, non sequiturs, and an extremely complex first-act finale. It is a truly funny score, as in "Tourist Madrigal," a laugh at the rudeness of New Yorkers. The aforementioned scene with the stereopticon is a love duet for the pure-hearted couple, Mark Livingstone (David Cryer) and Lucy Fairweather (Gail Johnston), "Aren't You Warm?" It ripples with exotic heat and the snap of finger cymbals (they're taking in views of India), yet is punctuated by laments from poor Mrs. Fairweather (Margot Hand), because someone opened a window and she's freezing. So it's a comedy number, yet its descending triplet that blossoms into an upward-rushing $^4/_4$ exclamation outlines a most unusual melody, the kind that, sitting in the theatre, one looks forward to hearing again on the cast album.

All the score plays thus, surprising and tuneful and so clever that it's a lot to take in at once. Though it ran 318 performances on excellent notices, it has not taken root the way *Little Mary Sunshine* and *Dames At Sea* have. Nor has John Clifton and Ben Tarver's *Man With a Load of Mischief* (1966), from Ashley Dukes' late-Victorian comedy. Clifton and Tarver were just as faithful as other authors in this genre, but their source was little more than a footnote by 1966, giving them a kind of prefabricated novelty. The six-character layout is a little too symmetrical—lord and lady, their two servants, two innkeepers—but the cast was unusually good. The Lady, Virginia Vestoff, was headed for a lead in *1776*; and Lord Raymond Thorne and servant Reid Shelton would meet again in *Annie*, as F.D.R. and Daddy Warbucks.

The score is uneven, with an irritatingly "touching" solo for servant Alice Cannon in "Little Rag Doll" and various floppo moments here and there. But the good numbers are very, very good. Better, one can visualize these performers singing this music on Broadway, had the authors decided to open Dukes up. Vestoff's establishing piece, "Goodbye, My Sweet," drips with honeyed irony to a clipped accompaniment, and her "Lover Lost" tenders unusually deep feelings for these so often precious little versions of old plays. (One sometimes wondered if the motivation for this entire genre was the fact that most of the source material lay in the public domain and thus could be "optioned" for free.) Raymond Thorne lacked a solo, perhaps to underline this Lord's lack of substance. But Shelton's two solos were star turns—the triumphant "Make Way For My Lady" and the angry "Come To the Masquerade." The latter, sung as Shelton made his way to Vestoff's bed to seduce her in disguise, encapsulates the show's overall distaste for deception and etiquette, its love of honesty and democracy. Lo, the manservant is the hero, tasting the bitterness of this forced impersonation in a sharply turned line, "Come as you like, but not as you are."

One thing that off-Broadway never lacked in the 1960s was satiric revues. A very few ran—*The Mad Show* (1966), for instance, in the style of the boys' humor magazine, with music by Mary Rodgers. But countless others shut down in weeks, even days. Barbra Streisand's first professional stage role was in a disaster lasting one night, *Another Evening With Harry Stoones* (1961). In fact, off-Broadway was where the variety show came to die. We've met up with two such on The Street, *From A To Z* and *Show Girl*. There were no others,* except two editions of Leonard Sillman's *New Faces*.

The 1962 *New Faces* was a horror. This series was supposed to introduce newcomers of major gifts, in material by the brightest writers. True, the early editions, in the 1930s, sometimes preserved used faces. (Imogene Coca appeared in the 1934 *and* 1936 entries; and the Duncan Sisters, très veteran by then, got into 1936 near the end of its run.) But Tyrone Power, Eve Arden, Henry Fonda, Van Johnson, and Alice Pearce were among Sillman's "discoveries," and the extremely high quality of *New Faces of 1952*, with Broadway debutants, solidified the series as a showcase for important new talent.

The contributors to 1962 were Sillman devotees, but the sketches were lame and the songs putrid. The usual grand spoof for the first-act finale,

---

*Some people think A *Thurber Carnival* (1960) was a musical, possibly because it got a cast album. No: it was all spoken, with interludes and bits by the Don Elliott jazz group. The show's success did invite the creation of another Thurber revue that *was* a musical, *The Beast In Me* (1963), with music by Elliott. Based on Thurber's *Fables For Our Time*, *The Beast In Me* offered Kaye Ballard, Richard Hayes, Allyn Ann McLerie, Bert Convy, and its lyricist, James Costigan, as hippos, moths, and such. It ran 4 performances. *Oh, Calcutta* ran forever—and some think this one, too, is a musical, because of a cast album. Now hear this: plays without vocal scores are not musicals. *Swan Lake* is not a musical. *Contact* is not a musical. Anyone who thinks otherwise is an illiterate idiot. Now, back to our story.

"Johnny Mishuga," was an Israeli western, with songs like "My Son the Marshall" and digs at *Milk and Honey*. It wasn't a bad idea, perhaps, but everything lies in the execution, and the execution failed. Marian Mercer sang "Freedomland," the complaint of a girl who wanted to go to the amusement park of that name (in the Bronx) and wound up on a southern civil-rights bus ride. Walter Kerr called the show "a disgrace," and it's amazing that it lasted 28 performances. Few knew that the cast harbored a graduate of *New Faces of 1956*, Jimmy Sisco. Appearing under a family name as James Corbett, he got his second chance mainly because he was a devastating redhead who was more than willing to come onstage in the briefest of Speedos to flex his biceps at a startled Travis Hudson, in a sketch lampooning high-tech beauty salons.

New Faces of 1968, though it lasted a bit longer, marked a return to form, barely. The familiar opening, "You've Never Seen Us Before," was rocked, and there was a lot of dithering fill. Worse, Sillman's just-made-it budget allowed only for a unit set of a living room, as Sillman pretended that the show was a backer's audition for itself.

But the cast included Madeline Kahn and Robert Klein; and the take-offs had wit. "Hullabaloo at Thebes" was a kind of swinging *Oedipus Rex*, with a wicked couplet at its heart. "He used to have eyes for his mother," it began. "But now he just used to have eyes." Kahn got the top spot, in what may be the best number ever written for a *New Faces*. It is certainly the best-ever spoof of Brecht-Weill: "Das Chicago Song" (by Michael Cohen and Tony Geiss). It's a blend of "Surabaja Johnny" and "Moon of Alabama," but, more, it's a demolition that could be brought off only by those who love the style. Sadly, *1968* was the last *New Faces*.

If off-Broadway claimed the variety revue from Broadway, it also invented the next exploitable revue form and sent it back to Broadway for our fifth genre, the Songwriter Anthology. *A Party With Betty Comden and Adolph Green* introduced this form on Broadway, true enough, in 1958. However, Comden and Green had been performers as well as authors, and were presenting their own material. The true Songwriter Anthology offers young people interpreting the work of older writers. Cole Porter and Leonard Bernstein were the first subjects, in 1965. Noel Coward joined them in 1968, and the following years turned a flurry into a storm—Porter, Bernstein, and Coward yet again, then Kurt Weill and the Gershwins, and others till the flash hit *Ain't Misbehavin'* (1978) moved from the Manhattan Theatre Club in its old home in the East Seventies (where *Man With a Load of Mischief* played) to Broadway.

This established the anthology format on The Street, where it has remained ever since, throwing off titles even on choreographers (*Jerome Robbins' Broadway, Fosse*). However, for many, the true breakthrough arrived in another of those tiny shows, but one devoted to new music, new to us. It was four singers, piano and drums. It ran and ran and developed a cult till, finally, even your Aunt Laura wants to go, even to the Village Gate: *Jacques Brel Is Alive and Well and Living in Paris* (1968).

Spurred, perhaps, by the Belgian writer-performer's Carnegie Hall concert in 1966, Eric Blau and Mort Shuman translated twenty-five of Brel's chansons, devising clever parallels for his sometimes untranslatable wordplay. Brel's songs are an odd lot, now romantic, now filled with social critique, now both at once. Moreover, they are given over to curious phrases that invade a song and nest there till, as the song concludes, the phrases become the song.

There had never been anyone like him. The closest I can come to describing Brel's style is: Edith Piaf writing Brecht-Weill to be sung by the title character of Jarry's *Father Ubu*, moonlighting as a vampire. Even that covers only about 8 percent of what Brel was. Blau and Shuman avoided for the most part Brel's most twisted songs, such as "Casse Ponpon," which starts as a comedy and closes as a savage attack on German militarism. No, in New York the concept of "Jacques Brel" was devoted to wistful-zany character pieces—"Jackie," "Mathilde" (in which a boy reconciles with his girl and the earth explodes), "Fanette," "Timid Frieda," "Funeral Tango" (sung by the deceased), "Madeleine."

Some of Brel's social criticism was heard, in "The Middle Class" and "The Bulls," with its running gag about who empowered grocers and English ladies imagine themselves to be on the day of the corrida—García Lorca, Carmen, and so on. But the main thing was the sheer novelty of the man. After all, there are just so many shows to be made out of the already familiar material of classic songwriters. Pop music had evolved, in the work of, say, Bob Dylan and the Beatles, to a level of great imaginative power. But even they could not create character the way Brel could.

Then, too, the space of two hours of Brel's art gave his interpreters a lot of "there" to work in. *Jacques Brel* popularized not only the Songwriter Anthology but a performing style we might call Cabaret Mannerist. Over the show's four-and-a-half-year run, many of the original and succeeding cast members were "vivid" and "unstinting" to their fans, "exaggerated" and even "twisted" to their detractors.

I take no sides. Let me state simply that the original cast was Elly Stone, Shawn Elliott, Alice Whitfield, and co-translator Shuman, that their replacements included June Gable, Robert Guillaume, Joe Masiell, Fleury D'Antonakis (of *Do I Hear a Waltz?*), Rita Gardner (of *The Fantasticks* and *A Family Affair*), John C. Attle, and George Lee Andrews, and that Stone and Masiell headed a limited engagement on Broadway at the Royale in the fall of 1972. Jacques Brel himself caught the piece then, though he disliked having to come to the United States, because like all the French he had no use for Americans except when we're bailing them out of World War I and World War II. We are told that he liked the show.

12

LOOK AROUND YOUR LITTLE WORLD

THE DARK SHOW

"Write colored," Sammy Davis told William Gibson. *Golden Boy* (1964) was in Boston Trouble, mainly because Charles Strouse and Lee Adams had written their fine score to a book not quite by Clifford Odets, based on his 1937 tragedy about a reluctant boxer. Odets had died *before*, and some other hands had cobbled him together *during*, and now Gibson was being asked to fix the script *just in time*.

Golden Boy told of one of American society's low-level guys who gets a chance and really could but then won't. In 1937, that guy was Italian. In 1969, that guy was black. It's the perfect Sammy Davis part; but the show as a whole must reflect the social background. So why was it directed by Peter Coe, the Englishman who staged *Oliver!* and *Pickwick*? These crazy Broadway deals.

Director Arthur Penn was brought in along with Gibson, who received the call less for his playwrighting expertise (on *Two For the Seesaw* and *The Miracle Worker*, not to mention an off-Broadway musical, *Dinny and the Witches*) than for his close friendship with Odets. And Gibson could indeed write colored. *Golden Boy* has a remarkable book—very, very lean and taut, just like the fighter that Sammy was playing. Aggressive, jumpy, a very boxing ring of a libretto in which everyone, from the money thugs and managers down to the fans, is fighting all the time. The script is also clearly aware that *Golden Boy* was presenting the first meaningful interracial romance in the musical.

Yes, Lena Horne and Ricardo Montalban were paired in *Jamaica* in 1957; but they were both supposed to be black, and in any case nobody said anything, so it didn't matter. There were similar combinations in *Flower Drum Song*; but almost nobody was playing his own race, so it also didn't matter. *Kwamina?* The lovers scarcely touched, and ultimately parted; and in *No Strings* race wasn't even mentioned till the very last scene. And still the lovers parted.

Golden Boy, however, strode forth boldly, coupling Sammy with the whitest woman ever seen, Paula Wayne, and featuring them embracing in the poster logo. Odets' original play is a tragedy, and so is the musical version. But the latter is more compelling, because the songs develop these difficult characters, explain why their needs have driven them to odd alliances—Sammy's with a crooked bully who wants to cut out Sammy's manager, and Paula Wayne's with the manager when she really loves Sammy. For once, race is not a problem. *People* are:

> LORNA: Joe, there's been a lot of men, went through me like—traffic in the tunnel, and the twice I was in love I took an awful beating, and he [the manager]—what he did—was pick me out of my filth, and wash my face and comb my—And once I tried to leave him, he drank some—
> (She is weeping.)
> —misery reached out to misery—Joe dear, you know that, in your own heart I *know* you know that—
> JOE: (Pause) I'll call Eddie [the crook] off.
> (He turns away, to the river.) Oh Christ, white or black, why's it so hard?
>
> · · ·
>
> Lorna, when I'm not with you I—*bleed*, I got a hole bleeding in my side nothing can stop but being with you because the other half is you, rotten, beautiful, the other half is you!—and I'm here on my feet, bleeding—for you—
> (His hand is out for her. Slowly she comes to it, black and white hands clasp, and the song begins.)

The song, "I Want To Be With You," is like all the others in the show, matching the book, amplifying it, articulating the softness that hard people are unwilling to show. Heavy with worry, the score is nevertheless full of hope, just as Sammy is till all goes awry in a knotty way and Sammy finds a simple solution in suicide. "Night Song" establishes the hero in a pensive mood. "Stick Around," to an ebullient Latin beat that grows emphatic as the lyrics do, is outstanding as a wedding of Sammy's natural style with how Strouse and Adams view the character. "Don't Forget 127th Street" is a neighborhood fiesta, especially comic when the on-the-rise Sammy says he'll miss the old place: "I'll miss it every chance I get!"

Like *Funny Girl* and *Flora, the Red Menace, Golden Boy* offered that somewhat rare chance for an exceptionally gifted singer to fill our ears with his or her music while playing a character in a book show. Yes, a Cesare Siepi or an Alfred Drake is a great pleasure; but that's opera, operetta. We want to hear *our* singers in *our* sound.

It was a fine production, too. Here's another great opening. No overture; the curtain rose on darkness. A spotlight picked up a boxer training. The drums imitated his grunts and wheezes, and, as he chanted some terse safety reminder, a second spotlight revealed another boxer hitting the heavy bag. He, too, was chanting, about the money he'll make on his next bout. A third boxer came into view skipping rope, then more men, all chanting, till a whistle pierced the space and the lights shrieked on and six boxers broke into three separate fights, reaching three K.O.s in a blast of violence. Then it all fell away, people entered, we were in a gym. Sammy asked his manager, "Where's my dough?" and the play was on.

At 569 performances, *Golden Boy* is our longest-running show so far not to pay off. But *Kelly* (1965) is the shortest, the first musical ever to close on opening night. This led many to assume that it was the worst musical ever produced. Walter Kerr called it "a bad idea gone wrong"; Howard Taubman wrote, "Ella Logan was written out of *Kelly* before it reached the Broadhurst Theatre on Saturday night. Congratulations, Miss Logan."

True, *Kelly* isn't a good show. Nor does it have a good score. It is, however, an unusual show, not another feeble mediocrity. It certainly went wrong during its frenzied let's-try-anything tryout, but it wasn't a bad idea. Its authors, composer Moose Charlap and word man Eddie Lawrence, had in mind an extravagant look at immigrant-Irish culture in late-nineteenth-century New York, centering on a feisty anti-hero who keeps trying and failing to jump off the Brooklyn Bridge. From back alleys to the headline makers' posh restaurant, from family ties to twisted friends, from his childhood sweetheart to tourists Frank and Jesse James (who plan to rob a bank during the latest jump), *Kelly* was to slice up life in an artful realism. The songs belonged to no established genre, and most of them included dollops of spoken lines, as if the characters were ad-libbing. Some of the lyrics had the quality of the arcane accusations that street loons scream at passing strangers.

The characters were all more or less flawed, even the mother that Ella Logan played out of town. The protagonist, Hop Kelly (Don Francks), got on one's nerves with his bluster, and others of the mostly male principals were scoundrels and cheats. Kelly's girl (Anita Gillette) was sweet, but her father, Stickpin Sidney Crane (Jesse White), was all for doing grave harm to Kelly while substituting a dummy for him in the next jump, thus to guarantee Kelly's dive and clean up in the betting. The only other woman lead after Logan was Eileen Rodgers, as a fancy dame who smokes a cigar and wants to be one of the guys.

At least Rodgers had the one song, "That Old Time Crowd," that is nearly enjoyable. *Kelly*'s is not a dull score: it's too strange to bore. It opens with Kelly's solo, "Ode To the Bridge." The curtain rises and he just comes out and starts . . . well, eructating in awe is one way to put it. It isn't really a melody. Nor is "Heavyweight Champ of the World," which sounds like a lot of people shouting one thing over and over. It's probably supposed to sound thus; but that's no excuse. The cut "Augie Masters' " is a restaurateur's patter song in praise of his place. It may be terrible, but at least it's breathless. Anita Gillette's second-act love song was "Ballad To a Brute," a salute to the sexual appeal of her bit of rough. She actually calls him a "snake" and a "bastard." But he's all man, it seems. The main other almost nearly enjoyable song, also cut, was the James Boys' "The Big Town," on the dangers of New York life ("a poet ran amuck"), set as a vaudeville duet with interpolated jokes.

Kelly's book is strange, too. When Kelly Senior makes a scene while defending his son, bystander Frank James rolls a cigarette and offers an opinion:

FRANK: Filial, Very filial. I remember *my* old man when Jesse tried to slug me one night from behind. Yuh know what Pop did? Shot Jesse inna back. Yesirree—damn near killed 'im. (Laughs.) Strong filial obligation. Runs in small families.

In the end, Kelly outsmarted the bad guys and made the jump. Director-choreographer Herbert Ross found a way to stage that, on Oliver Smith's clever catwalk set, and, as virtually the entire cast looked on, Francks tossed his derby, struck a pose, and leaped into the orchestra pit as the lights blacked out. Presently, a great *splash!* was rendered.

Charlap and Lawrence always maintained that *Kelly*'s unanimously bad reviews were the result of the producers' panicky "improvements." But the show is too odd ever to have succeeded in any form. It is an attempt, however flawed, to create something new, yes: it has a coherence that many successful shows lack. Its songs *sound* like the bizarre characters singing them; their very lack of glamour is why *Kelly* itself didn't have any.

Much less singular was *A Time For Singing* (1966), a show one might easily have anticipated: a setting of a well-liked novel about a big Welsh coal-mining family, Richard Llewellyn's *How Green Was My Valley*. There's plenty of feeling in it, ready for music. But here's another dark show, filled with death and despair and, more broadly, an exploited working class that has no future but to continue being exploited. In fact, though John Ford's 1941 movie version is inspiring despite all the disasters, Llewellyn's novel is a catalogue of tragedies that ends in utmost loneliness.

The novel is narrated by the youngest son in the Morgan family, Huw, but *A Time For Singing*'s authors, John Morris and Gerald Freedman, hoped to qualify the tragic ending by bringing two lovers together. They made a grown man, not the boy, the protagonist. That's sensible. Still, it takes the magic out of the tale. Huw's view of his ugly world is innocent, redemptive. Morris and Freedman's hero, the town minister, is smart; his view is knowing, and so we're stuck with all the awful facts of this life: the disgracefully underpaid and unspeakably dangerous mining work, the looting collusion of the mine owners, the ignorance of the men, and the helplessness of the women.

Right—another sixties musical that is bound to deflate even as it tries to inspire. A flop, too—41 performances. Its producer, Alexander Cohen, must have thought the Morris-Freedman score would carry it, for this is one of the decade's supreme achievements, a melodious, dramatic, and thrilling Big Sing that reminds us why operetta never quite vanished after its era had ended. There is nothing like a good story told with the power of opera; and this one has it.

There is plenty of choral singing, as the Welsh setting demands, in the grandly divided choirs with the intense high soprano and tenor lines that the 1960s loved. There is many a dirge, too, and those anthems sung by characters using music to assuage their pain. Comedy and charm songs are scarce. But then, there are too many people to delineate, in groups wherever possible. There is the Morgan family—Dada (Laurence Naismith, *Here's Love*'s Santa Claus); mother Beth (Tessie O'Shea); their five older sons and Huw (Frank Griso); their daughter, Angharad (Shani Wallis); and there are Bronwen Jenkins (Elizabeth Hubbard), in love with one of the Morgan boys; and Iestyn Evans (David O'Brien), son of the mine owner and Angharad's husband-to-be, though she loves the minister.

That's a lot of characters for one score to handle. Illustrating family life, the labor troubles at the mine, and the various marriages and deaths while trying to get something out of young Huw left Morris and Freedman with twenty-three separate numbers (besides reprises). It sometimes seemed as though characters had barely started speaking again before the orchestra was introducing the next number, common enough now but a novelty in 1966.

There may have been simply too much music for the critics to take in. The closer a work gets to opera, the farther it strays from the average American ear. This score was so big that the first male chorus, "Come You Men," served as a prelude as the houselights went down, and the minister's immediately following "How Green Was My Valley" begins on an upward-leaping ninth, that most ambitious and least employed of vocal intervals. (We recall Frank Loesser's use of it, somewhat comparably, on the third and fourth words of *Greenwillow*'s "The Music of Home.") It is true that Tessie O'Shea's entrance, to lead the ensemble in "What a Good Day Is Saturday," smacked of musical comedy simply because of the way O'Shea had entertained in *The Girl Who Came To Supper*. It is also true that Wallis' waltzing "When He Looks At Me" is a cliché, however pretty; and that young Frank Griso had such odd diction that it was difficult to follow him. These are flaws, no doubt. But the delicacy of the minister's "That's What Young Ladies Do," which Angharad thinks is a love song and he thinks is a character number; the almost psalm-like beauty of "Far From Home" and the caroling "Three Ships"; indeed, the great stack of deeply felt and fiercely sung ballads and choruses built this show not out of a balance of the traditional elements but almost entirely out of singing alone.

One might think that as well of *The Yearling* (1965), another adaptation of a beloved book and film about a boy's coming-of-age. This show, too, failed. Yet it threw off a slew of singles, including four by Barbra Streisand. For years, this show's numbers were staples of the audition room—"Why Did I Choose You?," "The Kind of Man a Woman Needs," "My Pa" (though this was cut), "I'm All Smiles," "One Promise Come True (he bought me a dress)," "Some Day I'm Gonna Fly," "Everything in the World I Love."

Yet *The Yearling* is no Big Sing. There is little chorus work, and the Michael Leonard–Herbert Martin songs are tidy little pieces, with almost no story context. Hearing the seven titles cited above, one would hardly guess them to be the vocal core of a show based on Marjorie Kinnan Rawlings' book, which is if anything loaded with context. In the Florida wilderness of the late nineteenth century, the little Baxter family tends a farm in poverty, contends with unscrupulous neighbors and a marauding bear, and allows young Jody to adopt an orphaned fawn. Yes, it's cute: but it eats their crops and must be killed. Jody's one friend, the whimsical Fodder-Wing, dies as well. In an odd exchange of gender stereotypes, Jody's father is sweet and forgiving, his mother tough and relentless.

It's even bleaker than *How Green Was My Valley*. But Rawling's rustic minstrelsy is beguiling, and the musical is as faithful as the movie. However, unlike *A Time For Singing*'s ecstatic chorale, *The Yearling*'s string of pop tunes cannot atone for the wicked turns of plot. Worse, producer Lore Noto and lyricist Martin co-wrote a book that could not possibly show what happens. The fawn, the bear, several dogs . . . why not just do a musical based on the Bronx Zoo?

In the days when shows previewed out of town as a rule, some of them went desperate for good notices and heavy ticket sales, having reached the limits of their budget just getting into costume and onto a dressed stage. *The Yearling*'s money was so tight that it began performances only partly orchestrated, and it had to come into New York earlier than scheduled. David Wayne and Dolores Wilson as Jody's parents were not names to attract many customers, so the critics had to bless the show. They didn't, and *The Yearling*, which opened on a Friday, played Saturday and closed.

At least *The Yearling* came in: a musical version of William Inge's *Picnic* gave up in Boston. It deserved to. *Hot September* (1965) had a book by Paul Osborn and a score by Kenneth Jacobson and Rhoda Roberts and was directed by Joshua Logan. Osborn was a playwright not known for expertise in musicals; Jacobson and Roberts were not known. But Logan had directed *Picnic* both as play and movie. Moreover, though Leland Hayward was the show's producer, David Merrick was Hayward's not entirely silent partner, and Merrick kept close links to Logan, who had directed Merrick's first hit, *Fanny*. (It was a nuance of the complexly creative-destructive Merrick psychology that he felt loyal to everyone connected with *Fanny* and always tried to Do It to anyone else first.) Yet *Hot September* was an amateurish mess with an almost off-Broadway cast and a largely floppo score. Why on earth did pros like Logan, Hayward, and Merrick ever agree to go ahead with it?

First of all, here was another "serious" subject, and that's what was happening in this decade. Fewer *How To Succeeds* were under option; more *Picnics* were. *Picnic*: drifter blows small town apart with his alpha-male power and runs off with local belle. The supplementary couple is an odd one, he a ditherer and she a phallic woman who would rather be dead than not married. They were Eddie Bracken and *Riverwind's* Lovelady Powell; but the belle was hard to cast, as ingenues so often seem to be. Kathryn Hays played the rehearsals, but Sheila Sullivan replaced her in Boston.

John Stewart played the nice college boy left in the lurch by the belle; like Bracken, he was sound professional casting. Stewart was one of the few kid actors who held Broadway right through adolescence into manhood. You enjoyed his Junior in *High Button Shoes* and *Love Life*, thrilled to his Chulalongkorn in *The King and I*. The drifter was a problem. This character is a boor, a braggart, and a loser who never stops trying to make it and only gets there—always momentarily—on sex appeal. William Holden, in the movie, is fakey Hollywood casting; Holden twenty years earlier would have played the college boy. Onstage, Ralph Meeker was perfect, unbearable yet magnetic. But how to put this guy into music? *Sondheim* couldn't. This man is beyond music.

Sean Garrison was hired, and did his best, but he was wrong and so was everything else. Jacobson and Roberts never caught Powell's man-hungry—really, marriage-hungry—intensity. (See Rosalind Russell in the film—in her greatest acting job ever—then try to imagine what songs this woman would sing.) Garrison and Bracken had a duet called "I Got It Made" that makes no sense—these two have nothing to sing together about, and neither has it made. "This Town" suggests a socially integrated community that Inge would not have recognized. "Show Me Where the Good Times Are" is a pathetic attempt to create a hit tune. When the authors played Powell's vapid $^6/_8$ happiness march, "Goodbye, Girls," for Leland Hayward, did Hayward ask them—as Hal Prince unfailingly did when he heard work of this caliber—"What high-school production did you intend that for?"

The trend toward formerly unlikely sources did create a hit here and there—*Fiddler on the Roof* is a fine example, but so is *Man of La Mancha* (1965). This is dark not so much because of its source, Cervantes' *Don Quixote*, but because book writer Dale Wasserman was more interested in Cervantes than in *Don Quixote*. Cervantes' highly vagabond life took in jail time and excommunication, and Wasserman brought into his script the terror of the Spanish Inquisition, in the form of a great drawbridge from on high to be lowered into Howard Bay's unit set of a prison common room, and in the person of black-clad and hooded men, officers of religious oppression. Every time the bridge came down, it was to add a prisoner to the jail or take one to judgment, and Wasserman wasted no time in making clear how helpless the prisoners are, whether thieves or nonconformists.

Man of La Mancha begins with Cervantes' arrival in the prison:

CAPTAIN OF THE GUARD: The cells are below. This is the common room,
　　for those who wait.
CERVANTES: How long do they wait?
CAPTAIN OF THE GUARD: Some an hour . . . some a lifetime.

For Wasserman, a musical *Don Quixote* would be no more than a satiric fairy tale. But a musical Cervantes would give us one of Western Civilization's heroes in a true story:

CERVANTES: I have lived nearly fifty years, and I have seen life as it is. Pain, misery, hunger . . . cruelty beyond belief . . . I have been a soldier and seen my comrades fall in battle. . . . These were men who saw life as it is, yet they died despairing. No glory, no gallant last words . . . only their eyes filled with confusion, whimpering the question: "Why?" I do not think they asked why they were dying, but why they had lived.

So *Man of La Mancha*'s protagonist is Cervantes, using the prisoners to enact the story of *Don Quixote* while the terror looms above and the drawbridge is lowered three times—at the start, as we have just seen; in the middle, to drag away some unknown unfortunate; and at the end, for Cervantes.

Surely this is our darkest show yet. The others had crime or death; this one has totalitarian oppression of individuals, a theme that the musical, to my knowledge, had never before tackled as directly as here. Keep in mind that the prison is no mere frame. The prison is the show's setting; the *Don Quixote* adventure is its decoration; and Cervantes' challenge to stand up to the torture chambers of the Inquisition is the show's content. Brother, that's dark.

Yet the show lacks reputation. It has popularity, to be sure; here was another of the many postwar American musicals to travel the world. But the relentless bleating of the show's theme song, "The Quest" (generally known as "The Impossible Dream"), by both pop singers and crossover opera guys has made the work ridiculous. Worse, its use in the almost insanely inspiring finale, as Cervantes walks up those stairs to his destiny, appalls the sophisticate. This is a show with an elemental appeal.

The staging, too, is very basic, though clever in its detail. No one seems to want to credit director Albert Marre with High Maestro talent, but this is one of the smartest of sixties productions. It occurs, without an intermission, in real time: Cervantes' two hours in the prison, during which he stands trial by the inmates' kangaroo court, his defense being vignettes drawn from his great novel. Lighting (also by Howard Bay) and costumes (by Bay and Patton Campbell) are extremely strategic, for the unit set is drab and there is next to no choreography. There isn't even an orchestra pit, the instrumentalists being broken into two groups, way

upstage left and right. Though *Man of La Mancha* debuted at the Goodspeed Opera House in Connecticut and was to play proscenium-bound
houses without problem, it opened in New York at the ANTA Washington Square Theatre. This had been the temporary home of the Repertory
Theatre of Lincoln Center before the Vivian Beaumont was ready, and
was thus a three-fifths "in the round" auditorium with a thrust stage. This
layout cannot accommodate a curtain: the action was established and
concluded entirely by the lighting.

So *Man of La Mancha* didn't look at all like most Broadway musicals in
this age when the rise and fall of the curtain was an essential part of the
theatregoing experience. In fact, before Jim Nabors got hold of "The
Impossible Dream," *Man of La Mancha* was considered somewhat revolutionary.

One odd note: at Goodspeed, this show opened a season of three musicals, all to be performed by a single group of actors. The leads in one title
would play supporting or even minor roles in another, in true repertory
fashion. All three works were composed by Mitch Leigh. *Man of La Mancha* had lyrics by Joe Darion; an adaptation of Sean O'Casey's *Purple Dust*
had—amazingly enough—lyrics by O'Casey himself; and *Chu Chem*, an
original piece about a Jewish family settling in eleventh-century China,
had lyrics by Jim Haines and Jack Wohl. The company included Richard
Kiley, Joan Diener, Irving Jacobson, Ray Middleton, and Robert Rounseville.

This is how *Man of La Mancha* ended up with such high-priced players
as the last two in small roles. Kiley was, obviously, Cervantes/Quixote.
Mrs. Marre, Joan Diener, was born not only to play Aldonza but to play
her in several foreign companies, as if protecting a copyright. Was Sancho
Panza written for a Jewish comic because Irving Jacobson was on hand
also to play the title role in *Chu Chem*, or was Jacobson hired because the
authors wanted a Jewish comic putting a spin on Sancho Panza? It's a disarmingly devious touch in a show that is otherwise very consistent in
tone. And note that Middleton and Rounseville were Broadway leads
(Middleton originated Frank Butler in *Annie Get Your Gun* and Rounseville was the first Candide), here in the very spotty roles of, respectively, the head prisoner and Innkeeper (in the *Don Quixote* scenes) and
an idiot prisoner without lines who becomes *Don Quixote*'s Padre.

Jacobson had a no more than capable theatre voice, but the other prin-

cipals were virtually an opera choir, crucial strategy in a score orchestrated to feature the solo voice over a rhythmic vamping from the players,
or even just voice and guitar. Remember, there are many different kinds
of singing on Broadway at this time, not just musical-comedy or musical-
play style. A *Time For Singing* was rhapsodic; *Kelly* was bellowed. *The Yearling* took in soprano Dolores Wilson, leprechaun David Wayne, and some
blasty kids. *Hot September* had not a single genuine singer in its entire cast
of principals.

Man *of La Mancha* must be *sung.* When Cervantes launches his *Don
Quixote* and Sancho helps them both into costume and introduces their
"horses" (actors in horse heads and wooden back-frames), the hero needs
vocal power to put over the charade. He has changed roles, gone from
author to character: entered that impossible dream.* We must hear the
sound of glory, however imaginary. Aldonza, the kitchen wench, must
belt aggressively yet keep in reserve the sumptuous head voice in her alter
ego as Dulcinea. The entire show is made of reverses, overturns, paradoxes. An old man becomes a vigorous knight. A predatory kangaroo
court acquits its victim. "Little Bird, Little Bird" is at first a flamenco
diversion, then accompanies a gang rape. Quixote changes Aldonza into
Dulcinea: for in the end she believes, too.

And The Enchanter is in actuality The Truth Teller. Cervantes' enemy
in the prison is the "Duke" (Jon Cypher), and, in the *Don Quixote* scenes,
he becomes Dr. Carrasco. This worthy, masquerading as the Knight of the
Mirrors, forces Quixote to face himself *as he is,* an old nobody without a
quest. It dissolves the adventure and kills the old nobody. The Enchanter
murders enchantment.

But fighting The Enchanter—the enemy? the Church?—is this show's
content. It explains why so many audiences go wild for it. Dark though it
be, it sees light. One has to believe to be, yes, inspired. But how else does
one survive in a world of Inquisitions? It was one of director Marre's

---

*A very little known fact: this number, in which Sancho follows Quixote with his own
chorus and the two then sing in counterpoint, is thought to be entitled "I, Don Quixote."
No. This is, by hap, the title of Dale Wasserman's 1959 television version of this material,
with Lee J. Cobb. In fact, this first number is *Man of La Mancha*'s title song. More trivia,
because my readers agree with Thomas Mann that "In art, only the exhaustive is interesting": Kander and Ebb's *Flora, the Red Menace,* which opened a month before *Man of La
Mancha* began its Goodspeed run, contains, in "Sing Happy," the secret of "how you realize an impossible dream."

choices that the prisoner who enacts Aldonza was always somewhat apart from the other prisoners, as if special. And so she is, once she meets Quixote—or, rather, Cervantes. When the prison drawbridge came down for the third and final time and Kiley and Jacobson began their ascent, it was prisoner Diener who started the last reprise of "The Quest."

The show doesn't tell us so, but Cervantes survived. He was pushing seventy when he died, and, more important, *Don Quixote* outlived the Inquisition.

Some readers may wonder if Broadway's dark musicals parallel the intensely fertile development of the American movie at this time, from the largely unexciting fifties fare into *Psycho*, *Splendor in the Grass*, *The Misfits*, *Dr. Strangelove*, *The Graduate*, *Bonnie and Clyde*, *Medium Cool*, *Midnight Cowboy*, *The Wild Bunch*. I think not. The cultural alliance between Broadway and Hollywood in the 1930s, when the two shared works and talent and acting style, was long over. Film and theatre were driven by different market considerations, different talent muscle, and different audience expectations; and they were supported by different infrastructures. There was some back-and-forth of works and talent, but no understanding.

Rather, the musical was pursuing a destiny first addressed in *Oklahoma!* in 1943: the musical play educates and then absorbs musical comedy, eventually to leave us almost nothing but dark shows. The sixties social input is niceties—flower children in *Your Own Thing* and *Hair*, anti-war numbers in *Mata Hari* and *1776*. The *1776* number is well known, "Momma Look Sharp." *Mata Hari*'s is very similar: a trembly young soldier singing of killing to his mother, "Maman."

Mata Hari: siren, spy, legend, Garbo, and now the lead in a musical, in 1967. We've seen heroes murdered; how about a heroine shot by firing squad, right on stage? If you don't place this show, that is because it closed after three weeks of tryouts in Washington, D.C. Nevertheless, it is an arresting example of the David Merrick–Gower Champion musical for three reasons. One, it told an extremely adult story, of a man who must control, in love with a woman who cannot be controlled. Two, its leads were Novelty Stars, and few in the rest of the cast could sing well, giving the work something of the Katzenjammer coarseness of *Kelly* and *Hot September*, as if to be certain that no one would mistake this period piece for an operetta. Three, though produced by Merrick, *Mata Hari* was directed not by Champion but by Vincente Minnelli, who had been in Hollywood for so long that he didn't know what a theatre piece even was. The production was lavish but incompetent.

Worse, *Mata Hari* has become a byword of disaster because of notorious technical problems and, especially, because at one performance the executed heroine wiped some irritation off her face. That may have happened. However, this is a show with a great story, two fascinating lead characters, and some accessory mess that could easily have been tidied up by anyone but Vincente Minnelli. Instead of bringing in someone to clean house, Merrick closed the production down.

Too bad: because Jerome Coopersmith's book, Edward Thomas' music, and Martin Charnin's lyrics combined most persuasively. There was atmosphere: Europe during World War I, with plenty of uniforms, street entertainers enticing recruits with a vaudeville number, even a scene in the trenches when the Yanks come over. Jo Mielziner and Irene Sharaff designed for spectacle, but the beauty was haunted by shadows, as the stupendous Mata Hari herself is. That trench scene, in which the French soldiers welcome the Americans with the rousing "Hello, Yank!," was in one way the typical second-act opener, the reinstitution of music after the intermission, so basic to all musicals. It's a nifty tune, starting most unusually on the fourth of the scale in the tonic (and falling, on the same harmony, to the second of the scale, which is unheard of). The brass blare out martial calls in between the vocal lines as the Americans call out their names and hometowns, and soon the stage is jumping with rough diplomacy. Then, just as the song nears its climax, an offstage voice cuts in brutally with *"Kill that match!"* and the men leap into battle stance. Yes, this is a musical: but it's also World War I.

Heading the cast were the American television star Pernell Roberts as a French army captain of intelligence and European film star Marisa Mell in the title role. Mell spoke her way through her numbers, in the husky *érotique* of the cabaret *diseuse*; Roberts could sing. There was little comedy, for the show centered on Roberts' martinet determination to seek and destroy. A patriot and family man, his Captain LaFarge was hurled at us in the first scene, at Headquarters. He is a believer; he is certain; he is for you or he wants you dead. The number is "Is This Fact? (This is fact!)," sung with his subordinates on a pounding idea in the minor as LaFarge dismisses the notion of ambiguity, gray areas, uncertainty. He already knows how the affair must end: "Mademoiselle, messieurs," runs the last line, "is a spy!"

With the next scene came Mata Hari's establishing number, "Everyone Has Something To Hide." It's very much of the Merrick-Champion genre, a lively $^4/_4$ that can't wait for the ensemble to jump in with the choral harmony. Note that this song maintains the opposite of LaFarge's song: you cannot ever be sure of anyone. Indeed, LaFarge loses his confidence when confronted by this enigmatic goddess. Not only is Mademoiselle possibly not a spy—*possibly*—but she is willing to *become* one to work for the French.

Is this fact? For, as the story develops, both LaFarge and we become confused about Mademoiselle's loyalties—she may be a double agent. One thing LaFarge is sure of (and by now it's the only thing) is that Mademoiselle threatens his way of life. She is bohemia itself, independent and unreliable. She is too fabulous to live amid the rules. So he destroys her. Coopersmith made sure that the war of establishing numbers held true throughout the show, the knowable facts versus the troublesome feelings. For we never do learn for certain whether Mata Hari is innocent or guilty.

The score is not entirely up to the brilliance of the book. Charnin's lyrics are of the second rank; some of the numbers generally are weak. But Champion, had he directed, would have replaced them. It's unlikely that any single title would have been a hit tune, but one number, "Not Now, Not Here," was one of the sexiest three minutes the musical has ever known.

It's the end of Act One. LaFarge and Mata Hari are alone in a dingy hotel room. They're in love. What better time than now? But no. It's her solo, in C minor. There's a vamp with a shiver in it, a touch of Kurt Weill, and Mell's delicate chant in her *chalumeau* register, bass clarinet. The harmony takes her to a G over f^7, an achingly hot touch, as if she had hardened him with a caress. But this is not the place, she says. Sex isn't dirty. It's lovely: "The feel of silk should be the prelude to our sin."

It's the beckoning wonder of her sin that causes LaFarge to have her shot; but why did Merrick shoot the show? William Goldman, on hand while researching his book *The Season*, noted that from rehearsals into the Washington tryout, Merrick was urgently requested to replace Minnelli. Goldman reasons that, with *How Now, Dow Jones* and *The Happy*

Time also in trouble, Merrick thought these two yet potential, and simply couldn't save all three.

But why didn't Merrick hand *Mata Hari's* direction over to its choreographer, Jack Cole? Cole had directed before (though never a hit) and had worked more than once for Merrick. So Merrick couldn't have mistrusted him. Cole also had the smarts to pull it off. Like Joe Layton, Cole never got his due for his talent, but in Cole's case it was because he was one of Broadway's most unpleasant characters. No one wanted to give him credit for anything.

Mata Hari's authors tried to revive their show off-Broadway, in 1968, under its original title, *Ballad For a Firing Squad.* But this is not a piece one can scale down. As we saw in the previous chapter, the off-Broadway musical is a little bundle of little genres populated mostly by little talents. A David Merrick spectacular with Mielziner and Sharaff and orchestrator Robert Russell Bennett (in the last solo credit of his life) cannot be dwindled into Theatre de Lys markdowns and ticktock accompaniment.

The shows discussed so far in this chapter are musical plays rather than musical comedies, and thus better suited to serious themes. But the darkness was beginning to stalk even the lighter form. *What Makes Sammy Run?* (1964), another latter-day *Pal Joey*, seems oddly meaner and tougher than the earlier show, with a final curtain that stings where *Joey's* last moment is an upbeat gag. Then, too, *Pal Joey* treats a show-biz underworld within which one cannot greatly rise or fall. *Sammy* tells how a snake becomes a powerful Hollywood producer. Yes, we know, it happens. But this show delights in showing us how.

With a score by Ervin Drake and a book by Budd and Stuart Schulberg, based on Budd's novel, *What Makes Sammy Run?* offered classy lady Sally Ann Howes and wisenheimer Robert Alda. First billed, however, was Novelty Star Steve Lawrence, as Sammy. It was an odd choice, perhaps, as Lawrence was a singer and not an actor, though in the end the critics felt he pulled it off. Director Abe Burrows may have thought that Lawrence's raw talent matched Sammy's, for Sammy does have a gift—for unscrupulously seizing an opportunity. Lawrence could realize that gift with his own self-assured vocalism.

"Only through music can the theatre handle this larger-than-life-size character," Burrows wrote in his introduction to *Sammy's* published text. "The music gives [the inarticulate protagonist] a capacity for saying things that he could never say in dialogue." Better, only through the dark show that gives its public a creep for a hero can the musical develop. It is as if musical comedy has run its course. The innocence is over.

True, some of *Sammy*'s script is sheer musical comedy. The Hollywood setting itself invites spoof, as when a few honchos scheme to imitate *Rain* with the genders switched:

SAMMY: (to the studio chief) Sir, you've just given us our title—*Monsoon.*

ASSISTANT DIRECTOR: What the hell *is* a monsoon?

DIRECTOR: It's a typhoon with a bigger budget.

STUDIO CHIEF: It'll never work. You cannot put Rita Rio in a missionary costume. She can't act with her clothes on.

DIRECTOR: Let's face it. She can't act with her clothes off.

STUDIO CHIEF: But somehow you don't mind so much.

There was also a good deal of musical-comedy dancing. Choreographer Matt Mattox's best number directly followed the scene quoted above. It was the movie, with Richard France as the studio hunk and Graciela Daniele as Rita Rio.* Lawrence narrated in voice-over as Mattox's crew lavished burlesque upon that most guilty of Hollywood pleasures, the South Seas Romance. Most nifty touch: at one point, Lawrence changed his mind about a plot turn and the dancers suggested the rewinding of film by their manic reverse actions. Even the orchestra played "backward."

Still, this is a somewhat dreadful show. One number, a witless goof on movie clichés, is called "Lights! Camera! Platitude!" But the score is almost nothing but platitude. "You Help Me" is the usual ironic list song. "A Tender Spot" is the usual solo for the heroine reluctant to fall in love. "My Home Town" is the newcomer's salute to Hollywood. (*Fade Out Fade In*'s "It's Good To Be Back Home" would be vastly better, later that same year.) "You're No Good" is the usual users-praising-each-other duet. "Something To Live For" is as empty as it sounds—and all this in music

---

*I hope my readers have caught this inside joke. The star's name is the title of an old Ziegfeld show with the two words in reverse order: *Rio Rita* (1927).

that is itself purest cliché. The show ran 540 performances; I can't imagine why. Even if there are over a year's worth of Steve Lawrence fans to fill the 54th Street Theatre, didn't the star's constant skipping of performances (unforgivably including the week right after Christmas, Broadway's most lucrative of the year) and onstage misbehavior warn them off?

We'll see Lawrence again, next time in a happy musical comedy; but songwriter Drake went on to an even more serious piece, *Her First Roman* (1968). Yet another *My Fair Lady*, with Shavian book (drawn from *Caesar and Cleopatra*), distinguished older thespian (Richard Kiley) paired with charming young lady (Leslie Uggams), *Her First Roman* called up far better things from Drake than *Sammy* had. This is almost, but not quite, a Type A flop, a real disaster at 17 performances. And the score, let me quickly add, is very variable.

Half of it is quite good, a crucial quality in a show that, like *My Fair Lady*, is essentially a spoken play cut down for the insertion of songs. Of course, mention of *My Fair Lady* and its matchless music somewhat embarrasses my praise of Drake's work. Still, Uggams had two winners in "Many Young Men From Now" and "Magic Carpet," the latter with an irresistible drum syncopation in the verse and clip-clopping "horse's hooves" (as percussionists call them) in the refrain. Kiley presented mostly patter songs but also the loving "Rome." In *Bravo Giovanni*, a song called "Rome" was a doting salute. Here, "Rome" is a love song, the city specifically feminized. Claudia McNeil, a commanding Ftatateeta, enjoyed a superb duet with Cleopatra and the deviously erotic "Pleasure Him." Best of all Drake's inventions was one for Barbara Sharma in a minor role, "Parable of the Monkey," a giddy Eastern hopscotch retailing news of Cleopatra's loss of vitality as the consort of Caesar—who is, after all, Egypt's conqueror.

None of this quite suited the script, unfortunately. Drake wrote for modern Broadway audiences in modern Broadway style, but the libretto was George Bernard Shaw, of the Problem Play grafted onto late-Victorian drawing-room comedy in the language of the eccentric wit. Shaw into "Magic Carpet" and "Pleasure Him" won't go.

Well, you say, *My Fair Lady* pulled it off. But *My Fair Lady*'s secret is how unmodern its score is—not outdated, just not in the vernacular. "Wouldn't It Be Loverly?," "I Could Have Danced All Night," and "On the Street Where You Live" inhabit their own out-of-time world. "Why Can't the English," "Ascot Gavotte," and "A Hymn To Him" sound like songs that Shaw himself might have collaborated on. And Doolittle's music-hall rave-ups only expand the class consciousness built into *Pygmalion*. All these songs mesh with My *Fair Lady*'s Shavian script in ways that do not allude to the Broadway of My *Fair Lady*'s 1956.

Her First Roman's songs are wedded to the Broadway of 1968. That, along with terrible reviews, was the show's undoing. It was a wrestling match, Shaw versus Drake. Worse, Drake's score was unfairly hacked about and humiliated with interpolations—both "Pleasure Him" and the Monkey Number were dropped in Philadelphia. It can't have helped that director Michael Benthall was replaced by Derek Goldby, and choreographer Kevin Carlisle by Dania Krupska. Or: it can't have mattered, because it had become a sixties usage that when a show was going to bomb, its director would be fired in Philadelphia or Boston. Can I tell you what shows did not lose their directors? *Bye Bye Birdie*, *Carnival!*, *How To Succeed*, *Fiddler on the Roof*, *Hello, Dolly!*, *Mame*, *Man of La Mancha*, *Cabaret*, *Sweet Charity* . . . I'll stop.*

Interestingly, all these dark shows failing to pay off did not discourage authors from writing dark. The misery kept coming. Even the choreographer of our next title thought it "classy, dull, and depressing." That was Ron Field on *Zorbá* (1968), from Nikos Kazantzakis' novel *Zorba the Greek*, and Hal Prince's encore after *Cabaret*. He was clearly under his own influence: a concept show with commentary frame (*Cabaret*: show biz; *Zorbá*: tavern philosophy); realistic young hero (*Cabaret*: Cliff; *Zorbá*: Nikos); oddball accessories (*Cabaret*: vital Sally Bowles, old lady Lenya, handsome Nazi; *Zorbá*: vital Zorbá, old lady Maria Karnilova, handsome young Widow); strange place (*Cabaret*: Weimar Berlin; *Zorbá*: Crete); crazed local traditions (*Cabaret*: men in drag; *Zorbá*: men kissing each other); and historical background (*Cabaret*: Nazi takeover leading to

Funny Girl, we know, more or less lost its director, Garson Kanin, when Jerome Robbins joined the production for a punch-up. However, by then *Funny Girl* was nearly ready for New York. *Nearly*, I emphasize. The show needed Robbins, yes: but he didn't reinvent it. A thorough last-minute reconsideration—new numbers, new dances, even new script—is virtually impossible to pull off. In fact, it was attempted only once in this era, so catastrophically that, as we'll see in the next chapter, this title became a byword of disaster, the show buff's most collectable flop musical ever.

World War II starts in five minutes; *Zorbá*: Greece invents Western Civilization three thousand years ago, after which nothing happens except *Illya Darling*).

Field may have been right. *Cabaret* is anything but depressing, though the events it records created the worst twelve years in history. *Zorbá* is depressing. Is it because all the fun people are old? Is it because so many people die? *Her First Roman* has a couple of murders, but at least it ends happily (unlike Shaw's original). *Zorbá* ends, as a modern musical of 1968 must, neither here nor there. "Embrace Zorbá!" Herschel Bernardi cries, to John Cunningham. What, and forget all the sadness and failed projects that have brought us to this embrace?

Yes. To enjoy *Zorbá*, one needs to share Zorbá's perspective, which is amoral and anarchic. "I Am Free" is his definitive song; but he defines freedom as not giving a flying heck about anything that happens. Credit the show with encompassing Zorbá's viewpoint in story and song: but it's a stupid and selfish viewpoint. The coal mine upon whose success all hopes depend collapses? *Embrace Zorbá!* Maria Karnilova dies hopeless and abandoned? *Embrace Zorbá!* The Widow is murdered because she wouldn't accept some jerk's advances? *Embrace Zorbá!*

I think *Zorbá* is one of the ugliest, most life-denying pieces of evil shit ever perpetrated as a Broadway musical, not least because it pretends to be beautiful and life-affirming. At least John Kander and Fred Ebb gave it a splendid score. They are always at their best when treating character and situation, steering the action from an event to its consequence, building throughlines and ever tightening them. They write the way Gower Champion liked to direct—with a fulfilling sense of detail, but centered. Like Bock and Harnick's cast albums, Kander and Ebb's always seem to end too soon. Yet that can't be true, because they follow the story so closely that story and score are always in perfect synch. Ron Field was forever appalled at how gently they took it whenever Prince rejected their latest composition. Wonderful stuff was being thrown away. But this team never runs out of ideas. Their concept number here, both the opening and finale (like "Willkommen" in *Cabaret*), is "Life Is," a preparation for the lesson, What is life? The song calls it "what you do while you're waiting to die." Zorbá caps the thought near the evening's end by saying that *he* lives "as if I'll die any minute."

Now, *that* is a typical musical-comedy message. It's what *Hello, Dolly!* is about very precisely, but what countless titles have been about implicitly. Of course, I speak here of light shows, of *enjoying* one's time. In *Zorbá*, people scrape by and make do. There's little to enjoy. As a post-*Cabaret* (or, to do history justice, a post-*Allegro*) show, *Zorbá* had its commentative chorus, shadowing the action, seemingly wondering about it even as they *must* know what's going to happen. A character billed as "Leader" (Lorraine Serabian), a belting Dramaturg, skillfully worked her way between all-knowing earth mother and simple referee. She helped structure Cunningham's hesitant tale of "The Butterfly," at once urging him on and interrupting his worried account with soothing refrains. Again, what is life? It is what happens. It must not be arranged, as Cunningham learns to his horror when he destroys life by trying to encourage it. Serabian also led a chorus of cawing women in "The Crow," a ghastly death song—but, as well, in the *Zorbá* manner, a life song. As Kander, Ebb, and book writer Joseph Stein see it, the two are not opposites but linked in symbiosis. "What doesn't die," Serabian crowed, exulting in the paradox of the logic, "never was born!"

At 305 performances, *Zorbá* was a failure only in the commercial sense, and was even revived in 1983, with the two leads from the movie *Zorba the Greek*, Anthony Quinn and Lila Kedrova. The film's director, Michael Cacoyannis, also directed the revival, with Graciela Daniele choreographing, Robert Westenberg in Cunningham's role, and Debbie Shapiro (Gravitte) as the Leader, now helpfully called The Woman. The work remained a difficult proposition for many theatregoers, not dull but, yes, classy and depressing. Herschel Bernardi had to figure out who Zorbá was and then enact him. Quinn doesn't figure out; he just is. It was an effective presentation, though his singing was extremely variable. Lila Kedrova was much better, because she was a charmer who, like her character, Madame Hortense, wanted only to be young and beautiful forever. All her life, Kedrova was a little girl just about to enjoy a triumph at her sixteenth birthday party. Amazingly, Kander and Ebb wrote the perfect song for her fifteen years before they knew she was to play the part, "Happy Birthday." As Karnilova sang it, a woman rises from her deathbed to dance about the stage in a touchingly creepy dream, her self-loving cries of "Happy birthday!" given dead echo by the chorus. But Kedrova played it as a music-hall specialty, or a spot on the Tony Awards show, or even as a sixteen-year-old triumphing at her birthday party. She was heartrendingly terrific.

Maggie Flynn (1968), which arrived just a few weeks before *Zorbá*, could almost have preceded it by a few decades. If *Zorbá* was a concept musical, *Maggie Flynn* was a fifties musical comedy—except one dealing with New York's Draft Riots of 1863, in which four days of street battles left as many as two thousand dead. The piece did not tiptoe around the subject. With the curtain up from the start, the audience was greeted by recruiting posters, and the overture never ended but broke into a military figure as soldiers marched down the aisles to the stage. This was prologue: two sergeants tried to pep bystanders into enlisting while chorus men took up the angry "Never Gonna Make Me Fight." While the stage cleared for Scene One, Shirley Jones bustled onstage to awaken her charges, the kids of an all-black orphanage, as their beds rolled onto the playing floor.

It was a state-of-the-art, smoothly maneuvered staging (by designers William and Jean Eckart and director Morton Da Costa). And, indeed, the ire of the draft resisters, so pertinent to the 1960s, was carried through the show quite honestly. Then, too, Jones' orphanage was burned down in the rioting, recalling the torching of the Colored Half Orphan Asylum on Fifth Avenue at Forty-fourth Street in 1863. Even Jones' opposite, her real-life husband, Jack Cassidy, was playing a serious role after a gallery of comic villains, in *She Loves Me, Fade Out Fade In,* and *Superman.* (One knew he was serious because he suddenly had a beard.)

Yet *Maggie Flynn* was otherwise a traditional cheer-up show, even a way-out-of-date one. The Irish humor and accents here had died out in the 1940s. The exposition of backstory was painfully coarse:

CASSIDY: Bein' a clown suits me just fine. Nobody has to take in laundry
    to support me.
JONES: I never complained.
CASSIDY: No, you wouldn't, but that didn't make it any easier for me.
    Seein' you breakin' your back to keep us alive while I lost part after
    part or was fired out of them. I wanted to do something on my own.
JONES: So you went off to play Hamlet and enjoyed your triumph alone.

It gets worse:

> CASSIDY: Why in God's name you bothered to track me down I'll never know, unless you're a glutton for punishment.
>
> JONES: It just so happens that I have certain obligations now.
>
> CASSIDY: As a matter of fact, I did hear a few years back your Uncle Sean brought you down from Albany to run his orphanage before he went back to Ireland.

One even gets the ancient Establishing of Jail Scene as the lights come up on lolling prostitutes and noisy drunks. One gets the yet more ancient (though still valid) gag in which someone addresses the tarts as "Ladies" and they look behind them to see whom he means. Positively nineteenth-century is the view of society women, characterized as stupid bigots who go all coquettish and comic when a man enters, and who have names like Vanderhoff and Opdyke.

Maybe this hurt the show, for it ran only 82 performances. Still, this is another one with a partway-to-Type-A score, not brilliant but characterful and melodious. The orphans boasted a number of stars-to-be, including Irene Cara, Giancarlo Esposito, and the Dorothy of *The Wiz*, Stephanie Mills, who even then fielded a dynamite belt. However, this was obviously a vehicle for the Cassidys, and perhaps a bit more for Shirley than Jack. She was billed first, and performed in particularly winning voice, giving plentifully of her high soprano extension. Cassidy had a rare chance to sing not the goofy ballads (think of "Ilona" or "The Man Who Has Everything") but heartfelt ones. He even got the show's hit, "Why Can't I Walk Away." Of course, both stars got into some of the foofoo numbers that musical comedy dotes on—her "I Wouldn't Have You Any Other Way" to a saloon of ragtag dumbos, or his "Mr. Clown," sung in jail with the prostitutes and drunks imitating instruments under the melody. The kids had their bits, and baritone Robert Kaye (as Cassidy's rival for Jones) sang "Look Around Your Little World," made extrapowerful when Cassidy joined in, watching from a balcony, for a self-hating descant.

Maggie Flynn was a good show—for, say, the early 1950s, when Jones was just coming out of the chorus and Cassidy had just made lead (in the sunny *Wish You Were Here*). It's a *simple* show, which makes one wonder why it needed Hugo Peretti, Luigi Creatore, and George David Weiss to write in collaboration with director Da Costa, this weighty enterprise "based on an idea by John Flaxman." To paraphrase Cole Porter, "It took five men to write *that*?" Perhaps the show's socio-historical background led them into thinking they had something trendy on their hands when what they really had was Mr. Peabody's WABAC Machine with a new coat of paint.

What is arresting here is how deeply the dark idea was penetrating the musical. *Golden Boy* and *A Time For Singing* and *The Yearling* were to be expected sooner or later. *What Makes Sammy Run?* and *Her First Roman* are not all that startling after *Pal Joey* and *My Fair Lady*. But with *Maggie Flynn* we see even the happiest kind of musical being overwhelmed by unhappy people and real-life events that no one is glad to remember. Yes, everyone got out of Jones' orphanage in time, and the Cassidys ended up together. We had to get through a lot of misery to reach the happy ending, however; and soon enough even the happy ending will grow unusual.

It's a long way from *Wish You Were Here*.

13

EVERYBODY HAS THE RIGHT TO BE WRONG

GOOD IDEAS AND BAD IDEAS

Skyscraper (1965) was a great idea. Elmer Rice's play of 1945, *Dream Girl*, about a young woman who daydreams to supplement the insufficient experience of her life, can open up beautifully. Reset in present-day New York, the show will challenge her with a construction project that threatens her brownstone; and she of course will be a kook attracted to lost causes. Her love interest will be integrally associated with the construction, her assumed ally will be in traitorous league with the construction . . . it all fits.

Better, the heroine's dream sequences will be one of the musical's favorite things, Hollywood pastiche, as hallucinative figures pop out of her shower, her armoire, even from under her bedclothes. We'll get tropes from *Gone With the Wind*, *The Three Musketeers*, any detective whodunit, and, best of all, we'll get Novelty Star Julie Harris. Beloved as Broadway's wistful heroine of Jean Anouilh, Carson McCullers, and *I Am a Camera*, Harris was also a sharp comic and fielded a slight but valid voice with some knowledge of how to shape a song. She even looked fetching in the very short nightgown they made her wear.

Peter Stone wrote the book and James Van Heusen and Sammy Cahn the score. Peter L. Marshall played opposite Harris, most creditably—he became famous as a game-show host but was the lead in London's *Bye Bye Birdie*. Charles Nelson Reilly was the Benedict Arnold and Dick O'Neill played Marshall's brother, also in on the construction project and one of those "I'm going to get an ulcer out of this" comic figures. As a Feuer and Martin production, *Skyscraper* was, technically, directed by Cy Feuer; but the real muscle was choreographer Michael Kidd.

It stank. A good idea needs more than a good cast and a good choreographer. It needs something lighter than Stone's clearly narrated but tedious book and Van Heusen and Cahn's mediocre songs. The first minute or so was wonderful—one could see why everyone wanted to do this show. The curtain rose on someone (Harris) asleep in bed. Into her apartment came: Renaissance duelists, a mad doctor and his female victim, a sultan and his houri, hooded men of the Inquisition and a martyr, and Parisian apache dancers. As they dueled, threatened, cringed, and danced, an alarm clock went off and everyone dropped what he was doing and left the stage. The alarm was Harris'. Still unseen, she silenced it. The dream figures came back in—but now the telephone rang, and Harris made her Star Entrance by coming out from under the covers as the figures walked off stage again.

Cute, sharp, and whimsical, it was why Americans loved musical comedy: but it was the only thing *Skyscraper* had that worked. The other dream sequences were uninspired, and while the songs struck appropriate positions—her apologia "An Occasional Flight of Fancy," his strongly felt ballad "More Than One Way," and an ode to that Manhattan fixture, the delicatessen—the score generally lacked delight.

Drat! The Cat! (1965) had no such problems. The score, by Milton Schafer and Ira Levin, is delightful. So is Levin's book. It's *funny*. *Skyscraper* was musical comedy without music and comedy. *Drat! The Cat!* was a fine new idea, as well: Little Old New York is plagued by an elusive and relentless jewel thief. Boy meets girl because he's the bumbling cop charged with the thief's capture and she's the thief. More fun: star comic Eddie Foy Jr. will play both their fathers, *his* in a comic deathbed scene early in Act One and then—with seconds to spare as Foy pulls off the nightshirt that had covered his other costume and dodges stagehands to get into the very next scene—*her* father for the rest of the evening.

And here's a smart move: the very inventive Joe Layton will serve as director-choreographer, working with set designer David Hays to fill the stage with bizarre surprises—characters popping up through trapdoors, scenery popping up through trapdoors, a candy box of lunacy. The two men's tour de force was the overture, staged, liked *Donnybrook*'s. Moving from The Academy of Music to Delmonico's and Tiffany's, it showed the Cat's white-gloved hands mooching her diamonds, even off the usual fat lady singing opera.

Lesley Ann Warren, having retrieved her middle name for professional use *and* having played the title role in the remake of Rodgers and Hammerstein's television *Cinderella*, will be the Cat and Elliott Gould her adorably pathetic swain. (His clumsiness is a running gag; after a series of crashes offstage, someone says, "That must be Bob now." He makes so little impression on Warren that she calls him "Tom" till the final scene.)

Like Sondheim's *Forum* songs, *Drat! The Cat!*'s score reflects the gaggy nature of the piece while beguiling with pleasing tunes. "She Touched Me" even did some hit-tune business. Some numbers were all for comedy. Foy's death scene, "My Son, Uphold the Law," got its mileage out of Foy's increasing commitment, his sermonizing, even his hysteria: which is of course what kills him. Gould's ballad "Deep In Your Heart" is pure melody when heard out of context. But onstage, it is his courtship of the Cat, just then holding a gun on him and angrily threatening to use it. She'll shoot on three, but he goes on singing, even as she reaches four. "Nine!" she finally wails, helpless in the grip of that all but insurmountable hazard, the love plot.

In Boston, the Cat's explanatory number was "Explanation," containing a political rationale for her criminal career: everyone's a thief. Lawyers. Brokers. Merchants. The song itself wasn't good enough, so Schafer and Levin replaced it with "Wild and Reckless," a Latin number complete with Rio Grande trumpet and—the hussy!—the flaunting of a lit cigarette. "Second one this week!" she gloats.

Doesn't this show sound winning? Unfortunately, there was no name on the poster to draw customers. There was no hook, no "based on" a familiar property, though in the end that failed to boost *The Yearling*. Having played nothing but flops since *The Pajama Game* in 1954, Foy feared that one more would destroy his career. He left the show in Philadelphia, to be replaced, catch-as-catch-can, by two different actors for the two fathers, ruining one of the show's cutest goofs. Worse, poor out-of-town business forced *Drat! The Cat!* into New York in fine shape but absolutely needing a rave from the man at the *Times*, Howard Taubman. It didn't get one, and immediately closed.

Maybe it wasn't a good idea, then. *Skyscraper* lasted over half a year because theatre parties booked it for Julie Harris—*that* was a good idea. *Drat! The Cat!* was horribly vulnerable despite having what were now the

Three Essentials of musical comedy: sharp script, good score, and clever staging.

Sweet Charity (1966) was another good idea, and it had star insurance: Bob Fosse and Gwen Verdon. It, too, got a bad review in the *Times* (now from Stanley Kauffmann), but weathered it with ease. *Charity* even had a "based on" hook, though the credit didn't state its source, Federico Fellini's 1957 film *Nights of Cabiria*. All it mentioned was "a screenplay" and named Fellini and his two co-writers. Still, everyone knew that this was Giulietta Masina's Roman prostitute transplanted to New York. Now she was a "social consultant"—actually a taxi dancer in the Fan-Dango Ballroom, though by 1966 that Depression phenomenon of the "ten cents a dance" girl was sheer fantasy.

Otherwise, *Charity* was extremely contemporary. A number of episodes from the film were faithfully retained, such as the opening robbery by the heroine's lover, who pushes her into the water, or her spending the night in the side room of a movie star's place as he reconciles with his girl friend. But nothing could be less black-and-white fifties neorealist Italian cinema than this latest Fosse stunt. It was a riotously colorful fantasy and a valentine to his wife and star, Verdon, and to her cohorts (Helen Gallagher, Thelma Oliver), and to a dancing chorus that seemed more important than such featured players as the movie star (James Luisi), a preacher-cum-hipster jazzman named Daddy Johann Sebastian Brubeck (Arnold Soboloff), Charity's boss (John Wheeler), and even the nerd (John McMartin) with whom Charity almost ends up.

This is a dancers' show. What other show's best number is a dance without a vocal? Orchestrator Ralph Burns gave the Cy Coleman–Dorothy Fields score the sound of this very morning in the mariachi trumpet of "There's Gotta Be Something Better Than This" and the bongo drums of "Rhythm of Life." For "Rich Man's Frug," Burns forced Broadway to consider the electric guitar* and Fosse made exhalations of cigarette smoke part of the choreography of disco swingers skittering across the stage in groups with their bodies bent like pretzels. Though Coleman and Fields

---

Bye Bye Birdie popularized this instrument in the Broadway pit, but only for generic authentication of Conrad's two rock-and-roll numbers. In "Rich Man's Frug," the electric guitar is meant as a noise of the times, its amplified anomie a kind of merit badge for being Where at exactly the right When.

had lavished a unique score upon the work, it was the "Frug" that centered the evening in its heartless self-absorption.

Because that is what Fosse brought to Fellini's tale. The film Cabiria is given a highly realistic context in which to show us how she lives and thinks.' Fosse gave Verdon a comic-strip background (complete with narrative captions) to protect her from reality. *Sweet Charity* is about a coarse but extremely likable girl's permanent failure to realize how crummy men are.' The ones who aren't outright criminals are nevertheless exploitative and unreliable. Fellini brought his heroine to such despair that, near the end, she begs her latest cheat to kill her, though, at the *very* end, she is half-smiling despite herself at the antics of a strolling band.

Fosse didn't want to bring Verdon to such a drastic pass. The worst that happens is her near drowning; but the worst she gets is exasperated. And Fosse's ending, pushing fantasy-reality into a corner of reality-fantasy, brought Verdon her Good Fairy (Ruth Buzzi, later the angry spinster smacking the Walnetto man on television's *Laugh-In*), though this character proved to be part of a commercial promotion.

So Fosse leaves Verdon where we met her: in the time of her life. Their show gave us the American musical in a comparable time: where any show is possible, any subject matter in any one of a number of styles, all in such fluid motion that *Sweet Charity* is almost still a movie. By now, the blending of spoken dialogue and song in a musical number is so acute that one marvels at the lack of such cohesion in the old days, when characters sang a verse, then a refrain, another verse and refrain, and then pranced to the music of the refrain.

How could stories be told in such a stilted manner? Or remember when shows were locked into a limited number of sets, with the dainty little interscenes holding up progress while the stagehands assembled the next big scene? In *Sweet Charity*, after the near-drowning incident, Verdon is telling a cop about it while the view changes behind her to the Fan-Dango locker room. Thus, right in the middle of her speech, without pausing for even a breath, she is suddenly addressing not the cop in the park but her pals at work. A movie, I tell you! Act One ends with a sign reading "To be continued," and Act Two starts in exactly the same place with a sign reading "Meanwhile."

Note that musical comedy is still obsessed with New York as the place where all the excitement occurs. Except now the musical's city is starting to look scummy. It's not the low-down New York of On the Town: that's a cute New York all the same. Sweet Charity's Fan-Dango Ballroom, Barney's Chili Hacienda, and even the upmarket Club Pompeii are a dirty New York. Both shows have scenes in Coney Island, and On the Town's Coney is no Garden of Eden. Still, On the Town is a romantic show and its New York a dreamland, while Charity's New York is where men keep scamming Charity. On the Town's Ivy Smith wins a beauty contest and takes singing lessons, but Ivy is working-class with middle-class aspirations. Charity is without class, so rootless that when her friends consider her options, "that nice obstetrician" is cited as someone she'll never meet, and the mere mention of the PTA makes Helen Gallagher snicker.

Sweet Charity is what Cy Feuer called "a mug show." Let others idealize women; Fosse loved hot-and-down women, prostitutes wherever possible. He was the most womanizing figure in the musical's history since Florenz Ziegfeld—but I mean "womanizing" in the best sense: he loved women. To Fosse, a highlight of the show was not the serious character stuff (such as "Where Am I Going?") or the, for once, unassuming title song, but something like "There's Gotta Be Something Better Than This." The plot doesn't need it, but Verdon, Gallagher, and Oliver do, as they envision holding down respectable jobs in a comically raffish manner and then tear the music apart in an abandoned Latin dance. Even better, to Fosse, is "Big Spender," an exhibition piece for the Fan-Dango girls, posing and beckoning at a bar that they hold, sit on, straddle, pet, and all but make love to while the music gets so merrily filthy that it does in sound what Fosse does in movement.

Sweet Charity was a staging triumph; but it did have an imposing writing team. Neil Simon was originally to have no more than improved Fosse's own book. Fosse quickly realized, however, that the show needed not a Simon edit but a Simon libretto. The Coleman-and-Fields score found both at their best. From Little Me on, everything that Fosse did was suffused with lampoon, so Coleman could exploit his penchant for lampoons of genre: in the movie star's overblowing self-dramatization in "Too Many Tomorrows," in the jazz-fugato chorale "Rhythm of Life," in the Sousa-fied list song "I'm a Brass Band," which found Verdon in leotard and the boys upstage bearing trumpets.

As for Dorothy Fields, this wonderful talent may be the only lyricist in musical-theatre history who sounded more youthful as time ran on. Her first show had come along in 1928, when Cy Coleman was running around in a propeller beanie. Yet, in *Sweet Charity*, Fields has the ear of a teenage prodigy. Moreover, like Oscar Hammerstein and Stephen Sondheim (but unlike most Golden Age lyricists and especially unlike Cole Porter and E. Y. Harburg), Fields changes voice from character to character. She's great with slightly demented women of no education, such as Ethel Merman's Jeanette Adair in *Stars in Your Eyes* or Shirley Booth's roles in *A Tree Grows in Brooklyn* and *By the Beautiful Sea*. *Charity* would be right up Fields' alley, as we hear in "You Should See Yourself," Charity's eulogy of the boy friend who pushes her into the lake. He's a creep, but he's her creep; so she's glowing, building, praising—especially his dressing style, that "college-type, rah-rah-dee-da tweed." I ask you, is even Fred Ebb sharper?

Sweet Charity was the great Verdon-Fosse achievement. Their *Chicago*, in the next decade, is a more substantial work, for its satiric look at how everything in America conduces to show biz. Moving back to the 1950s, their *Redhead* is a unique accomplishment because the show was an unexciting composition that, through their work, wowed the town and avalanched the Tonys in a way that has never been fairly equaled. And *Damn Yankees*, on film, is their documentary, preserving his choreography and her performance. (He even appears with her, in the number "Who's Got the Pain?")

But *Sweet Charity* is something none of those others is: a first-class piece of writing that nevertheless could not have existed without Fosse and Verdon. *Damn Yankees* was a George Abbott show, *Redhead* is not first-class writing, and someone or other would have got to *Chicago* sooner or later. *Sweet Charity* belongs to Verdon and Fosse.

A hit, if not quite a smash, the show went to London (with Juliet Prowse) and even Paris (with Magali Noël), which normally disdains American musicals. Fosse filmed the work himself, unfortunately without Verdon. The Hollywood powers believed that the film would succeed only if its star was someone who had been reincarnated. This left a very narrow casting field: Shirley MacLaine and Bridey Murphy. Fosse went with the former, as the latter was an indifferent singer, an awkward dancer, and (temporarily) dead.

Good ideas and bad ideas. It says a great deal about the early years of the Golden Age that there were no bad ideas. There were inadequate authors, uncharismatic performers, and the breaks. But musicals of the 1920s and 1930s were for the most part so generic that there weren't "ideas" in any real sense. The worst that could happen was that Ziegfeld would lavish his usual munificence upon a vehicle for Marilyn Miller and the Astaires, with music by Vincent Youmans, and a lifeless book would sabotage the piece. *Smiles* (1930) was a flop. But its premise—the Astaires are society playkids mixed up with Miller of the Salvation Army—was not the problem. Most musicals had such silly premises that everything lay in the execution. There were no adaptations of cumbersome novels, bites of history, rotten mothers, gang wars, Bambi getting shot by Dolores Wilson. There was nothing to figure out; nobody had to know what the show was. Operettas went this way and musical comedies went that way.

Then *Oklahoma!*, *Allegro*, *Love Life*, *A Tree Grows in Brooklyn*, *The Golden Apple*, and especially *Candide* proved that anything could be a musical. Now one had to count on not only authors, performers, and the breaks, but a good idea in the first place. Because, in fact, not *everything* can be a musical.

Not a good one, anyway. *Breakfast at Tiffany's* (1966) was the worst one of the decade, judging by its reputation. This is based on a tryout so vexed that producer David Merrick had the book not rewritten but *totally junked* in favor of a *wholly new book*, reconceived around the existing score. Then, after 4 New York previews, Merrick closed the production, though it could have run six months on its advance sale, and even had a potential hit tune to spur ticket sales.

The show's reputation is based also on the poster credits, because they promised an easy hit: television stars Mary Tyler Moore and Richard Chamberlain in the roles that Audrey Hepburn and George Peppard had originated in the screwball comedy that writer George Axelrod and director Blake Edwards made of Truman Capote's dour story. The contracts specified that credit go to Capote, as is usual in these matters. But no one wanted to see a musical of his off-kilter tale, in which heroine Holly Golightly is more selfish than zany and in which the winsome young author that Peppard played doesn't even exist. On the contrary, Capote's narrator is a watchy, listeny little telltale: Capote himself, making revelation, it is generally believed, about Marilyn Monroe.

So this is Moore and Chamberlain making a musical of the film, with songs by Bob Merrill and book and direction by Abe Burrows. Let us join audiences at Philadelphia's Forrest Theatre, at the start of the show's shakeout, when Merrick is billing it as *Holly Golightly*. Philadelphia critics were terrible and Philadelphia's theatregoers knew it, so they went to shows for their own reasons, either by subscription (as here) or through word of mouth (as when *Funny Girl* extended its tryout). Philadelphians knew they were seeing work still in process and thus yet to be judged. But they knew when they had a good time: *Mame*. They knew when they had a rotten time: *Illya Darling*. They knew when a show seemed okay but needed improving: *Superman* or *Sherry!*. But they didn't know what to think of *Holly Golightly*, because it was neither quick nor dead, and certainly not compelling but sort of maybe amusing in a kind of spotty if-you-know-what-I-mean way.

It was, in fact, a misconceived mediocrity. Clearly, none of the team knew what the show *was*—not even Bob Merrill, so perspicacious in creating *Funny Girl*'s heroine. *Holly Golightly*'s heroine went unwritten, giving Mary Tyler Moore nothing to play. Nor was Richard Chamberlain's role fleshed out. She had a Wanting Song, "I've Got a Penny"; he had the jazzy title number; she had a relatively attractive character number called "Travelling," which was much too self-analyzing for a woman who runs on instinct, not policy; the two had an empty quarrel duet called "Who Needs Her" . . . But for the clichés of genre, these people wouldn't have been there at all.

At least Merrill got Doc Golightly (Art Lund). There was an excellent plot number, "Lulamae," in which the calmly overbearing Doc kept pressing Holly to give up her fantasy Manhattan identity to return to him and the farm. But Holly's fellow dash-around doll (Sally Kellerman) eluded Merrill. She had an unfunny comic number, "My Nice Ways," and a dainty and absolutely unnecessary duet with Moore, "Home For Wayward Girls," sung at a party consisting of Moore and Kellerman and nothing but male guests, who glared at each other in "Lament for Ten Men." This number's one joke was the repeated singing of the then popular buzz term "dirty old men." But they weren't. They were Broadway gypsies in three-piece suits.

The whole show was like that—not terrible, just not about anything and completely lacking the film's glamour and charm. One thinks of *its* party scene, truly funny ("She's . . . a *real* phony") or of Hepburn and Peppard encountering the stately yet Thurberesque Tiffany's clerk John McGiver, or of Patricia Neal, with her clipped diction and control freak's power smile, so dykey that a generation of lesbians grew up harboring a secret crush on her.

Like *Sophie*, *Holly Golightly* had no content of its own, and thus had to borrow it from tradition. "So Here We Are Again" found Holly waking up her neighbors in the wee hours because she can't ever find her house key. The set showed the brownstone's exterior, bulging with chorus people singing a humdrum waltz while Moore just stood there, grinning. It was exactly the number one might have expected of the show as one filed into the Forrest and took a look at the program. Yes, there's the number wherein she explains why . . . And that song will give his view of . . . And that's the irrelevant chorus number to open the second act, with references to crime and other local events, "Nothing Is New in New York." (That should have been the show's title.) Desperate for a hit, Merrill put in "Ciao, Compare," for a minor character, the gangster Sally Tomato, whom Holly visits in prison. There was no reason for this guy to be singing a ballad, but at least some of the gypsies can back him up harmonically, dressed as cops. "Ciao, Compare" is smooth and appealing, a "parting" number of such nice sentiment that it would surely have become a standard. The Philadelphia audience stirred in their seats at this sudden intrusion of something special into a nondescript evening. So the show *is* good?

Truman Capote hated it. He caught it in Boston, dismissing it all with a wave of that dear little hand and telling everyone that Tuesday Weld would have been perfect for the part, or maybe the young Tammy Grimes.

The then-current Tammy Grimes was supposedly in Boston, too, waiting to replace Moore. But Merrick was no idiot. The cast wasn't wrong: the show was. So he loaded up the longest shot ever fired in tryout hell, bringing in Edward Albee for the aforementioned new script. One's first thought is, What does Albee know of musicals? Well, Burrows was supposed to be an expert in musicals, and his adaptation was worthless. Maybe the material is so weird that it needs a neophyte's hand—someone who, not knowing the bromides, won't utter them.

As the show played Boston, eight numbers listed in the opening week's program in Philadelphia were discarded and eight new ones added. The losses included some of Merrill's better numbers, but he gamely stayed on.

Burrows gave up, presumably exhausted and unhappy at being demoted from author-director to merely director, though the official line is that he resented a comment Albee made about the nature of Burrows' sense of humor. When Merrick asked Joseph Anthony to take over, Anthony pointed out that he had spent no little time after *110 in the Shade* promising everyone on The Street that he would never, never, never work for David Merrick again. What could he say to them now if he took on the renamed *Breakfast at Tiffany's?*

Merrick said, "Tell them you did it for the money."

That is so Merrick, and so Broadway—so "My profession obeys different rules than your profession"—that it must have happened. Anthony took over the show's steerage, readying everyone to put in the Albee version when they all reached New York. And there, blaming no one but himself, Merrick put an end to what he called "an excruciatingly boring evening."

Again: it wasn't. Either in its light Abe Burrows reading or in the darker Albee initiative, *Breakfast at Tiffany's* didn't work because it was a bad idea for a show. Capote's Holly is tough and Paramount's Holly is Audrey Hepburn; neither one would adapt well to the musical, not at this time, anyway.

Illya Darling (1967) was another musical based on a movie of the very early 1960s, *Never on Sunday*. This was an even worse idea than *Holly Golightly*. The story of a Greek prostitute resisting a *Pygmalion*-like education by an American, *Never on Sunday* was filmed in great hunks of Athens and Piraeus. Most musical adaptations open up their source; this musical closed its source down. The sea, the ships, the Acropolis: gone. In their place were the film's writer, director, and costar, Jules Dassin; the film's star, Dassin's wife, Melina Mercouri; some other of the film's actors; and the film's composer, Manos Hadjidakis.

Retaining Hadjidakis was *Illya Darling's* one creative move. A wonderful composer, he would obviously bring the bona fide *bouzouki* sound to Broadway. Working with lyricist Joe Darion, Hadjidakis all but marinated the songs in *ouzo*, especially in the more atmospheric numbers, such as Mercouri's "Piraeus, My Love" and the comic "Medea Tango," in which she turns the classic horror story into a plot for Disney; or the ballad "After Love," for Mercouri's on-and-off boy friend (Nikos Kourkoulos); or the Farewell Song, "Ya Chara," when the reforming foreigner (Orson Bean) leaves Mercouri and Greece, his work unfinished.

So there are good numbers; but it's not a good score. There are floppo pieces like "Heaven Help the Sailors on a Night Like This," and there is the intrusion of the film's title song. As *Carnival!* demonstrated, it is preferred style to write a new hit tune for the stage version. It shows your valor. The *show's* title song, led by Titos Vandis, was another of those extraneous salutes infesting the sixties musical. The worst of them were sounding floppo—and, even if the song itself was pleasing, it created floppo atmosphere ceaselessly to fall back on what was fast becoming a desperation genre. *Illya Darling* even had a floppo role, that of Despo Diamantidou, playing mononymously under her own name as Despo. Though she had held a proud place in the film, in the show her every line was an embarrassment and her solo, "I'll Never Lay Down Any More," was the worst song of the decade.

To add to these problems, Jules Dassin seemed determined to keep the entertainment down, to delete anything that might detract from Mercouri. Kourkoulos had a terrific number in Philadelphia, the launching vocal in the show, after he encountered Mercouri for the first time. One of those "I Met a Girl" numbers, it gave vocal opportunities to both Kourkoulos and the male chorus in dense harmony. Dassin cut it, as he cut plenty more, to guide the New York critics to his only goal, rhapsody for his wife.

It worked, for by the time *Illya Darling* reached Broadway, there was nothing to praise but Mercouri. The show ran an absurd 320 performances (entirely on the advance), but no one knows anyone who liked it, including Bette Midler. Of course, she was there. "I never miss an Orson Bean–Nikos Kourkoulos–Joe E. Marks musical," she told excited friends.

Breakfast at Tiffany's was a bad idea and a misconceived execution, and *Illya Darling* was simply an aberration. What to call *The Happy Time* (1968), a Merrick-Champion show built around Robert Goulet? This one should succeed, with a Kander and Ebb score, with David Wayne joining Goulet over the title as trusty father to Goulet's errant son, a glamorous photographer. The source must be Samuel Taylor's life-loving family comedy of French Canadian culture, by the same title, from Robert L. Fontaine's nostalgic stories: grandpapa, uncles and aunts, a young boy wrestling with the secrets of life. A little trouble and a lot of joy. It should be a musical: this is a good idea.

Yet it wasn't. Although Merrick did have the rights to set Taylor's play to music, Merrick's book writer, N. Richard Nash, had his own story in mind. He used Taylor's characters only, not Taylor's dramaturgy. He made Goulet a sham hero, an idol to his nephew (a teenage Michael Rupert) but a reproach to Wayne. Champion wanted to bring photography into the production—his credit read "Directed, filmed and choreographed by." True, projecting all those stills would satisfy Champion's need to keep his shows restless. But wouldn't those stills play hell with replacement performers if the show ran any amount of time?

It didn't matter, because once Champion dropped Samuel Taylor's play as inspiration, he lost the substance of the entire project. One can't make a musical out of a title and photo stills. Nash's script did not excite Kander and Ebb. We sense in their better numbers a wish to have written a score for Taylor's play and in their less interesting numbers a dispirited attempt to give Champion what he wants while knowing that no one else wants it, including the audience.

The Happy Time was a superfluous show. Fred Ebb describes it as "*The Glass Menagerie* at Radio City Music Hall." Another way of putting it is Arrogance of Production. This had come creeping in—in *Cabaret's* curtain call, perhaps, when all the players stood unmoving, not acknowledging the applause and thus rejecting the traditional socialization of thespians and their public. Or in Big Lady titlesongitis. Or in the very notion of using *The Happy Time's* characters but not *The Happy Time's* content.

No matter, says Champion. The play's the thing—stepladders, clusters of dancers on the big open stage, those back-projected photos constantly appearing, transforming, reappearing. As the family scapegrace, Goulet is always on the move yet, like those photos, ever returning. "He's Back," the family's number establishing their relationship to him, is wary. Nephew Rupert adores him but father Wayne manages to love and dislike him at once. Well, there's a story in that, surely.

The Happy Time started its tryout in Los Angeles. Why? Because Champion insisted. So there were all those movie people urging movie expedients upon the creative team. Robert Goulet disliked? A sham? Even a loser? But he's your Gary Cooper!

So, on bad advice, Goulet's character was reinstructed. Now he really was a glamorous photographer, not a failure pretending to be one. It was ever Fred Ebb's regret that this demoralized the song "Please Stay." Rupert's platonic love song to his uncle, it ran on a dramatic subtext: Rupert is begging Goulet to abjure the golden kingdoms that Goulet in fact has no access to. The number worked on two levels: to show how much Rupert loved his uncle, and to show how unworthy his uncle was of that love. That's sound dramatic writing. Making Goulet a big deal drained the scene of its humiliating honesty.

Worse, is there even such a thing as a glamorous international photographer? A glamorous international dancer, yes: Baryshnikov. A glamorous international widow: Jackie Onassis. A glamorous international musician: Leonard Bernstein. Who's a photographer? Friedman-Abeles?

What makes one irritated about *The Happy Time* is the reckless waste of Taylor's very potential play and of Kander and Ebb, who would have found lovely music in it. Merrick could have had a hit. By 1968, however, a Merrick-Champion show wasn't a smallish, book-oriented piece, as *Carnival!* had been for them and as *The Happy Time* would have had to be. No, a Merrick-Champion show was a production of such arrogance that it could try to run on no material under the guidance of Hollywood idiots.

14

WHAT DID I HAVE THAT I DON'T HAVE?

MUSICAL COMEDY II

And here's another Merrick-Champion show of no great import, though this one was a sixteen-month hit: *I Do! I Do!* (1966). Its source was unlikely, a two-person comedy following thirty-five years in the marriage of Michael and Agnes. It takes them from their first night together in their new house to the day they move out to make room for the next pair of newlyweds. Called *The Fourposter*, after the huge bed that dominated the set when Hume Cronyn and Jessica Tandy played Jan de Hartog's play in 1951, the work covers the expected issues. The two raise kids, have arguments (including a near divorce), see their kids married (to an "ape," a "pie face," says Michael, of his daughter's intended), and grow old.

With a score by Harvey Schmidt and Tom Jones and a book by Jones, *I Do! I Do!* could easily have been opened up—but then, why do *The Fourposter*? Its charm lies in how much of the world we see through just two pairs of eyes. The Cronyns, by all reports, played with great verve; all Champion had to do was find the musical's equivalent of the Cronyns. That's right: Mary Martin and Robert Preston. (They were billed in that order, probably out of Preston's gallantry.) In the event, Champion *did* open up *The Fourposter*, not by adding cast and scenes but by filling the stage with stuff—balloons, toys, musical instruments (which the stars actually played), startling costume changes for solo numbers (his night-shirt for a barefoot soft "shoe," her sneaking-out-on-the-town finery with a bird-of-paradise hat), an endless supply of tricks and stunts. Merrick loved it: only two salaries to pay and another of those unit sets. The critics loved it, too, mostly, though Walter Kerr thought it all an amiable cliché and Norman Nadel was at pains to remind readers how much of the material came from Hartog's play.

It did. What was new was the score, the least arresting one of all Schmidt and Jones' shows. Some of it is boring and some only serviceable. The best number, "Thousands of Flowers," was cut out of town, because Champion wasn't satisfied with the staging. This reminds us that the real cliché here is not *I Do! I Do!*'s script but the creative power of the director-choreographer. At least Champion allowed Mary Martin to sing the melting "What Is a Woman" unmolested by show-shop didoes.

Hair (1967) had even less plot, though "the American Tribal Love-Rock Musical" made such an occasion of itself that it fooled some into thinking it was a breakthrough of some kind. It started at Joseph Papp's Public Theater, with music by Galt MacDermot and words by Gerome Ragni and James Rado. "Ain't Got No," "Dead End," "Electric Blues," "Walking in Space," "Exanaplanetooch," and "Climax!" typify the tune-stack. There was no plot but rather a throughline: Claude Bukowski (Walker Daniels) is so Beatled that he prefers to be from Manchester, England, than from Flushing, Queens. Dad (Ed Crowley) and Mom (Marijane Maricle) oppose him. Berger (co-author Ragni) supports him. Eventually, he is drafted, and the show ends.

There was not a lot of action, for *Hair* wasn't about people but about attitudes. A wildly enthusiastic reception drew the work on, at first to a discothèque and then to Broadway in 1968, wholly rewritten, recast, and restaged. Ragni still played the hippie Berger, but Rado now played Claude, various cast members faked his parents (usually in transgender shock style), and director Tom O'Horgan filled the Biltmore Theatre's stage with trendy cult insignia—beads, long hair, "pot smoke," and even nudity. Direct contact with the public was elemental in the ethos, so when Ragni wanted to queen Rado up to defy the draft board, Ragni went into the house to borrow makeup sticks from hapless seat holders.

The score was greatly expanded for Broadway. This was a smart move, because MacDermot's music is tuneful and the Ragni-Rado lyrics, though often dumb, are just as often cagily right and smart and even poetic. *Hair* was trendy novelty with genuine talent behind it. That's rare. The book cuts right to the chase:

MOM: What are you going to do with your life?

    Besides dishevelled . . . what do you want to be?

CLAUDE: Kate Smith.

MOM: Start facing reality . . .

CLAUDE: Which one?

and the score fills out the stage picture of a "tribe" of hippies bloviating on grass and issues. At the close of "Air," everyone coughs. "Initials" brings together LBJ and LSD—the ultimate authority versus the ultimate subversion. "Colored Spade" exorcises racist epithets simply by using them. At 1,836 performances (from downtown through uptown), *Hair* was a hit and its score seemed to be rock. What did that mean?

It meant that *Hair* was a one-time-only stunt that could not be turned into genre. *The New York Times'* theatre idiot, Clive Barnes, had been pushing for "rock scores." However, the first critic (and the last fair one), Aristotle, teaches by his example that critics don't dictate to creators. Creators make the art. The correct critic merely describes what they are creating. Barnes, whom the *Times* had flown in from a foreign clime, knew and cared nothing of the American musical's history and destiny; he just attached himself to a handy piece of hip. In fact, rock's intrusive beat and usually illiterate lyrics made it useless on Broadway—to everyone except Barnes. Savaging traditional Broadway scores and rewarding authors who flattered his demands, Barnes helped destroy the musical's confidence by bombing decent shows and pushing for that jackass's ideal, the rock musical.

There were no rock musicals, in fact, including *Hair*. *Hair*'s songs were, yes, late-sixties pop. They had a beat. You could dance to them. But Mac-Dermot's intelligence placed them way above Top 40. To hear "Manchester, England," "Black Boys/White Boys," or "Frank Mills" today is to realize how poverty-stricken most late-sixties American pop was. *Hair*'s songs use the pop sound while transcending it, to create something new. Sophisticated, literally: made of diverse sources. There was never to be a rock musical worth hearing,* and there was no need for rock to make it to Broadway, except in the mind of Clive Barnes.

*One arguable exception is Richard O'Brien's *The Rocky Horror Show* (1973). However, this spoof uses its score as part of the lampoon, and the music is thus not meant to be taken seriously.

While *I Do! I Do!* and *Hair* were hits, some worthier fare lost money. I offer a quartet of shows whose failure is hard to explain: *Baker Street* (1965), *The Apple Tree* (1966), *Hallelujah, Baby!* (1967), and *George M!* (1968). Two are adaptations of short fiction and two are originals, but each offers typical sixties uniqueness.

Baker Street, "a musical adventure of Sherlock Holmes," suggests at first moment something better left untried. Sherlock Holmes singing? And where's the romance? But, remember, it's an *adventure*, a rare chance to use the musical's technology on a thriller. Jerome Coopersmith drew his libretto more or less from Arthur Conan Doyle. But this really was a novelty in every respect, from its Sprechstimme Holmes (Fritz Weaver) and Moriarity (Martin Gabel) to the giant electrified sign of crimes in progress that producer Alexander Cohen erected on the façade of the Broadway Theatre for all to see.

Inga Swenson supplied some heart interest, as the American actress who starts as Holmes' foe and quickly becomes his confederate, Peter Sallis played the ever clueless Dr. Watson, the Bil Baird Marionettes presented Queen Victoria's Diamond Jubilee parade, and Oliver Smith designed an ingenious series of twisty visuals, peaking in a confrontation on the Dover cliffs when both Holmes and Moriarity went flying over the edge. Hal Prince directed, Lee Becker Theodore (the original Anybodys in *West Side Story*) choreographed, and Cohen spent the money. All this led to *Baker Street*'s being a genuine "spectacular," lavish and fast and suspenseful, as a mystery must be.

The notices were of course mixed—when weren't they now?—but there was that talk-of-the-town sign over the marquee, not to mention a temporary hit tune, Watson's wistful "A Married Man," sung while he and Holmes, bound, wait out the minutes before a bomb carries them off; Richard Burton recorded the number, perhaps thinking it an encore to "How To Handle a Woman."

That brings us to *Baker Street*'s flaw. In terms of its songs, this is no *Camelot*. Cohen entrusted the score to the unknown Marian Grudeff and Raymond Jessel, and they produced an unknown score. It's not terrible, exactly. Inga Swenson inspired them; her numbers are valid. An ensemble number when the good guys are setting off in disguise, "What A Night This Is Going To Be," is lively. The first number, a setting of the famous Holmesian deductive process, "It's So Simple," is correct.

A hit musical needs more than valid, lively, and correct in its score, though, and Cohen attempted to control the damage with interpolations by Bock and Harnick. But their Holmes (in "Cold Clear World") and Moriarity (in "I Shall Miss You") are as boring as Grudeff and Jessel's. Captivated by Swenson like everyone else, Bock and Harnick gave her a wonderful establishing number, "I'm in London Again." (Another Harnick zinger: "I know your critics," the actress sings, "and already I feel a chill.")

Still, *Baker Street* was not the kind of show that needed a strong score. Its energy lay in plot and pacing and the eye-filling designs; and one could not ask for more faithful impersonations than those of Weaver and Gabel, not to mention la Swenson. Why didn't it run on sheer theatricality? It was that horrible sixties paradox: people were patronizing the biggest hits almost relentlessly while neglecting everything else.

Baker Street gave up after nine months, but *The Apple Tree* got halfway through its fourteenth month. That's impressive, for if *Baker Street* was unexpected, *The Apple Tree* was impossible—three one-act musicals on the battle of the sexes. Barbara Harris and Alan Alda played the First Couple (Eve and Adam), then the Worst Couple (they're barbarians, so she loves but may have to kill him), and at last the Odd Couple (Marilyn Monroe meets Mick Jagger). Mark Twain, Frank R. Stockton, and cartoonist Jules Feiffer were respectively the sources, and while there were a few unifying elements (especially mention of the color brown as a running gag), the show reveled in heterogeneity. Bills of one-acters are extremely rare in the Broadway musical,* and the chance to see Harris in particular, leaping from a bewildered Eve through the nearly topless, prowling-panther Princess Barbara to the pathetic chimney sweep who turns into a frosty love goddess, should have been irresistible. After all, Harris was one of the great newcomers of the early 1960s, first in the comedy revue *From the Second City* and then both on and off Broadway, most notably in Jerome Robbins' staging of Brecht's *Mother Courage* with Anne Bancroft and *On a Clear Day You Can See Forever*. In this age when the

---

*There have been some off-Broadway. The only instances of the mixed grill that I can cite on The Street before 1966 are Victor Herbert's *Dream City* and *The Magic Knight* (1906), Jerome Moross' *Ballet Ballads* (1948), and *A Day in Hollywood A Night in the Ukraine* (1980).

musical was clearly in transition, Harris' abilities as singer, actress, and bizarre comic should have been sine qua non.

Yet not only did *The Apple Tree* lose money, but it isn't even a cult musical. What, with a Bock and Harnick score? Relieved of their *Baker Street* chores, they're in superb form, developing separate *tinte* for each title in the triptych. Twain's "The Diary of Adam and Eve" is a musical play, culminating in a number on a Hammersteinian concept that Richard Rodgers must have admired, "What Makes Me Love Him?"

But then, after the first intermission, Stockton's "The Lady or the Tiger?" is a goof. The Twain explores the differences between the genders—his wanting to get a thing over with, her taking the time to understand it. The songs all pursue such differences. (Another ultra-Harnickian line, in her "Here in Eden": "I find the apples especially exciting.") "The Lady or the Tiger?," however, is set up by the very nature of Stockton's tale to be a stunt with a twist ending—or, rather, without a proper ending at all. Alda has to open one of two doors. Behind one: a ravenous tiger. Behind the other: a beautiful girl, guests, rice, an immediate shotgun wedding. Harris must lose him—or lose him. She knows the secret of the doors. She subtly points. He chooses that door. Just before he opens it, the curtain falls.

One odd thing about *The Apple Tree* is that humor increasingly infected the show as it progressed. "Adam and Eve" was more sentimental than funny. "The Lady or the Tiger?" was funny and also fast-paced—so much so that one of Bock's loveliest melodies, "Forbidden Love," got as lost in plot development as *Camelot*'s "Follow Me." And the third segment, "Passionella," was an outrageous spoof—of the American fame fantasy, of grisly rock musicians, of sex symbols, of television, of the very notion of two stars playing three musicals. (There was a third star, Larry Blyden, with much less to do. In Eden, he was the snake; in the barbarian kingdom, he knew the secret of the doors; in "Passionella," he narrated.)

Mike Nichols directed (along with choreographers Herbert Ross and Lee [Becker] Theodore), and everything seemed set to roll to success. In the 1950s, *The Apple Tree*'s 463 performances would have marked a hit. Even *Hallelujah, Baby!*'s 293 would have promised some profit. A show wins the Best Musical Tony—as the latter did—and loses money? That's the 1960s. At least, here is another work that, in 1967, sought to reflect the social situation of the times. *Hallelujah, Baby!* is the civil-rights musical. Arthur Laurents, to a Styne-Comden-Green score, looks at sixty years of American race relations.

As in *Love Life*, the principals do not age, but grow along with the events they experience. Leslie Uggams was the protagonist, an idealistic young black woman torn between white and black suitors (Allen Case, Robert Hooks) as she makes her way in show biz. As we watch, the twentieth century passes—in, for instance, Hooks' move from Pullman porter to civil-rights leader, or in a change of setting from speakeasy to the New Deal's Federal Theatre Project, putting on a "jazz" *Macbeth*,* with Uggams as one of the witches.

With Kevin Carlisle's choreography and Burt Shevelove's direction keeping things smart and speedy, *Hallelujah, Baby!* should have been a sure thing: sound liberal politics, an enjoyable (though not excellent) score, and especially the enchanting Uggams. She gave real substance to her character, who goes about the usual musical-comedy heroine's business—Wanting Song ("My Own Morning"), spoof tap number ("Feet Do Yo' Stuff"), angry-at-my-boy-friend number ("I Wanted To Change Him")—while undergoing the character development typical of a musical-*play* heroine.

Perhaps *Baker Street*'s substandard score really did dampen its gleam. Maybe *The Happy Time* was just too much staging of too little story. But *Hallelujah, Baby!* ran right down the center of what Broadway traditionally wanted from a musical. Even more surprising, at least to me, is the failure of *George M!* (1968) to run four or five years. A bio of George M. Cohan starring Joel Grey under super-director Joe Layton, *George M!*, certainly acted like a hit. At 427 performances, it even computes as a hit. It just happened not to make back its money.

Yet it had that ageless song catalogue to build on, not only "Yankee Doodle Dandy," "Over There," "You're a Grand Old Flag," and "Forty-

---

*This more or less happened: in 1936, Orson Welles staged *Macbeth* for the so-called "Negro Division" of the Federal Theatre. Jack Carter and Edna Thomas played the leads, with Canada Lee as Banquo; and the play was moved from Scotland to, as the program stated, "Jungles of Mythical Island Resembling Haiti." The cast wore ballroom finery and the witches' magic was turned into voodoo. It must have been the real thing, too, for some of the actors held an all-night *cérémonie vaudou* in response to a bad notice from Percy Hammond of the *Herald Tribune*. He died three days later.

Five Minutes From Broadway," but a trove of wonderful songs. Not all of Cohan is worth hearing. Some of it is trite, and much of the later work, from the 1920s, is simply horrible. But musical supervisor Laurence Rosenthal (or someone not thus credited) selected the very best music of this much misunderstood figure and filled the show with it. Think of it all: *The Little Millionaire, Fifty Miles From Boston, The Governor's Son, Little Johnny Jones, Mother Goose, Hello, Broadway,* even an unproduced show, *Musical Comedy Man* . . . a lost chapter of theatre history came rushing back as the unstoppable Georgie pushed his family act into the big time, went on to promote his own gifts, then faced failure as times and styles changed on him.

Michael Stewart seems to have conceived the show, along with Layton, to let a talented bunch of kids double, triple, or quadruple in various roles, now doing an important specialty, now a walk-on, and all serving as their own chorus. The overture, Stewart directed, would be "Give My Regards to Broadway" in a brilliant sonata-allegro rondo like that of *Candide*'s overture—Stewart specifically cited that piece as his model—and the show would race from each joke, number, and event to the next. Telling of America's ultimate show-biz legend, *George M!* must naturally be the ultimate backstager, rich with the spit-out comebacks and sudden dejections that this most American of genres lives on.

For instance, early on, the Four Cohans present their act to vaudeville magnate E. F. Albee (the real-life grandfather by adoption of the playwright, by the way). Seniors Jerry and Nellie give us "Musical Moon." Daughter Josie delights with "Oh, You Wonderful Boy." All four hot up the stage with the rousing "All Aboard for Broadway." They're done. Three beats, then:

ALBEE: I'll take the girl.

Jerry talks fast, but Georgie's fuming at Albee's second offer, to take all four Cohans, but in Poughkeepsie:

GEORGIE: Nobody starts in Poughkeepsie, Pop! That's where you finish!

Georgie tells off Albee but good:

GEORGIE: You'll come begging for this act someday . . . and the Four
Cohans will never play any theatre of yours as long as we're in this
business! . . . Remember that, Mr. Albee—*never!*

ALBEE: Add thirty days to that, sonny, and you've got a deal.

Most of *George M!*'s book scenes didn't last this long. As Walter Kerr
observed, Layton was "prodigal with lively mechanics: headlong hoofers,
hair-breadth tumblers, dogs flipping skyward over table tops, caterwauling
maidservants, manic managers, race and stomp and furious rat-a-tat-tat.
The whole show is a photo finish, except that the race never ends."

Trickery, you might say. But of a very clever sort. The show's highlight
typifies how Layton's crew seemed to craze their way through the story:
Georgie and his producing partner, Sam H. Harris, try to get Fay Templeton to star in *Forty-Five Minutes From Broadway*. Rather than spell it out
in book scenes capped by songs, or even interspersed with songs, Layton
combined dialogue, song, and dance in a fluidly shifting action, cutting
cinematically from the Cohan & Harris office to Templeton's apartment.
For much of it, Templeton is *hounded* by the show's title song. Her maid
sings it (as Kerr just noted), her agent sings it, her *mother* sings it. At one
point, the lights came up on a sight gag: Templeton lying on a chaise, a
lace square covering her features. She'd rather die than be in this show, or
even hear that darned tune again. Indeed, Cohan & Harris appear determined to employ her or kill her. She gives in at last, and walks across the
stage to their office, joining in on the last line of the song as she signs the
contract.

Some onlookers resented all the arranging, the finessing, the technical
electricity. But that's theatre, especially musical theatre in the 1960s. Like
Follies and *Grand Hotel*, *George M!* is a show that buffs returned to several
times during the original run and that, for them, can never be adequately
revived.

George M!'s cast was gifted, but not entirely irreplaceable. Besides
Grey, Jerry Dodge, Betty Ann Grove, and Bernadette Peters as the Four
Cohans, the ensemble took in Jill O'Hara, Harvey Evans, Jacqueline
Alloway (as the tempestuous Templeton; also Draper's Assistant and
Wardrobe Lady), Loni Ackerman (as Templeton's maid; but also Dog
Trainer and Second Pianist), Jonelle Allen, Janie Sell, and John Mineo.
Every one of them drew greater distinction to various other parts in their

careers. Nevertheless, this was a one-of-a-kind show, notwithstanding the familiarity of some of its score and the well-known facts of Cohan's life.

We know them largely from the James Cagney Hollywood bio, *Yankee Doodle Dandy*. This left out the central event in Cohan's life, his championing of The Corporation against the individual during the 1919 actors' strike and the martyred bitterness that he suffered ever after. However, the film's sense of the show biz that Cohan knew is surprisingly faithful, so it is unfortunate that it got one thing entirely wrong: Cohan himself. The real George M. was nothing like the strutting dynamo that Cagney, Mickey Rooney (on television), Joel Grey, and others have as a rule presented. Yes, Cohan was cocky, a smart aleck. He called everyone "kid," as if he were the boss. He was the typical aggressively compensating short guy, albeit with the talent to back it up and the self-invention to pull it off.

But that self-invention was not noisy, not busy. Cohan was above all an underplayer. He spoke very, very quietly. He could prance around when necessary, but mostly he hypnotized the public, pulled them in, hardly moved at all. An eyebrow, maybe. All this Yankee doodling obscures the Cohan style just as the now uncorrectable *Co-han* obscures *his* pronunciation, the more truly Irish *Co-an*. Still, to go into legend is to become a fantasy, and a *George M!* centered on something less pugnacious than Grey—and Layton's whole Yankee Dandy production—would have been only deflatingly authentic.

If this quartet of failures demonstrates how easily one could lose money on a good show, what are we to say of such second-raters as *It's a Bird It's a Plane It's Superman* (1966), *Henry, Sweet Henry* (1967), and *Sherry!* (1967)? These are okay shows; okay shows aren't doing so well any more. Call them even pleasurable. Say that *Superman* was an attempt to extrapolate something in American culture by linking two distinct pop forms, the musical and the comic book. Consider *Henry, Sweet Henry* as another instance of the sixties show seeking to improve upon a decent movie by harmonizing its emotional discords, like *Carnival!* and *She Loves Me*. And imagine how delightful *Sherry!* must have been to theatergoers unfamiliar with the classic lines of its classic source, Kaufman and Hart's *The Man Who Came To Dinner*.

This was an age that liked its hits high-powered. The time of *Up in Central Park, Make Mine Manhattan, Me and Juliet, Plain and Fancy*, and other titles that made bank without becoming cultural jackpots was the 1940s and the 1950s. *Superman* would have been a hit in the 1950s; in 1966, it lasted four months. The other two averaged out at ten weeks each.

Producer-director Hal Prince wanted his *Superman* young. Or, at least, hip, media-young. His librettists were Hollywood screenwriters (David Newman and Robert Benton) and his choreographer a television specialist (Ernest Flatt). Strouse and Adams wrote the score in a somewhat pop vein—the near-title song, "It's Superman," is out-and-out rock and roll, and the Man of Steel smacked bad guys around in "Pow! Bam! Zonk!" There was even one set, reminiscent of the "Telephone Hour" boxes in Strouse and Adams' *Bye Bye Birdie*, laid out as the panels of a comic-book page, with a "Meanwhile" at the upper left and a song helping the plot to thicken.

True, the bulk of the score is standard Broadway—scientist comes on to girl reporter in scientific terms to a vamp glowing like the Milky Way in "We Don't Matter At All"; heroine sings Wanting Song—called, in fact, "What I've Always Wanted"; evil columnist opens Act Two in front of blowup of newsprint chortling through "So Long, Big Guy."

This is traditional expertise. Maybe the show would have been more interesting if it had broken out of tradition—if it had made a musical into a comic book instead of the other way around. Maybe the authors should have brought in the zany side of the super-hero's rogues gallery in the DC comic books—his clumsy doppelgänger Bizarro, or his childish antagonist Mr. Mxyzptlk, who can't be got rid of till Superman tricks him into pronouncing his name backward. In fact, the musical used almost nothing of the comic besides its premise and its two most famous characters, the hero (Bob Holiday) and Lois Lane (Patricia Marand). There was no Jimmy Olson, Perry White had no more than a bit, and the expectable mad scientist was a somewhat colorless clown, physicist Abner Sedgwick (Michael O'Sullivan). The second villain, modeled on Walter Winchell (Jack Cassidy), his assistant (Linda Lavin), and the other guy in the triangle with Superman and Lois (Don Chastain) filled out the cast of a Broadway musical rather than amplified any vision of what this ageless good-versus-evil fantasy means to Americans.

Call it routine, then: but good routine. Superman actually flew, and Holiday's height and looks made him ideal, once the padding filled out the familiar red, blue, and yellow suit and a dashing comma of forelock was isolated. It was an impossible role to play, and probably to write. Newman and Benton did much better with Cassidy's insidious columnist; and Lavin got the show's best three minutes in "You've Got Possibilities," her seduction of Clark Kent in the newspaper office. One of those quiet little belt jobs that keep getting louder and broader, the song was a comic number, but you'd never guess as much from the cast album. It was all visual: as Lavin pulled at Holiday's tie and unbuttoned his shirt, she unwittingly began to reveal those super-tights underneath his street clothes.

Nunnally and Nora Johnson wrote the screenplay for the 1964 movie *The World of Henry Orient* (based on Nora's novel), and George Roy Hill directed it. So it made sense for Nunnally and Hill to recombine for the musical version, with Bob Merrill doing the score. Better yet, the choreography was by Michael Bennett, though his name meant nothing at the time. Don Ameche played the title role, that of a gimmicky pop-classical musician (Peter Sellers in the movie) pursuing adulterous affairs while being stalked by two schoolgirls. A spectacular young talent named Robin Wilson played the more important of the two. She, in fact, not Ameche, was the show's protagonist, an unloved and virtually orphaned rich kid who runs around in a fur coat inventing dramas and escapades. Neva Small played her confidante and Alice Playten their nemesis, a money-crazed wheeler-dealer. All three were girls of the Norton School, along with the female ensemble, and the male gypsies were the Knickerbocker Greys. A few grown-ups flitted in and out of their lives—teachers, parents, the evasive Orient. But the show clearly sided with the kids.

It's kind of a white *Flower Drum Song*—musical-comedy generation war. Besides Ameche, the other main grown-ups were the dithering Louise Lasser and the classy Carol Bruce—Wilson's mother, which helped bind the picaresque story line. It was an entertaining show and a good idea, for the movie is stuffed with emotional content. But Merrill was not at his best, Playten's adorable rascal stole the show from the plangent Wilson, and perhaps the notion of a pop musician who fills Carnegie Hall with his *sinfonia* was premature in 1967. There was no John Tesh then— even if musical comedy often creates a prescient reality, as in *Damn Yankees*' woman sportswriter or *A Family Affair*'s telephone-answering tape. We should at least recall a charming curtain at a school dance, when the Greys pair off with the Nortons. The anxious Wilson reprises her Wanting Song, "Here I Am," is asked to dance, and, shyly smiling, joins in the waltz.

Shouldn't *Sherry!* have been a natural? It was filled with the original Kaufman-Hart put-downs and comebacks, the dizzying catalogue of celebrities of the 1930s, and the relentless discoveries and tortures of farce. Some of the celebrities are impersonated in the action—Alexander Woollcott, of course, but also Gertrude Lawrence, Noël Coward, and Harpo Marx. Except for a score that varied from good to ordinary, *Sherry!* had not just the primer but the finish of a hit. Audiences loved it, giving it genuine ovations, but it couldn't get that all-important *Times* rave and went down after 65 performances.

James Lipton wrote the book and lyrics, to Laurence Rosenthal's music. Morton Da Costa, a good director of surefire material but useless at reordering a chaos, left during tryouts with choreographer Ron Field, the pair replaced by Joe Layton. He worked wonders: an out-of-town mediocrity began to play with style and dramatic power and, above all, comedy. It was no longer an insipid show, but a hot one. I call *Sherry!* the one sixties bomb that in most respects behaved like a hit.

It had a hot cast. The unhappy George Sanders also left during the tryout, replaced by Clive Revill, a taut comic and, surprisingly, a good singer. Better than any Sheridan Whiteside I have seen, Revill defined the very strange relationship with his secretary (Elizabeth Allen). Are they friends? Conspirators? Platonic lovers? Layton jumped at the last possibility, adding in one of the era's last dream ballets (and one of the few comic ones ever), in which Revill considered marrying Allen and saw himself as Fred Astaire partnering a chorus woman billed in the program as Ginger. Their music even spoofed "The Continental." Of course, the dance must be a lampoon. Whiteside is ultimately . . . well, what? Gay? Sexless? What was Alexander Woollcott, sexually?

It's an odd question for the musical version to deal with. But then, this formerly okay musical grew so formidable in Layton's overhaul that it tried to answer questions that the play never bothered to ask. *Sherry!* had plenty of smart musical-comedy things—the villainess' phone conversation with her stuttering English-lord fiancé, his lines played in the pit by a hilariously inarticulate trumpet; a first date for the secretary and a local newspaperman (Jon Cypher) that becomes an ensemble dance built into and around her "Maybe It's Time For Me"; an insistent use of song to convey plot matter, even the mundane dialogue of Whiteside and his irritating doctor; the use of "With This Ring" as *two* plot numbers to the same melody and title, one Cypher's proposal to Allen and the other Whiteside's telephone call to the Waldorf-Astoria to the villainess to lure her into destroying the Allen-Cypher romance.

I ask you, does this sound like a flop? The Roundabout Theatre's 2000 revival of *The Man Who Came To Dinner* gave us in Harriet Harris a secretary very clearly in need of the newspaperman's love. Harris played an insecure woman blessed by the interest of a secure man—very much how Allen and Cypher played these roles in *Sherry!* The Roundabout's villainess, Jean Smart, tried to humanize her. But this isn't a human role. Lorraine Sheldon is, as Gertrude Lawrence was, explosively wonderful when on stage and an all-devouring terror when off. In short: Dolores Gray, not least while singing the belt-purring "Putty in Your Hands" to Cypher and undergoing screwball choreography in Layton's spicy reediting of the original humdrum dance.

Our next group of flops comprises sheer duds, though one boasted one of the decade's best scores: Burton Lane and Alan Jay Lerner's show about ESP, *On a Clear Day You Can See Forever* (1965). There are three things to say about this piece—economically, artistically, and historically.

Economically: this was the attraction that broke the ten-dollar limit on the Saturday-night ticket top, jumping to $11.90.

Artistically: the writer James Kirkwood once found himself seated with *Clear Day* librettist Alan Jay Lerner on a panel. Noting the proliferation of shows based on plays, films, and novels that he was already familiar with, Kirkwood told Lerner how much he enjoyed the intermission of *On a Clear Day*, because he honestly didn't know what would happen next. Lerner said, "I didn't, either. That was the problem."

Historically: Louis Jourdan, as the ESP doctor treating a patient who has been reincarnated, was relieved of his part in Boston. Lane insisted: because if the show was going to bomb—and it obviously was going to— at least let the music be properly sung. John Cullum took over as the doctor, aggressively pealing out in the title song, the creepily intense "Melinda" (a love song to a woman who died over a century before), and "Come Back To Me." He was a neat match for the absurdly comic Barbara Harris, nerdy quicksilver to his solid grandeur. (He had been one of Guenevere's favorite bodyguards in *Camelot*, though, quite oddly, he took over the part of not Lancelot but Mordred.) Perhaps Lerner hoped that the extensive flashbacks to Regency England (the place of Harris' former life) would fatten his thin story line. It certainly gave Lerner a chance to show off his gift for Gilbertian twisty-pun patter, in Clifford David's "Don't Tamper With My Sister." David also got a ballad, "She Wasn't You," that reminded one how well Lerner's wit could subside into an almost purely musical structure without losing its identity.

Still, for all Oliver Smith and Freddy Wittop's visual spectacle, the antique sequences failed to reflect, comment on, or embellish the main story line. As if conceding as much, Lerner considerably revised them in his screenplay for the film version, with a miscast Barbra Streisand and the noted French zombie Yves Montand. Even thus pointedly revised and yet more spectacular, the flashbacks remain unintegrated. Lerner was right in what he said to Kirkwood—Lerner had a premise for a show. He didn't have a show.

Chu Chem (1966), Mitch Leigh's encore to *Man of La Mancha*, has been footnoted in these pages as having closed in Philadelphia. It did, at least, have an eye-opening unit set, with the back wall of the theatre decorated as a giant scroll, its pages "turning," to the marvel of the house.

But then, every musical has something. *A Joyful Noise* (1966) had John Raitt, Karen Morrow, and a pleasing taste of the country sound, a much more useful pop idiom for theatre music than rock. *Golden Rainbow* (1968) had Steve Lawrence and Eydie Gorme in an adaptation of Arnold Schulman's *A Hole in the Head,* removed to Las Vegas (from Miami). Ron Field jumped at it—showgirls, spangles, show-biz super-kill so tasty that one doesn't know whether it's parody, demi-parody, or meta-parody. Suddenly, during tryouts, Eydie turned prudish. That next-to-naked pas de deux typical of acts in every Vegas hotel—out! Those louche double-meaning jokes—out! The one-step-from-topless chorus girls' pasties—out!, to be replaced by Song of Bernadette *cache-poitrine* halters. And Ron Field says, "Eydie, why don't we cancel this show and do one about the Pennsylvania Dutch?" On second thought, Field left the show before it came in.

Worst of all these flops is *How Now, Dow Jones* (1967). Its producer, David Merrick, completely threw the history off when he closed *Breakfast at Tiffany's* in previews but let this stiff come in, for the former show ever after took the rap as the ultimate sixties bomb while *How Now, Dow Jones* merely stupefied helpless audiences for nearly seven months. It was Carolyn Leigh's idea: the voice announcing the Dow Jones Industrial Average belongs to a woman whose fiancé won't marry her till that average reaches the level of 1,000. She becomes pregnant (by another man) and, with absolutely no foundation, simply makes the announcement.

What? Were book writer Max Shulman, lyricist Leigh, composer Elmer Bernstein, and that overrated director of stupid fluff George Abbott (replacing Arthur Penn) out of their minds? A man won't marry till the Dow Jones average hits a certain level? His fiancée dares to register a fake announcement? On Wall Street? And *lives?*

This is the sort of plot premise one accepted in the twenties musical because twenties musicals weren't sensible. By the 1960s, musicals were sensible, even the daffy ones. They didn't try to get away with the legacy-with-a-catch or stolen-diamonds plots popular when Jerome Kern and George Gershwin were writing the music. *How Now, Dow Jones* was a sixties musical with a twenties sense of reality and a score so bad that I don't know a worse one; and I've emptied parties singing my way through *The Gingham Girl* (1922). But then, *How Now, Dow Jones'* casting gave its lead roles exclusively to Anthony Roberts, Marlyn Mason, Brenda Vaccaro, and Hiram Sherman, a quartet of somewhat less than golden voices.

Am I being too hard on a show that innocently tried and failed? No. *Greenwillow, Tenderloin, Jennie, Flora, the Red Menace,* and *Sherry!* tried and failed. *How Now, Dow Jones* didn't try. Carolyn Leigh had a stupid idea and a bunch of people ran with it with nowhere to go. Let's sample the script, remembering that Max Shulman also wrote one of the worst books of the 1940s, to *Barefoot Boy With Cheek.* Here's mogul Hiram Sherman dictating letters:

WINGATE: To the chairman of the Securities and Exchange Commission: Sir: your allegations about Wingate and Company are base, cowardly, and communistic. Let's have lunch when you're in town. . . . To the National Association of Manufacturers: Happy birthday. . . . To the Federal Reserve Bank: Can you let me have eighty million dollars till Tuesday? Love, Bill.

Again, almost no musical has nothing. *Alive and Kicking* had spectacular Jack Cole dances. *Hit the Trail* had Irra Petina. *Jekyll & Hyde* had eerie Eurotrash erotica at the sides of the stage. *How Now, Dow Jones* had nothing. It was something new in the musical's history, a major producer's major production without a shred of anything except a snappy title.

Merrick also produced *Promises, Promises* (1968), a different case altogether—and, we should note, an instance of Broadway's absorbing a pop-music style of genuine theatre potential. The Burt Bacharach–Hal David score was ultra-contempo, especially in Bacharach's slithery mixed-meter rhythms and Jonathan Tunick's woodwind-bright orchestrations, which included four women's scat lines in the pit. Based on Billy Wilder's film *The Apartment*, *Promises, Promises* had a book by Neil Simon, so the unsuspecting might have anticipated another zany musical comedy like *Little Me*, or a dancey super-production like *Sweet Charity*—Simon's two earlier book shows.

But *The Apartment* is a serious comedy. Jack Lemmon, in one of his most characteristic roles as the well-meaning schnook, lends his flat to adulterous executives (especially Fred MacMurray) for career advancement. When MacMurray's latest (Shirley MacLaine) attempts suicide, she and Lemmon become involved. They eventually become a pair, though we are haunted by the notion that Wilder wants to show us how women must choose between the destructive power of the alpha male and various consolation-prize schnooks.

The almost-suicide alone makes *Promises, Promises* another of our dark shows. But a dark musical *comedy*? With a schnook hero, an oxymoron that works better in sixties film than in the sixties musical? And where in all the music and fun is the MacMurray character to fit?

First, *Promises, Promises'* authors gave their schnook a lot of power. He has the best comedy lines and some very outgoing songs. Moreover, Jerry Orbach, while playing schnook, wasn't a schnook type like Lemmon. Seven years before *Promises*, he was *Carnival!*'s embittered puppeteer; seven years after *Promises*, he was *Chicago*'s sly lawyer. Other than the clueless hat that Orbach wore in a *Promises* bar scene on Christmas Eve, he was every bit the hero—just, maybe, a New York kind of hero.

Edward Winter, in MacMurray's part, was a suitably honey-tongued villain. He even had a solo, sort of a Villain's Wanting Song—called, in fact, "Wanting Things." Jill O'Hara, one of the few leads in a musical to be succeeded by her own sister (Jenny O'Hara), made an admirable heroine, and A. Larry Haines enjoyed a comic tour de force as Orbach's doctor neighbor, ever speculating on the meaning of the comings and goings in The Apartment. A surprising number of later prominent names claimed small roles or ensemble work—Ken Howard, Graciela Daniele, Carole (Kelly) Bishop, Robert Fitch; and an office-party entertainment, "Turkey Lurkey Time," offered Donna McKechnie, Margo Sappington, and Baayork Lee in Michael Bennett choreography.

As so often, Merrick had unveiled not just another hit, and not just a smash hit, but a show that seemed the latest of all shows, so state-of-the-art in Simon's storytelling and Bacharach's sound. The piece was not a breakthrough in design and hardly a super-director's achievement—Robert Moore may be the least familiar name among those who staged major sixties musicals. Yet *Promises* was very major, running 1,281 performances. The score threw off two hit tunes, the title number and "I'll Never Fall In Love Again," and "Knowing When To Leave" knew some currency, too.

Still, what strikes one most about this show is how far musical comedy has come from *le genre primitif et gai*, as Jacques Offenbach called musical comedy when he invented it. Before Offenbach came to Paris from his native Cologne in 1833, Western Civilization's music theatre was either opera or its derivatives, or fairground playlets strung with new lyrics to traditional melodies. What we call "the musical" operates between these two camps, in music less grand than opera's but more dramatic than that of the fairgrounds, and in entirely new composition.

So a German invented musical comedy in France. His form, too, had its derivatives. But the key line ran from such works as *Orphée aux Enfers* and *Les Brigands* in their English adaptations through the Offenbach-influenced Gilbert and Sullivan and their disciples, whose shows had tremendous influence in the United States at around the turn of the century. Most of the dominant composers at the time were from Europe; but the word men were Americans.

Then Jerome Kern and Irving Berlin invented American music, and the Golden Age began. Indeed, the musicals spawned at its start, roughly from 1915 to 1925, were, as Offenbach said, *le gai primitif*: raw dramaturgy and crazy fun.

In *Promises, Promises*—in virtually any sixties musical comedy—the dramaturgy is not raw. It at least aspires to craftsmanship, and the fun is more than fun. The stories aren't crazy any more, as they were for Offenbach and his followers, or for Kern, Berlin, the Gershwins, Rodgers and Hart, and Cole Porter.

The stories are now intelligent. When did this happen, yesterday? Six years before *Promises, Promises*, Simon was writing crazy in *Little Me*. Two years before *Promises, Promises*, Simon was writing crazy in *Sweet Charity*.

No more. This is the decade in which the American musical renounced *le gai primitif* for what we might call a Rodgers and Hammerstein version of it, a *Me and Juliet* or *Flower Drum Song* musical comedy, in which everything makes sense. Isn't that true of all this chapter's titles? *Baker Street* makes sense the way Sherlock Holmes makes sense. *Superman* made too much sense. *Henry, Sweet Henry*, which should have gone totally screwball, made sense. Even *Golden Rainbow*—a Steve Lawrence–Eydie Gorme production—made sense. Isn't that absurd? The one moment in the last show that satisfied was when story and character were tossed aside so that the two stars could try out what was in effect a nightclub-style takeoff on Jeanette MacDonald and Nelson Eddy, complete with a goof on "Stout-hearted Men," a bit of Jewish humor, and Gorme's high B. "Desert Moon," they called it.

There is some of *le gai primitif* left, but it's spotty—*Skyscraper*'s off-the-wall dream sequences, the Looney Tunes zip of *The Apple Tree*'s "Passionella," the pace and surprise of Joe Layton's *George M!* antics. But there is none in *Promises, Promises*. It's very funny, but it's so . . . reasonable. Giving the villain a solo is symmetrical, well-wrought, correct. But is this guy singing because we need to know him or because he's the second male lead in a musical and it would look odd if he weren't in the score?

Yes, but odd is what the musical used to delight in being. *Promises, Promises* is so loaded with symmetry that O'Hara has a solo called "Whoever You Are" that gives us *her* impression of the villain. It's a beautifully intense ballad. A Streisand song, one might say. The lyric really edges into the heroine's romantic difficulties; one almost can see why she might want to throw her life away for this man. "You're two different people," she observes, as countless women have noticed about problem men. It's a superb piece of theatre writing, a disturbing number—the antidote, say, to all the trusting innocence of Barbara Cook's "Magic Moment" in *The Gay Life*.

That's the trouble. A late-sixties musical comedy offers the antidote to early-sixties musical comedy. That quickly, it happened.

15

I Don't Want To Know

Three Shows of 1969

Certain factors bearing upon the history of the American musical but pertaining especially to the form in the 1960s are apparent:

One, with expenses greatly on the rise, shows must attract unnaturally large audiences in order to make money; and most shows don't, even shows counting what had once been called "long runs."

Two, musicals are becoming more serious, so much so that projects impractical in 1959 are smash hits in this decade. *Fiddler on the Roof*, once again, is the obvious example, but so are *No Strings, I Can Get It For You Wholesale, Golden Boy, Man of La Mancha, The Apple Tree, Cabaret, Zorbá*, and *Promises, Promises*. Some of these were succès d'estime, true: but all of them ran.

Certain technical advances are also obvious: one, scene changes are now accommodated almost instantly and in full view of the house, relieving the musical of that drain on plot energy, the scene in one before a traveler curtain.

Three, the unit set—acculturated in *Carnival!*, *A Family Affair, Forum, Man of La Mancha*, and even *Chu Chem*—is gaining popularity, for economic as well as artistic reasons.

Four, there is suddenly a lot less dancing. This is partly because the more intelligent and realistic the shows become, the less they can use a form as abstract as dance. In the second act of *Bloomer Girl*, in 1944, the action abruptly paused for a stylized Agnes de Mille ballet on the Civil War. Imagine that occurring in the middle of . . . what? *No Strings? Cabaret?* Stylized dance was outdated, as Gower Champion and Jerome Robbins demonstrated in, respectively, *Hello, Dolly!* and *Fiddler on the*

Roof: with dance placed strictly within the action, as in the parade of waiters celebrating Dolly's return, or the bottle dance at Tzeitel and Motel's wedding. The Dream Ballet, so basic to the Rodgers and Hammerstein era, is over; *Mata Hari's* was the last—and it might well have been cut had the show come in.

Five, the director-choreographer's super-production is becoming so habituated that many shows have no desire to be anything else. It used to be: a star and a good score. Then it was: a good story and a good score. Now it is: razzle-dazzle.

Certain other factors are less apparent. One: the national music is changing, in this very decade, from Tin Pan Alley to rock, so the population as a whole is becoming less attuned to Broadway. Hit shows will sell fewer cast albums, radio gives less and less airplay to this music, and the extinction of the television variety show—those of Ed Sullivan, Perry Como, Carol Burnett, Judy Garland—will cut a willing audience off from the dissemination of this music. All of this undermines the economic base of a form whose expenses already overwhelm much of its potential profit.

I wonder if airplay of the score would have boosted *1776*. Not that it needed any, at a run of 1,217 performances. But the Sherman Edwards songs are oddly utilitarian for a smash. Has there ever been another musical hit that made it solely on a superb book (by Peter Stone) and direction (by Peter Hunt)? Actually, Edwards had wanted to write the entire show himself, in the Meredith Willson manner. A onetime history teacher, actor, and pop tunesmith (including "See You in September"), Edwards had a brainstorm one day—all Americans know what happened on July 4, 1776, but almost none knows how it came about or what antagonistic forces very nearly forbade its happening at all.

Producer Stuart Ostrow brought Stone in, and the cast was headed by William Daniels, Ken Howard, Howard da Silva, Virginia Vestoff, and Betty Buckley: as John Adams, Thomas Jefferson, Ben Franklin, and the Adams and Jefferson wives. These are fine performers, but what characters to find listed in one's program! What a risky venture! Yet Edwards was right—this is a thriller whose narrative intrigue triumphs over the fact that everyone in the audience already knows the surprise ending.

But then, one had no idea what a concerto of oppositions the Continental Congress really was. It is North versus South, liberals versus conservatives, adventurists versus stay-at-homes—even, at one point, "land-lord" versus "lawyer." There is a running gag in that, at every vote, New York State's response is always "New York abstains—courteously." But the intensity with which Adams pursues his dream of American independ-ence is no jest, and author Edwards gave him powerful antagonists in Pennsylvania's John Dickinson (Paul Hecht) and South Carolina's Edward Rutledge (Clifford David).

The reason why I call attention to a dramatis personae filled with names of such ring is that they are much harder to present than purely invented characters. They must convince us of their reality without par-taking too much of ours. Their language, for instance, must tread care-fully between phony antiquing and intrusive modern idioms. Then, too, the historical background of mercantile colonialism and regional differ-ences must be filled in organically, without the use of blatant expository speeches or minor characters serving as human trots. And where do the women fit in?

Jefferson's wife visits Philadelphia from Virginia, and Abigail Adams appears only in Adams' imagination, as his correspondent and inspira-tion. Has a musical ever seen a more enchanting duo who never meet in any real sense for the entire action? Has there ever been another such duo at all?

But this show is autonomous in its use of the Essentials. First of all, there was virtually no dancing, except for a minuet so stingy of movement that it could have been a frieze. There was no chorus: the Congress was the chorus. There was no intermission. There were no set changes. True, the unit set was, by 1969, almost convention, and the elaborate lay-out of the Congress's assembly room, with its members arrayed in chairs and at tables, made this main set and attendant "bit" sets necessary. Still, strongly narrative shows did not use unit sets. In this decade, story shows still employed the time-honored program of large playing areas giving way to smaller playing areas and back again, with the backdrops and wing pieces of the 1930s, '40s, and '50s replaced by three-dimensional parts slid in on wagons.

Indeed, *1776* made its book its First Essential. It's almost too good a one, so obsessively following the trail of independence—like John Adams himself—that at one point it forgoes all music for more than twenty minutes. It had to be an extremely intelligent book, for here were gathered some of the nation's brightest minds—including, in Franklin, a genuine wit. And Franklin does shine:

ADAMS: Damnit, Franklin, you make us sound treasonous!
FRANKLIN: Do I? (thinking) Treason . . . "Treason is a charge invented by winners as an excuse for hanging the losers."
ADAMS: I have more to do than stand here listening to you quote yourself.
FRANKLIN: No, that was a new one.

Most interesting are the tortuous ways to independence, the plot surprises; as when John Hancock (David Ford) of Massachusetts appalls his fellow New Englanders by insisting that the vote for independence be carried not by a simple majority but unanimously:

HANCOCK: Don't you see that any colony who opposes independence will be forced to fight on the side of England—that we'll be setting brother against brother? . . . Either we walk together or together we must stay where we are.

The libretto is so keyed to the action that one can never tell when a song is about to start. There is none of the lead-in dialogue suggestive of wee-hours desperation in Boston, when new numbers are floated into a show and somehow never genuinely anchored as it is rushed into town. On the contrary, *1776* is frighteningly well integrated. Yet its songs function very differently from the songs in other shows—in the lift that "Dancing" gives to *Hello, Dolly!*, say, or the folkloric investigation of "The Tailor, Motel Kamzoil" in *Fiddler on the Roof*. Does *1776* even need its songs at all?

This is the first time in the decade that I've asked this question. Back in the enjoyably bad old days of the unintegrated musical, one would more likely ask, Does it really need its script? As we look over outstanding titles of the 1960s—*Bye Bye Birdie* and *Mame* as pure musical comedy; *She Loves Me* as musical comedy becoming musical play; *Camelot* as the end of the last era and *Cabaret* as the start of the next; *Hello, Dolly!* and *Sweet*

Charity as staging triumphs; and *Fiddler on the Roof* as the unique show, defiant of lists—we find works that, for all their coordinated alchemy, would be nothing without the music.

Can that be said of *1776*? Certainly, it makes use of its score. John Adams' two songs with his wife humanize him. In the Congress, he is "obnoxious and disliked"; to his wife, he is treasure. The double-tongued "He Plays the Violin" does comparable work for the reflective Jefferson, as *his* wife dotes upon his music-making in sighs suggestive of love noises.

On another level, the snorting, stamping Dixie march "The Lees of Old Virginia" faces down "Cool, Cool Considerate Men" as if confronting the impulsive and life-affirming nature of the rebels with the smug detachment of the conservatives. It's a way of reminding us that the right is as arrogant as the rambunctious Adams.

It is not a dramatic score. The aforementioned "Momma Look Sharp" never quite surpasses the horror of the spoken lines preceding it, about mothers going out at dinnertime to find their sons' corpses:

> COURIER: Miz Lowell—she foun' Tim'thy right off. But Miz Pickett— she looked near half the night f'r Will'm cuz he'd gone 'n' crawl'd off the green 'fore he died.

There is but one genuinely dramatic number, the ghoulishly dazzling "Molasses To Rum," provoked by a passage in Jefferson's draft of the Declaration of Independence that specifically criticizes slavery. South Carolina's Rutledge wants it out, but the North refuses. "It's a stinking business, Mr. Rutledge," says Adams. "A stinking business."

Comes then Rutledge's solo, based on what American high schools used to teach as "the triangle trade": New England merchant ships taking rum and other goods to the Guinea coast of Africa, where a victorious local tribe would sell prisoners taken from the losing tribe to the horror of the "middle passage" to the West Indies. There the slaves were traded for molasses and sugar to take home to New England, part of this final cargo to be converted into rum for the next voyage. "Who stinketh," Rutledge cries, "the *most?*"

It is the show's one dangerous moment, not only because it reminds us of the anti-democratic paradox left in the compact of democracy from its inception, but because it amply expresses Rutledge's hatred. Not for

blacks—for the white North that hypocritically wears the robe of innocence. Then Rutledge imitates the voice of the slave auctioneer, going on
in such scathing abandon that Adams finally has to beg him to stop.

"Molasses To Rum" is dramatic also in its use as a climax in the overall
debate. For, with the offending passage removed from the Declaration
and the South mollified, the vote is near the needed unanimity. A dele-
gate from Delaware is hauled from his deathbed, Pennsylvania's Dickinson is overruled by a worm terrified of making history . . . and it's done.
(New York still abstains—courteously.) Throughout the show, a calendar
upstage has been used to frame the time for us; now one last page is
pulled, to reveal July 4.

It's a thrilling moment, perhaps the most spectacular piece of throwaway business in the musical's history. In a finale that must have been in
Edwards' head from the day he conceived the piece, the delegates take
turns signing the Declaration of Independence, to the pealing crescendo
of the Liberty Bell. At length, all freeze in a semblance of the famous
painting of the moment by John Trumbull (who was, by the way, a
colonel in the Revolutionary War). As the audience absorbs the almost
religious communality of this experience, a secular Mass for Americans, a
scrim falls over the scene. The figures dim from view and the scrim now
reproduces the original Declaration, with the signatures lined up at the
bottom, clearly spelling out for His Majesty who would hang if the war of
separation failed. And the curtain comes down.

One expects mixed notices for a show this odd. But except for one
character whose work throughout the decade was a relentless homopho-
bic rant, every critic gave the show a rave. One review included among its
adjectives "striking," "gripping," "exciting," "entertaining," "literate,"
"urbane," and among its nouns "style," "humanity," "wit," and "passion,"
Another wrote, "Often, as I sat enchanted in my seat, it reminded me of
Gilbert and Sullivan in its amused regard of human frailties; again, in its
music, it struck me as a new opera."

You may wonder what Walter Kerr thought. I seldom do, because I find
him absurdly overrated, given to an almost morbid love of silly rather
than serious musicals and the first of Broadway's theatre critics with
absolutely no ear for music. Among the scores he hated were those to *The
Most Happy Fella* and *West Side Story*.

However, it keeps one spry to test one's dislikes by debating from the

other side. Kerr's admirers like his suave use of the language and his ability to sense movements and epochs in theatre history as they are happening. He was also, uniquely among his colleagues, a theatre veteran, not a
writer of unproduced plays but a working thespian.

And Kerr really got this show's number. Playing with the word "independent," he noticed how self-defining *1776* is. "It will not do things anybody else's way," he observed, "even if everybody else has always been
right. . . . Book and music do what they want to do, not what musical-
comedy custom dictates. . . . An original, strangely determined,
immensely pleasing evening."

So *1776* marked a culmination of the movement to tinker with the
musical's form while reinforming the musical's content. This movement
dates back to *Show Boat* in the 1920s but had influence only after *Oklahoma!* in the 1940s. Musicals had been "independent" for decades—but
now *1776* was being independent of even *those* shows.

Harvey Schmidt and Tom Jones' *Celebration* was another independent
show. It was to be a less appreciated one, lasting 110 performances to the
1,217 of *1776*. At that, *Celebration* held out for those three months only
because of its low-rent maintenance, in a unit set that gave little to look
at, with four principals and a chorus of twelve. Having learned from *The
Fantasticks*' very gradual word-of-mouth success, the authors and their
producer, Cheryl Crawford, deliberately budgeted the production to survive losing weeks.

There is a *Fantasticks* feeling to the composition itself, a kind of little-
show mentality that seems to want to reproach the Big Broadway that
Schmidt and Jones had, perhaps unhappily, toiled in during the years
between *The Fantasticks* at the decade's start and *Celebration* at its close.
There was a lot of David Merrick in their dossier. Could *Celebration* have
marked an attempted retreat from money, from the theatre-party ladies
who differentiate the shows that are to live from those headed for death?
Celebration's villain is a plutocrat and a maker of artificial things. Flowers
that don't smell, for instance.

It is worth remarking that Schmidt and Jones had by this time set up a
laboratory for the creation of little musicals, the Portfolio Workshop, in a
brownstone in the West Forties, developing and then presenting works
such as this *Celebration*, *Philemon*, and *The Bone Room*. Their idea, appar-

ently, was to reinvent the musical as an entity devoid of show-shop extravaganza. What, in the age of *Cabaret*?

On the other hand, *Celebration* could be seen as simply a revolt against Big Broadway's increasingly prohibitive economy. A popular art had grown too expensive to be popular. Edgar Allen* Rich is *Celebration's* bad guy, and he was cast as fat and awful and treated with such derision that his entrance scene involved his gobbling down and then vomiting up a lobster. This is an angry show.

It doesn't have much story. A cute boy loves natural things, such as flowers that smell and shows with small overheads. A cute girl wants to sell out to show-biz success; she eventually settles for the boy. A Narrator called—again, can anyone explain this?—Potemkin is cynical, as befits the age. Ted Thurston (the old guy), Michael Glenn-Smith (the boy), Susan Watson (the girl), and Keith Charles (the narrator) did their best. But this "musical parable," staged by Jones and choreographer Vernon Lusby, was largely sixties leftist slogans turned into a musical. In effect, *Celebration* was the show that everybody had mistaken *Hair* for: late-sixties Zeitoper on the theme of "We're here; we're rebellious and counter-cultural; get used to it."

Hair's safety clause was its clever score. *Celebration*, too, had a good score, in the established Schmidt and Jones style. As in *The Fantasticks*, the two wrote more arrestingly for the kids than for their elders. A single number framed the action, as so often now, loosely creating the feel of a primitive people enacting ritual theatre while waiting out an eclipse of the sun. This number was the title song, a macabre anthem whose imagery combines world creation with world's end. Jim Tyler's orchestrations, for nine percussionists, emphasized the song's driving pulse, giving *Celebration's* first few minutes—as a good opening number can give many a flop—the misleading impression that it is a major and even influential show.

Actually, *Celebration* was that; but I'm getting ahead of myself. Because *The Fantasticks* also had a Boy and Girl (though they had names, and in

*If this is meant as a reference to Poe, that's Edgar Allan. Otherwise, why the name at all? Because "rich" is the opposite of "poor," as it would be pronounced in Schmidt and Jones' native Texas ("po' ")?

Celebration they were technically Orphan and Angel), one might anticipate similar numbers for *Celebration*'s pair. On the contrary, in this show
she is cynical, only dimly aware of romance, where *The Fantasticks'* Luisa
was a full-blown romanticist. And now he's dumbly naïve, where the earlier show's Matt was precocious. Her establishing number began, "At
twenty, man you've had it!" and his was directed to "Mr. Somebody in the
sky." Her song is the wickedly jiving "Somebody," his the wistfully swinging "Orphan in the Storm," both good pieces that sounded the way the
characters looked, she a dirty sylph and he a farm boy.

With the lively music, the honking, bonking orchestration (for an
entr'acte, the chorus performed as a kind of grown-up kindergarten
rhythm band), and Ed Wittstein's disturbing costumes, *Celebration* had
everything it needed but a plot. Instead, it had "the battle of winter and
summer." Traditional musical-comedy planning brings two kids together,
but in this version they have first to kill some rich old man, as if inspired
by hippie theory and *Wild in the Streets*. Isn't another of traditional musical-comedy precepts Live and Let Live?

Celebration was a terrible idea, but it was executed well. More important, while working out the relationships among the three characters, the
narrator, and the chorus, the authors forged the all-but-essential link
among the first generation of concept shows (*Allegro* and *Love Life*), the
central sixties concept show (*Cabaret*), and all the rest of the history from
Company and *Follies* on. The first generation invented the commentative
numbers and out-of-real-time dramaturgy. *Cabaret* reinaugurated the program by integrating the realistic and commentative zones into one playing "area." But it was *Celebration* that integrated the *performers*. Now
anyone could "comment" to anyone else on any event at any time. This
was never true in earlier concept shows; each of them observed certain
limits.

For instance, *Allegro*'s chorus could remark on the action and "advise"
the protagonist—but it could never converse with a real-life character,
never function within the action per se. *Love Life* had two scores, one for
the characters and one for the specialty players *about* the characters.
Cabaret merged its two scores in that Sally Bowles is both a character and
a specialty player; and it had that shivering moment when the girl in the
cabaret simply appeared in Cliff's room; or, rather, in his imagination; or,

better, in the novel that will tell of his adventures and eventually become the musical *Cabaret*. Life *is* a cabaret.

But *Cabaret*'s Emcee had places he was not allowed to go to. He has them even in Sam Mendes' "I am Wunderkind, hear me roar" revision. *Celebration*'s narrator has no forbidden places. He controls the show's Ice Age cabaret but is also a person of sorts in the story. He even has a character song, "Survive." This effortlessly confident use of the Greek chorus–specialty player–Emcee as a figure as much *in* the show as *of* it may have been the last liberating act in the concept show's history. One can define this mercurial form in any number of ways, Perhaps the least useful—but truest—way is as "the show without limits."

Celebration was that show—"independent," as Walter Kerr said of *1776*. *Dear World*, the third of our definitive shows of 1969, was anything but. This was the most conventional of the decade's musicals, yet another Merrick-Champion Big Lady vehicle with titlesongitis put on by others than Merrick and Champion, another adaptation of an intractable play, another eagerly awaited behemoth that couldn't have sold a ticket after the ghastly reviews, and a show so insecure of its identity that it went through four *Playbill* covers during its four-month run in a pathetic determination to "look" like a hit. Maybe they should have printed a photo of *Oklahoma!* or *The Music Man*; but the smart money knew that *Dear World* was doomed from the first reading.

Flop collectors, for example. They thrilled to the announcement of the signing of Carmen Mathews in a featured role, for Mathews had never been in a musical that lasted more than a few weeks. Even in high school, her shows were fiascos; at her third-grade Easter pageant, some parents demanded their money back, though admission had been free.

Amateurs of French drama, for another example. Those acquainted with *Dear World*'s source, Jean Giraudoux's *The Madwoman of Chaillot*, know Giraudoux as one of those unadaptable writers. In language, worldview, and structure he is absolutely *spoken theatre*, brittle, abstract, delicate. *The Madwoman of Chaillot* is funny, and presciently bears the anti-corporation politics so trendy in the 1960s. It is, all the same, a fragile piece with little action and a very odd leading part. Aurelia, the Madwoman, is as apt to go on obsessively about a lost feather boa as to express correct politics, and she plays a love scene with a boy three generations off her dance card. Remember, too: she saves the world. Anything less than *Promenade*'s stream-of-consciousness score would misrepresent her; and Jerry Herman is writing the songs, not Al Carmines and Maria Irene Fornes.

Who else knew *Dear World* was headed for bomb heaven? Angela Lansbury didn't, because she starred in what had been Giraudoux's title role and gave it her greatest performance ever. Her part in *Anyone Can Whistle* was written to be ersatz, and *Mame* didn't need a greatest performance, or Jane Morgan wouldn't have been one of the Broadway replacements. But Lansbury's Aurelia somehow read her way through Jerome Lawrence and Robert E. Lee's unknowing book and Herman's sometimes inappropriate songs to center the character in musical-comedy charm while fondling her crazy edges. Moreover, Herman's score was at least lovingly made on Lansbury, tuned to her voice to the point of anchoring the climactic note in "Each Tomorrow Morning" to Lansbury's refulgent A above middle C, letting the natural glow in her timbre shine forth in the following phrase. Then, with the accordion going full-blast, the chorus took over, building the number for dance and joy in Herman's personal view of musical shows as essentially exhilarating.

Still, to understand how undignified and mistaken *Dear World* was, we must backtrack to Giraudoux and his play. The writer, professionally a diplomat, knew a lifelong love of German culture and fear of German belligerence. There is a lot of this in some of his work, especially so in a piece written in 1943. When *La Folle de Chaillot* was first performed, posthumously, in December 1945, France was only recently rid of Nazis, collaborators, and black-market profiteers, so the targets of Giraudoux's criticism were very real to his audience. True, his villains are various presidents of companies, oil prospectors, unscrupulous reporters, and even a few society women—all part of what Giraudoux terms "the machine" of destruction. They detect oil under Paris and would turn the city into a drilling field; the Madwoman lures them into a downward-driving stairway from which none returns. Where are they now? "They have evaporated," she answers. "They were evil. Evil evaporates."

Who are they, exactly? In Maurice Valency's translation:

THE RAGPICKER: In the street they go bareheaded, and indoors they wear hats. They talk out of the corner of their mouths. They do not run.

They do not hurry. You will never see one perspire. They tap their cigarette on their cigarette case when they wish to smoke. A sound of thunder . . . They manage everything, they spoil everything. Look at the shopkeepers . . . The butcher depends on the veal pimp, the service station on the petrol pimp, the fruit-vendor on the produce pimp.

So it is more than Nazis or predatory businessmen. It is all the anti-humanist oppressive destructive forces in the world, neutralized forever by a loony who is in fact the most reasonable person onstage. "A Sensible Woman," Lansbury's establishing song, tells us how easy it is to save the world. One has only to rise above what one reads in newspapers and identify harmful people by how they behave.

Like his contemporary Jean Anouilh, Giraudoux wrote his comedies in a zany mode that makes them funnier than Feydeau's farces; *La Folle de Chaillot* had its original public helpless with delight. It's easy to see why so many have loved this work, and why, sooner or later, it had to be a musical. But it shouldn't have been a formula show, because the play itself is anti-formula. Like so much of twentieth-century French drama, it has an odd structure. There are too many speaking parts, for one thing. There are also too many madwomen—four in all. (The musical dropped one.) It has a romantic subplot that comes and goes on pretexts. It has the *jeune premier* playing that love scene with the Madwoman, something only the French would fail to find embarrassing.

Dear World's Big Lady formula was its undoing. All Broadway had been ready to enjoy the work, the encore to *Mame* with the added intellectual glamour of a modern French classic. But the authors did what Rodgers and Hammerstein had warned authors never to do: they shoved the material into a preexisting genre. Mame as a bag lady. Dolly saves the world. The book used a lot of Giraudoux yet didn't know what to do when his tone clashed with Big Lady convention. The play was not adapted but mashed, even contaminated, especially when Peter Glenville replaced director Lucia Victor (Gower Champion's protégée) and then Joe Layton replaced both Glenville and choreographer Donald Saddler out of town. Layton knew how a hit musical worked, but he didn't know how Giraudoux worked—at least, not Giraudoux as Big Broadway. A trimming of the original play's text with a few embellishing songs might have succeeded: adding, say, the accordion but not all those big-number dancers. Layton had easily restirred the elements of star-turn musical comedy when he perfected *Sherry!* But *The Man Who Came To Dinner* was perfect musical-comedy source material. What is not perfect source material is a witty and ironically pirouetting historical document by a Frenchman punctuating the German surrender with a slap in those fucking Nazi faces. That is the beginning of a bad-idea musical.

Titlesongitis was the worst aspect of the bungling. "Dear World" found the ensemble, costumed in every conceivable profession and hobby, going through a marche militaire while singing outré lyrics on the theme of an ailing planet in emergency-room treatment. This is not Giraudoux! Remember the "veal pimp"? The "petrol pimp"? The "produce pimp"? The earth isn't ailing. It's under assault by crooks. One doesn't heal the world: one eliminates the crooks.

It's almost irritating to report that most of the score is wonderful as sheer music. With orchestrator Philip J. Lang supplying Instant Paris with that accordion, Herman moved with surprising care through the show, trying to balance his theatre with Giraudoux's. The Sewerman utterly defeated him, in a list song called "Garbage" and in "It's Really Rather Rugged To Be Rich." But Herman caught the bad guys in "The Spring of Next Year." It's an evil lyric set to a carefree waltz, with the singers howling most beautifully in high tenor, hypocrisy in three-quarter time.

Herman's version of the Countess, as Aurelia is called, is variable. Nothing that he wrote matches the grotesque look that Lansbury affected, nor even her low-camp Star Entrance, up from the basement through a manhole. A typical Jerry Herman ⁶/₈ pep-up tune, "One Person," was ridiculously incorrect, generical in the wrong genre. The Countess shouldn't be singing Jerry Herman format numbers any more than Eliza Doolittle should sing, say, "I'm Not at All in Love."

The Countess was graced with the two aforementioned establishing numbers, but that's one too many even for Lansbury in a Tony-baiting performance. "A Sensible Woman" was dropped (along with the Sewerman's "Really Rather Rugged" solo) in favor of "Each Tomorrow Morning." Moreover, Herman outdid himself in what seems to be everyone's favorite number in the score, the Countess' "I Don't Want To Know." Whirling with the quirks and tizzies of a woman called "mad" because she is living in a vanished age rather than in the morally devolved current one, it survives in cabaret. It's still vital, even inspiring. It suggests what madder music Herman might have composed had he broken just that much out of his accustomed matrices. Instead, he returned to the quodlibet of *Mame's* "Fox Hunt" in the teatime meeting of the three madwomen. Each of them got a solo—"Dickie," "Voices," "Thoughts"—that she then sang in synch with the other two.

In short, here is another misleading cast album, forgiving the sins of a corrupt adaptation. One hint of how badly *Dear World* played lies in that Ben-Hur of an overture. Giraudoux asks for a big cast, true: but his play is tidy, a mocking little piece about how vast is the evil in the world. They are, as the musical calls them, The Establishment. If they went to the theatre, isn't *Dear World* exactly the kind of show they would see?

Jane Connell and, as said, Carmen Mathews were the other madwomen. Kurt Peterson and Pamela Hall played the spotty romance. Milo O'Shea was so unhappy as the Sewerman that he managed to leave the show before its short run was up, And while Lansbury won her Tony, the show did nobody any good—not even Miguel Godreau, who won a lot of notice as the Mute, here made into an elaborate dance role. The critics fell on *Dear World* with such appetite that one expected never to hear of it again.

One was wrong: Goodspeed at Chester mounted it in 2000. Sally Ann Howes (unusually intense in "I Don't Want To Know"), Diane J. Findlay, and Georgia Engel were the madwomen, in a revision by David Thompson. His script moves songs around and retrieves "A Sensible Woman" (which now very sensibly opens the show, in utmost simplicity) but also "It's Really Rather Rugged To Be Rich," the worst Jerry Herman song alive. Thompson further makes far too much of the villains, personified in three money bosses and given an excruciatingly unnecessary scene in their office. This sabotages Giraudoux's presentation of them as ghoulish demonic exploiters. They don't inhabit places; they invade them.

It was not necessarily Herman who retained that hopelessly immiscible title song, here a trio for the *folles*. It remains a jabbering horror of a number, a pleasant tune saddled with bad lyrics. But then, the problem, from the start, is that Giraudoux, like Anouilh, defies musicalization, which is why both men have seldom been so treated. Their arch and epigrammatic prose sings as it is.

By 1969, big hit musicals tended to become Hollywood movies. So

1776 was filmed, happily with almost all its original leads, in a faithful rendering. That may suggest a vitality in the stage musical's relationship to mass culture. No. Every year, Broadway was losing more of its lock audience, more media coverage, more importance. It was almost, maybe, disappearing.

That, at least, is what some inferred from the dismal 1969–70 season, a garden of flowers that don't smell. *Jimmy*, on New York's Jazz Age mayor, was scandalously unworthy as a follow-up to the intrepid *Fiorello!* of ten years earlier. *Buck White*, based on *Big Time Buck White*, was raving black racism. *Coco* was a nearly tuneless piece saved by an amusing book and lavish revolving-stage fashion exhibits. *La Strada, Gantry, Georgy*, and *Look To the Lilies*, all associated with popular films, lasted a combined total of 31 performances. *Purlie* and *Applause* were hits of no special quality. *Company*, at least, made history. But this was largely a time of extremely questionable Novelty Stars—Frank Gorshin, Muhammad Ali, Katharine Hepburn, Robert Shaw, Shelley Winters, and Lauren Bacall. True, some had charm, or could act, but none belonged in a musical. It was a time also when such sure shots as Lionel Bart, Jule Styne, and Charles Strouse and Lee Adams did their least impressive work. Musicals in tryout hell can lose much of their original book, but Bart's *La Strada* was so rewritten that it opened with almost no Bart in it.

Something was wrong. This wasn't just a poor season, but a revealingly poor one. The one previous bad season that anyone knew of was that of 1955–56, which saw in a few one-man shows and minor revues, an extensive visit by the D'Oyly Carte troupe in their trademark Gilbert and Sullivan, and only five book shows. Three of them were failures—but failures with Carol Channing and Sammy Davis Jr., or with a score by Rodgers and Hammerstein. The two successes were *My Fair Lady* and *The Most Happy Fella*.

If *1776* confirms that the musical continues to develop its independence, and if *Celebration* points us toward the modernist reality-fantasy stagings that we now take for granted in such works as *Chicago, Sweeney Todd*, and *Grand Hotel, Dear World* unveils the bankrupt heart of superproduction. It even worries independence: it is a paradox that the more unusual the musical gets, the more unusual it wants to be, leading it to tackle difficult projects that possibly should not be musicals—*Greenwillow, The Yearling, Breakfast at Tiffany's, The Madwoman of Chaillot*.

Absurdly, the musical has become most liberated just when it is growing short on talent and losing its security as the national amusement.

But then, it isn't an amusement any more. Yes, it's *Hello, Dolly!*, but it's also *Cabaret*. It's nervy, opinionated, and tensely finding itself. Hit-length runs lose money. Tickets are sold on the *Times* review. Gwen Verdon will die in thirty years. But hold. The thrill and the fun and even the goodwill are running out like the audience at *Chu Chem?*

Embrace Zorbá!

INDEX